Ant

The Definitive Guide

Ant

The Definitive Guide

Jesse Tilly and Eric M. Burke

Foreword by James Duncan Davidson

O'REILLY®

Beijing · Cambridge · Farnham · Köln · Paris · Sebastopol · Taipei · Tokyo

Ant: The Definitive Guide
by Jesse Tilly and Eric M. Burke

Published by O'Reilly & Associates, Inc., 1005 Gravenstein Highway North, Sebastopol, CA 95472.

O'Reilly & Associates books may be purchased for educational, business, or sales promotional use. Online editions are also available for most titles (*safari.oreilly.com*). For more information, contact our corporate/institutional sales department: (800) 998-9938 or *corporate@oreilly.com*.

Editor: Jonathan Gennick

Production Editor: Colleen Gorman

Cover Designer: Hanna Dyer

Interior Designer: David Futato

Printing History:

May 2002: First Edition.

ISBN: 0-596-00184-3

[M] [7/02]

For my grandmother, Dorothy Tilly.

—Jesse Tilly

For Mom.

—Eric M. Burke

Table of Contents

Foreword

I have to confess that I had absolutely no idea that Ant, the little build tool that could, would go as far as it did and make such a mark on the Java developer community. When I wrote the first version of Ant, it was a simple hack to help me solve a cross-platform build problem that I was having. Now it's grown up and being used by thousands of developers all over the planet. What's the magic behind this? How did this little program end up being used by so many people? Maybe the story of how Ant came to be holds some clues.

Ant was first written quite some time before it was checked into Apache's CVS servers. In mid-1998, I was given the responsibility at Sun Microsystems to create the Java Servlet 2.1 specification and a reference implementation to go with it. This reference implementation, which I named Tomcat, was to be a brand new codebase, since the previous reference implementation was based somewhat on code from the Java Web Server, a commercial product that was migrated from JavaSoft to iPlanet. Also, the new implementation had to be 100% Pure Java.

In order to get the 100% Pure Java certification, even for those of us working on the Java Platform at Sun, you had to show Key Labs (an independent certification company) that you could run on three different platforms. To ensure that the servlet reference implementation would run anywhere, I picked Solaris, Windows, and the Mac OS. And not only did I want Tomcat to run on these three platforms, but I wanted to be able to build and develop on all three platforms as well as on Linux. I tried using GNU Make. And shell scripts. And batch files. And God knows what else. Each approach had its own unique problem. The problems stemmed from the fact that all of the existing tools had a worldview rooted in building C programs. When these practices were applied to Java, they worked, but slowly. Even though Java programs themselves can perform well, the startup overhead associated with the Java Virtual Machine is lengthy. And when Make creates a new instance of the VM with every file that needs to be compiled, compile times grow linearly with the number of source files in a project.

I tried many approaches to write a make file that would cause all of the source files in a project that needed to be recompiled to be passed to javac in one go. But, no matter how hard I tried, and how many Make wizards I consulted with, I couldn't get an approach that would work the same way on multiple platforms. I got very, very tired of the *!&#$%#ing* tab formatting of make files. As much as I've been a proponent of Emacs in my life, any tool that requires Emacs to properly write its files so that you can make sure that no unintended spaces creep in should not be tolerated.*

It was on a flight back from a conference in Europe that I finally got fed up once and for all of trying to create some make file that would work the same way everywhere. I decided to "make" my own tool: one that would examine all the Java source files in a project, compare them with any compiled classes, and pass the list of sources that needed to be compiled directly to *javac*. In addition, it would do a couple of other things like stuff all the classes into a JAR file and copy some other files around to make a distributable version of the software. In order to ensure that things would work the same way on every supported platform, I decided to write the tool in Java.

A few hours later, I had a working tool. It was simple, crude, and consisted of just a few classes. It used the functionality of `java.util.Properties` to serve as its data layer. And it worked. Beautifully. My compile times dropped by an order of magnitude. When I got back to the states and tested it out on Solaris, Linux, and Mac OS, it worked just fine on all of them. Its biggest problem at that time was that the number of things it could do was limited to compiling files and copying files—and that this functionality was hardcoded.

A few weeks later I showed the tool, which I had named Ant because it was a little thing that could build big things,† to my friend Jason Hunter (author of *Java Servlet Programming*, published by O'Reilly). Jason thought that it was a decent enough tool, but didn't really think it was a big deal. That is, until I mentioned that I was thinking of using Java's reflection abilities to provide a clean way to extend Ant's abilities so that a programmer could write their own tasks to extend it. Then the light bulb went off over his head and I had my first Ant user as well as evangelist. Jason also has an uncanny ability to find a bug in any piece of software within moments and helped me stomp out quite a few problems.

Once the reflection layer was in place, I wrote a few more tasks and Ant became useful to other groups at Sun. However, the build file format was getting a bit bulky. Properties files don't really lend themselves to hierarchical grouping well, and with the introduction of tasks came the idea of targets (collections of tasks). I played around with a few different ways of solving the problem, but hit on the solution when I was on another flight back from Europe. This solution structured the project-target-task

* I've been told that the original designer of the make file format knew after the first week that the tab thing would be a problem. But he already had dozens of users and didn't want to break compatibility.

† Also, the letters ANT could stand for "Another Neato Tool." Silly, I know. But true.

hierarchy to follow an XML document hierarchy. It also leveraged the reflection work I had done earlier to associate XML tag names with task implementations.

Evidently I do my best coding while flying over the ocean. I wonder if there's something about the increased radiation at high altitude that helps. Or maybe trips to Europe bring out something creative in me. Only more experimentation will tell.

Ant, as we know it, had come into being. Everything that you see in the version of Ant that you use today (the good and the bad) is a result of the decisions made up to that point. To be sure, a lot has changed since then, but the basics were there. It was essentially this source code that was checked into Apache's CVS repository alongside Tomcat in late 2000. I moved on to other things, principally being Sun's representative to the Apache Software Foundation as well as working on XML specifications such as JAXP from Sun and DOM from the W3C.

Amazingly enough, people all over the world started talking about Ant. The first people to find it were those that worked on Tomcat at Apache. Then they told their friends about it. And those friends told their friends, and so on. At some point more people knew about and were using Ant than Tomcat. A strong developer and user community grew up around Ant at Apache, and many changes have been made to the tool along the way. People now use it to build all manner of projects, from very small ones to incredibly huge J2EE applications.

The moment I knew that Ant had gone into the history books was during JavaOne in 2001. I was at a keynote presentation in which a new development tool from a major database software company was being demoed. The presenter showed how easy it was to draw lines between boxes to design software, and then hit the build button. Flashing by in the console window were those familiar square brackets that every user of Ant sees on a regular basis. I was stunned. Floored.

The number of Ant users continues to increase. Evidently the little itch that I scratched is shared by Java developers world wide. And not just Java developers. I recently stumbled across NAnt, an implementation of Ant's ideas for .NET development.*

If I had known that Ant was going to be such a runaway success, I would have spent a bit more time on it in the first place polishing it up and making it something more than the simple hack it started out as. Yet that might have defeated exactly the characteristic that made it take off in the first place. Ant might have become over-engineered. If I had spent too much time trying to make it work for more than just my needs, it might have become too big a tool and too cumbersome to use. We see this all the time in software, especially in many of the Java APIs currently being proposed.

* You can find NAnt at *http://nant.sourceforge.net/*.

It might be that the secret to Ant's success is that it didn't try to be successful. It was a simple solution to an obvious problem that many people were having. I just feel honored to be the lucky guy who stumbled across it.

The book you now hold in your hands will guide you in using Ant as it exists today. Jesse and Eric will teach you how to use Ant effectively, extend it, and tell you how all the various tasks, both the built-in ones as well as widely used optional ones, can be used. In addition, they will give you tips to avoid the pitfalls created by some of Ant's design decisions.

Before placing you in their capable hands, I want to leave you with just one last thought: always scratch your own itch where possible. If a tool out there doesnt do what you need it to do, then look around for one that will. If it doesnt exist, then create it. And be sure to share it with the world. Thousands of other people might have just the same itch that you do.

—James Duncan Davidson
San Francisco, CA, April 2002

Preface

Compilation of all Java™ source files is no longer the only step necessary to build many Java-based projects. For the typical `HelloWorld` program, book examples, and simple applets, source file compilation is sufficient. Complex Java-based projects, like web applications or Swing-based programs (such as JBuilder), require much more. Up-to-date sources must be retrieved from source control. Dependencies not automatically handled by the Java compiler need to be managed. Various classes must be bundled and delivered to multiple locations, sometimes as JAR or WAR files. Some Java technologies, such as Enterprise Java Beans (EJB) and Remote Method Invocation (RMI) classes, need separate compilation and code generation steps not performed by the Java compiler. While shell scripts and GNU Make are often the first choice tools for performing these alternative tasks—in terms of "getting the job done," these tools perform adequately—they turn out to be poor choices in the long run.

As functional as it may be, GNU Make leaves a lot to be desired in terms of ease-of-use. Makefiles have their own language syntax, requiring a separate knowledge set for their authors. GNU Make lacks platform-independence, requiring multiple versions of the same makefile (one for each target platform) to be maintained and distributed. The nature of shell scripts and GNU Make (remembering that GNU Make is simply a language extension on top of an existing shell) makes moving from operating system to operating system, and even from shell to shell, difficult or impossible for anyone but an expert user. While it is not unusual to use GNU Make, the time and maintenance required to follow this path is too high for modern Java-based projects.

Sun provides Java versions of all their SDK tools. Executables such as *javac* are simply wrappers executing the Java code. Other vendors' tools, like BEA's EJB compiler for WebLogic, JUnit, and the Jakarta tools and libraries are all written in Java. GNU Make can only call executables from the command line. For example, to invoke a Java class, GNU Make must use the *java* command to invoke the JVM, and pass the class name as a command-line argument. Make is incapable of programmatically using any of the Java tools' libraries, such as exception and error objects. These libraries allow for a more flexible build process. A tool written in Java (such as WebLogic's *ejbc* compiler) can share information from exceptions and errors with other objects (such as Ant task objects) available inside the same JVM. This serves to enhance the build process beyond command-line return codes and after-the-fact error-message string parsing.

The problems with GNU Make and the possibilities of a build tool written in Java influenced James Duncan Davidson to write Ant. Ant runs the Java compiler as a class, not as a call from the command line. Remaining inside the JVM allows for specialized code to handle errors, and for action on results Sun provides through its compiler. Ant uses XML as its buildfile syntax, therefore enhancing, rather than straining, developers' and project managers' skill sets. Ant extends the build process beyond just running programs, and is more properly termed a build *environment* than a build tool.

Structure of This Book

Ant: The Definitive Guide contains all of the knowledge a newcomer to Ant needs. For the Ant expert, *Ant: The Definitive Guide* is a reference, providing detailed definitions of Ant's core tasks, discussing the main features of Ant, providing some best practices for managing projects with Ant, and explaining workarounds for some of Ant's problems.

Chapter 1, *Ant Jumpstart*, walks through a very basic Ant buildfile example, with the intent of getting you up and running quickly. We show how to create directories, compile code, and generate a JAR file, but do not delve into the details of how everything works. The chapter also includes detailed information on Ant's command-line usage. We conclude with a rough outline of a buildfile for use as a starter template.

Chapter 2, *Installation and Configuration*, shows how to get Ant, install it, and configure it on Windows and Unix platforms. We list some of the pitfalls found with these development platforms, as well as provide workarounds and solutions.

Chapter 3, *The Buildfile*, shows an example Ant buildfile in the context of a sample project. We dissect and describe the major parts and structures of the buildfile, explaining such things as the general flow of the Ant engine and the benefits of Ant using XML, highlighting the major parts of a buildfile.

Chapter 4, *Ant DataTypes*, describes each of the Ant DataTypes in detail. While DataTypes are used in earlier chapters, this is where we really dig into them. We show how to use environment variables and pass command-line arguments to processes, as well as how to work with lists of files and patterns.

Chapter 5, *User-Written Tasks*, covers one of Ant's best features: the ability to extend Ant. With the capability to write extensions, you are able to handle anything a particular project may require. As a bonus, you can reuse your tasks in future projects, reaping benefits from your effort well beyond the initial implementation. Your tasks can even be shared and distributed publicly so that people you don't even know can benefit from your work.

Chapter 6, *User-Written Listeners*, covers how to design and develop your own build-event listeners. With these, you can write classes that perform operations based on the flow related to buildfile processing. These operations range from sending emails when certain complex tasks complete, to redirecting the same events to a centralized "build-listening framework." The possibilities, just like with user-written tasks, are endless. The chapter also covers a further extension to listeners: user-written loggers. With these, you can augment or even replace Ant's default logging system.

Chapter 7, *Core Tasks*, is a comprehensive reference to the entire set of core Ant tasks. For each task, you'll find a description, a list of Ant versions supporting the task, and definitions for all task attributes. You'll also find helpful samples of task usage.

Chapter 8, *Optional Tasks*, provides a reference, similar in form to Chapter 7, for Ant's rich library of optional tasks.

Appendix A, *The Future of Ant*, discusses just that. We cover future directions and expected new features, as well as suggest steps you can take to avoid using soon-to-be-obsolete features.

Appendix B, *Ant Solutions*, delves into some of the more common ways Ant is used to solve various build problems. Additionally, we talk about using buildfiles with cascading project structures. These are project structures with a primary project directory and many subproject subdirectories. Each subproject contains its own buildfile, and the master project has a master buildfile capable of building all of the subprojects.

Audience

This book is targeted primarily at Java developers, especially those who develop enterprise-level Java applications and need a robust build tool that can do more than just invoke command-line compilers and utilities. This book will also be useful to build managers on large projects, and to project managers who have responsibility for build-management.

What You Should Know

For most of the book, only a basic understanding of Java and XML is required. The chapters on writing extensions for Ant ask that you also have a firm understanding of Java inheritance and interfaces. Ant is best used as a system for building and deploying Java-based projects. While some Ant tasks are available that provide the ability to compile and run other languages such as Perl, Python, C, and C#, this book focuses on Ant's use with Java.

Which Platform and Version

As an open source project under Apache's Jakarta project, Ant undergoes nightly code revisions and builds. These nightly builds create Ant's "non-stable versions." Every so often, the primary maintainers declare the functionality and stability of a nightly build as *release quality*. As of this writing, there have been five such releases: 1.1, 1.2, 1.3, 1.4, and 1.4.1. This reference's main focus is on 1.4.1, released in October of 2001. Some tasks, `copydir` for example, are deprecated as of Release 1.2, but are still covered in this book since they have not been completely removed from the list of core tasks.

Conventions Used in This book

The following typographical conventions are used in this book:

Italic
: Used for Unix and Windows commands, filenames and directory names, emphasis, and first use of a technical term.

`Constant width`
: Used in code examples and to show the contents of files. Also used for Java class names, Ant task names, tags, attribute names, and environment variable names appearing in the text.

`Constant width italic`
: Used in syntax descriptions to indicate user-defined items.

`Constant width bold`
: Used for user input in examples showing both input and output.

Terminology

For consistency, in this book we refer to an Ant instruction file as a *buildfile*. In other Ant-related forums and documentation, you may encounter the terms *build.xml* and *antfile*. These terms are interchangeable, but *buildfile* is the preferred term.

When referring to XML, we use the convention that a *tag* refers to a bracket-delimited markup in the buildfile. For example, `<path>` is a tag. The term *element* refers to both a tag and its children, should it have any. The following XML markup is an example of a `<path>` element. The distinction between tag and element is that the term tag refers only to `<path>`, while element refers to everything from `<path>` through `</path>`.

```
<path>
    <fileset dir="src">
        <includes name="**/*.java"/>
    </fileset>
</path>
```

XML elements and tags define Ant tasks and DataTypes in the buildfile. *Tasks* perform operations and act as the modular part of the Ant engine. *DataTypes* define complex groupings of data, typically paths or file sets, for the Ant engine.

Filename and Path Conventions

Ant is a Java program and adopts Java's "agnostic" viewpoint towards filesystems. When run, Ant checks for the path separator and directory separator characters, provided by the underlying JVM, and uses those values. It successfully interprets either the ';' or the ':' inside of the buildfile. For example, when run on a Unix machine, Ant interprets the path *dir;dir\\subdir* (note the escaped '\') correctly as *dir:dir/subdir*. Separators must be used consistently within the same value type; the string *dir;dir/subdir*, combining a Windows path separator (;) and a Unix directory separator (/), is not good form. Throughout this book, Unix and Windows file path conventions will be interspersed in the examples to emphasize the fact that Ant does not care which you use.

Ant does not handle drive letters across platforms. Using drive letters in Ant path elements will restrict a buildfile's use to Windows environments.

Comments and Questions

We have tested and verified the information in this book to the best of our ability, but you may find that features have changed or that we have made mistakes. If so, please notify us by writing to:

O'Reilly & Associates
1005 Gravenstein Highway North
Sebastopol, CA 95472
(800) 998-9938 (in the United States or Canada)
(707) 829-0515 (international or local)
(707) 829-0104 (FAX)

You can also send messages electronically. To be put on the mailing list or request a catalog, send email to:

info@oreilly.com

To ask technical questions or comment on the book, send email to:

bookquestions@oreilly.com

We have a web site for this book, where you can find examples and errata (previously reported errors and corrections are available for public view there). You can access this page at:

http://www.oreilly.com/catalog/anttdg/

For more information about this book and others, see the O'Reilly web site:

http://www.oreilly.com

Acknowledgments

From Jesse

I'd like to begin by thanking my wife, Melissa, and my two kids, Natalie and Peter, who had to put up with many lost family weekends. Without their love and support I could have never finished this book. Thanks also go out to Keyton Weissinger, who inspired me to write a book in the first place. The entire Ant community played an important role in support of the knowledge effort Eric and I went through to write this text. In particular, I'd like to thank Stefan Bodewig and Conor MacNeil, who took time from their busy schedules to help me understand some of the deeper functions of Ant. They always offered their information gladly, and I thank them for their time.

In addition, I'd like to thank our tech reviewers: Diane, Dean, Jeff, and Paul. Your contributions to the book made quite a difference. I had to keep telling myself "critiques only serve to make the book better"...and they did.

Finally, I'd like to thank the employees at Caribou Coffee in Roswell, GA, who had to put up with me for 4–8 hours every Saturday while I commandeered a table and electricity. Good coffee and friendly people made writing the book there very enjoyable.

From Eric

I want to thank my family for helping to make this book possible. To my wife, Jennifer, thank you for enduring all of those evenings and weekends while I was writing this book. To my son Aidan, I'll always find time to take you to the zoo, no matter how much work I have to do. I love you both.

I'd also like to thank each of the tech reviewers for the contributions they made to this book. Diane Holt, Dean Wette, Jeff Brown, and Paul Campbell took a great deal of time out of their personal schedules to help with this book, and I am grateful for that.

CHAPTER 1

Ant Jumpstart

It is likely that you have already downloaded and installed Ant and are ready to see an example of how it works. If so, then this chapter is for you. Here, we walk through a very basic buildfile example, followed by a full description of Ant's command-line options. If you prefer to walk through the step-by-step installation procedure first, you might want to skip ahead to Chapter 2 and then come back to this material.

We do not attempt to explain every detail of the buildfile in this chapter. For a more comprehensive example, see Chapter 3.

Files and Directories

For our example, we start with the directory and file structure shown in Figure 1-1. The shaded boxes represent files, and the unshaded boxes represent directories.

You can download this example from this book's web page, located at *http://www.oreilly.com/catalog/anttdg/*.

The Ant buildfile, *build.xml*, exists in the project base directory. This is typical, although you are free to use other filenames or put the buildfile somewhere else. The *src* directory contains the Java source code organized into an ordinary package structure. For the most part, the content of the source files is not important. However, we want to point out that *PersonTest.java* is a unit test that will be excluded from the generated JAR file.

Our sample buildfile causes Ant to create the directory tree and files shown inside the shaded, dashed block in Figure 1-2. It also compiles the Java source code, creates *oreilly.jar*, and provides a "clean" target to remove all generated files and directories.

Now let's look at the buildfile that makes this possible.

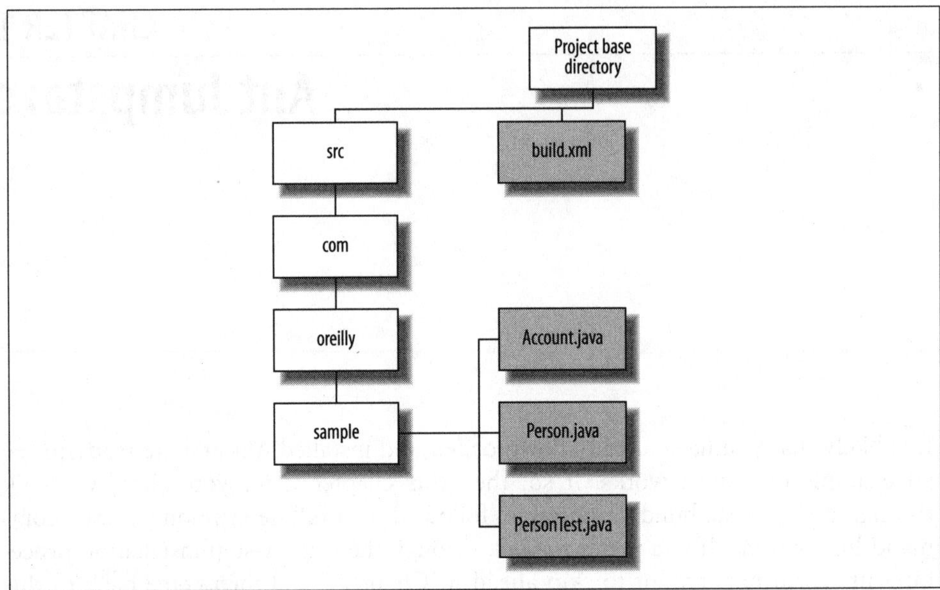

Figure 1-1. Starting point for our example buildfile

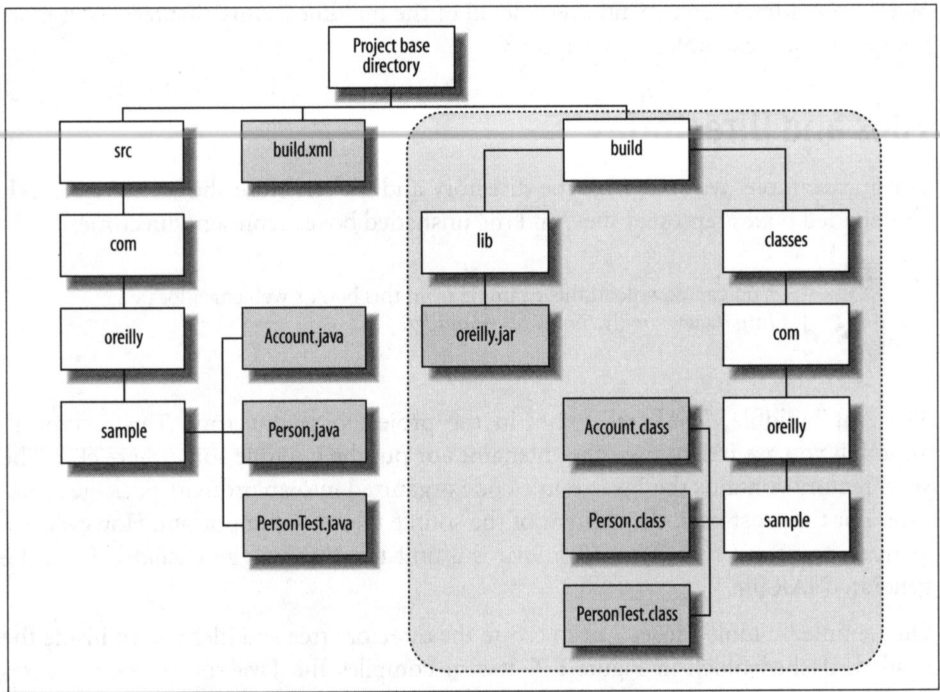

Figure 1-2. Directories and files created by our sample buildfile

The Ant Buildfile

Ant buildfiles are written using XML. Example 1-1 shows the complete Ant buildfile for our example. This is simpler than most real-world buildfiles, but does illustrate several core concepts required by nearly every Java project.

Example 1-1. build.xml

```
<?xml version="1.0"?>

<!-- build.xml - a simple Ant buildfile -->
<project name="Simple Buildfile" default="compile" basedir=".">

  <!-- The directory containing source code -->
  <property name="src.dir" value="src"/>

  <!-- Temporary build directories -->
  <property name="build.dir" value="build"/>
  <property name="build.classes" value="${build.dir}/classes"/>
  <property name="build.lib" value="${build.dir}/lib"/>

  <!-- Target to create the build directories prior to the -->
  <!-- compile target. -->
  <target name="prepare">
    <mkdir dir="${build.dir}"/>
    <mkdir dir="${build.classes}"/>
    <mkdir dir="${build.lib}"/>
  </target>

  <target name="clean" description="Removes all generated files.">
    <delete dir="${build.dir}"/>
  </target>

  <target name="compile" depends="prepare"
          description="Compiles all source code.">
    <javac srcdir="${src.dir}" destdir="${build.classes}"/>
  </target>

  <target name="jar" depends="compile"
          description="Generates oreilly.jar in the 'dist' directory.">
    <!-- Exclude unit tests from the final JAR file -->
    <jar jarfile="${build.lib}/oreilly.jar"
         basedir="${build.classes}"
         excludes="**/*Test.class"/>
  </target>

  <target name="all" depends="clean,jar"
          description="Cleans, compiles, then builds the JAR file."/>

</project>
```

XML Considerations

Ant buildfiles are XML files that can be created with any text editor. Keep the following points in mind as you create your own buildfiles:

- The first line is the XML declaration. If present, it must be the very first line in the XML file; no preceding blank lines are allowed. In fact, even a single blank space before `<?xml` causes the XML parser to fail.
- XML is very picky about capitalization, quotes, and proper tag syntax. If any of these items are incorrect, Ant fails because its underlying XML parser fails.

Here is an example of an error that occurs if the `</project>` end tag is typed incorrectly as `</Project>`:

```
Buildfile: build.xml

BUILD FAILED

C:\antbook\build.xml:41: Expected "</project>" to terminate
element starting on line 4.

Total time: 2 seconds
```

Buildfile Description

Our buildfile consists of several XML comments, the required `<project>` element, and many *properties*, *tasks*, and *targets*. The `<project>` element establishes the working directory for our project: ".". This is the directory containing the buildfile. It also specifies the default target, which is "compile." The purpose of the default target will become apparent shortly when we describe how to run Ant.

The property definitions allow us to avoid hardcoding directory names throughout the buildfile. These paths are always relative to the base directory specified by the `<project>` element. For example, the following tag sets the name of our source directory:

```
<property name="src.dir" value="src"/>
```

Next, our buildfile defines several targets. Each target has a name, such as "prepare," "clean," or "compile." Developers interact with these when invoking Ant from the command line. Each target defines zero or more dependencies, along with an optional `description` attribute. Dependencies specify targets that Ant must execute first, before the target in question is executed. For example, "prepare" must execute before "compile" does. The `description` attribute provides a human-readable description of a target that Ant will display on command.

Within targets we have tasks, which do the actual work of the build. Ant 1.4.1 ships with over 100 core and optional tasks; you can find all of the tasks described in detail in Chapters 7 and 8. These tasks perform functions ranging from creating directories to playing music when the build finishes.*

Running Ant

We are going to assume that Ant is installed properly. If you have any doubts on this point, now is the time to read Chapter 2 and get everything up and running.

Examples

To execute the tasks in the default target, `compile`, type the following command from the directory containing our sample *build.xml* file:

```
ant
```

Ant will open the default buildfile, which is *build.xml*, and execute that buildfile's default target (which in our case is `compile`). You should see the following output, assuming your directory is called *antbook*:

```
Buildfile: build.xml

prepare:
    [mkdir] Created dir: C:\antbook\build
    [mkdir] Created dir: C:\antbook\build\classes
    [mkdir] Created dir: C:\antbook\build\lib

compile:
    [javac] Compiling 3 source files to C:\antbook\build\classes

BUILD SUCCESSFUL

Total time: 5 seconds
```

As Ant runs, it displays the name of each target executed. As our example output shows, Ant executes `prepare` followed by `compile`. This is because `compile` is the default target, which has a dependency on the prepare target. Ant prints the name of each task within brackets, along with other messages unique to each task.

In our sample output, [javac] is the name of the Ant task, not necessarily the name of the Java compiler. If you are using IBM's Jikes, for instance, [javac] is still displayed because that is the Ant task that is running Jikes behind the scenes.

When you invoke Ant without specifying a buildfile name, Ant searches for a file named *build.xml* in the current working directory. You aren't limited to this default;

* See the sound task in Chapter 8.

you can use any name you like for the buildfile. For example, if we call our buildfile *proj.xml*, we must type this command, instead:

```
ant -buildfile proj.xml
```

We can also explicitly specify one or more targets to run. We can type **ant clean** to remove all generated code, for instance. If our buildfile is called *proj.xml*, and we want to execute the clean target, we type **ant -buildfile proj.xml clean**. Our output would look something like this:

```
Buildfile: proj.xml

clean:
   [delete] Deleting directory C:\antbook\build

BUILD SUCCESSFUL

Total time: 2 seconds
```

We can also execute several targets with a single command:

```
ant clean jar
```

This invokes the clean target followed by the jar target. Because of the target dependencies in our example buildfile, Ant executes the following targets in order: clean, prepare, compile, jar. The all target takes advantage of these dependencies, allowing us to clean and rebuild everything by typing **ant all**:

```
<target name="all" depends="clean,jar"
        description="Cleans, compiles, then builds the JAR file."/>
```

all is dependent on clean and jar. jar, in turn, is dependent on compile, and compile is dependent on prepare. The simple command *ant all* ends up executing all our targets, and in the proper order.

Getting Help

You may have noticed that some of our targets include the description attribute, while others do not. This is because Ant distinguishes between main targets and subtargets. Targets containing descriptions are main targets, and those without are considered subtargets. Other than documentation differences, main targets and subtargets behave identically. Typing **ant -projecthelp** from our project base directory produces the following output:

```
Buildfile: build.xml
Default target:

 compile  Compiles all source code.

Main targets:

 all      Cleans, compiles, then builds the JAR file.
 clean    Removes all generated files.
```

```
    compile  Compiles all source code.
    jar      Generates oreilly.jar in the 'dist' directory.

Subtargets:

    prepare


BUILD SUCCESSFUL

Total time: 2 seconds
```

This project help feature is particularly useful for large projects containing dozens of targets, provided you take the time to add meaningful descriptions.

For a summary of the Ant command-line syntax, type **ant -help**. You will see a brief description of Ant's command-line arguments, which we cover next.

Ant Command-Line Reference

The syntax to use to invoke Ant from the command-line is as follows:

```
ant [option [option...]] [target [target...]]

option := {-help
          |-projecthelp
          |-version
          |-quiet
          |-verbose
          |-debug
          |-emacs
          |-logfile filename
          |-logger classname
          |-listener classname
          |-buildfile filename
          |-Dproperty=value
          |-find filename}
```

The syntax elements are as follows:

-help
: Displays help information describing the Ant command and its options.

-projecthelp
: Displays any user-written help documentation included in the buildfile. This is text from the description attribute of any <target>, along with any text contained within a <description> element. Targets with description attributes are listed as "Main targets," those without are listed as "Subtargets."

-version
: Causes Ant to display its version information and exit.

-quiet
: Suppresses most messages not originated by an echo task in the buildfile.

-verbose
: Displays detailed messages for every operation during a build. This option is exclusive to *-debug*.

-debug
: Displays messages that Ant and task developers have flagged as debugging messages. This option is exclusive to *-verbose*.

-emacs
: Formats logging messages so that they're easily parsed by Emacs' *shell-mode*; i.e., prints the task events without preceding them with an indentation and a [`taskname`].

-logfile `filename`
: Redirects logging output to the specified file.

-logger `classname`
: Specifies a class to handle Ant logging. The class specified must implement the *org.apache.tools.ant.BuildLogger* interface.

-listener `classname`
: Declares a listening class for Ant to add to its list of listeners. This option is useful when integrating Ant with IDEs or other Java programs. Read more about listeners in Chapter 6. The specified listening class must be written to handle Ant's build messaging.

-buildfile `filename`
: Specifies the buildfile Ant should operate on. The default buildfile is *build.xml*.

-D`property=value`
: Defines a property name-value pair on the command line.

-find `filename`
: Specifies the buildfile on which Ant should operate. Unlike the *-buildfile* option, *-find* causes Ant to search for the specified file in the parent directory if it is not found in the current directory. This searching continues through ancestor directories until the root of the filesystem is reached, at which time the build fails if the file is not found.

Buildfile Outline

Shown next is a generic buildfile good for using as a template. A buildfile consists of the `<project>` element with its nested `<target>`, `<property>`, and `<path>` elements.

```
<project default="all">
  <property name="a.property" value="a value"/>
  <property name="b.property" value="b value"/>
```

```
  <path id="a.path">
    <pathelement location="${java.home}/jre/lib/rt.jar"/>
  </path>

  <target name="all">
    <javac srcdir=".">
      <classpath refid="a.path"/>
    </javac>
  </target>
</project>
```

Some notes about buildfiles to remember:

- All buildfiles require the `<project>` element and at least one `<target>` element.
- There is no default value for the `<project>` element's `default` attribute.
- Buildfiles do not have to be named *build.xml*. However, *build.xml* is the default name for which Ant searches.
- You can have only one `<project>` element per buildfile.

Learning More

We have only scratched the surface in this chapter, but this does give you an idea of what Ant buildfiles look like and how to run the command-line *ant* script. As mentioned earlier, Chapter 3 presents a much more sophisticated example with a great deal more explanation of what is going on in each step.

CHAPTER 2

Installation and Configuration

This chapter describes where to get Ant, explains the differences between the various distributions, and covers the most common installation scenarios. As a portable Java application, Ant works very consistently on many different platforms. This should not be a surprise, given that Ant was written as an alternative to platform-specific *make* utilities. Most differences manifest themselves in the Ant startup scripts, which are understandably different on Windows and Unix systems. Once Ant is installed and configured, it does a remarkable job of insulating you from differences between platforms.

The Distribution

Ant is open source software from the Apache Software Foundation, available in binary and source forms.* It is available from the Ant home page located at *http://jakarta.apache.org/ant/*; you can choose either a release build or a nightly build. To ease installation, different distributions are provided for Unix and Windows systems.

The direct link to the list of nightly builds is *http://jakarta.apache.org/builds/jakarta-ant/nightly/*. The nightly builds include the latest bug fixes and features, and are a constantly changing target. The vast majority of software development teams should opt instead for a release version of Ant, available at the following URLs:

http://jakarta.apache.org/builds/jakarta-ant/release/v1.4.1/bin/
: The binary distribution.

http://jakarta.apache.org/builds/jakarta-ant/release/v1.4.1/src/
: The source distribution corresponding to the current binary distribution.†

* The Apache Software License can be found at *http://www.apache.org/licenses/LICENSE/*.

† The very latest Ant source code is available from a publicly accessible CVS repository. Retrieving the latest source code is useful if you need recently committed bug fixes and features, or wish to see a complete history of changes to files comprising Ant. See Ant's web site for detailed instructions on how to access the repository. Be warned that no one guarantees the latest source code to run or even compile!

For earlier releases of Ant, merely substitute 1.1, 1.2, or 1.3 for the version number in these URLs.

Each directory contains *.tar.gz* files for Unix users, *.zip* files for Windows users, *.asc* files, and a *.jar* file. The *.asc* files contain PGP signatures, useful for determining the authenticity of the distributions. Usually, you can safely ignore these files. The *jakarta-ant-1.4.1-optional.jar* file contains Ant's optional tasks, and is described later in this chapter. We recommend that you download this file.

Installation

Regardless of platform, downloading Ant is the first step to installing the software. The files can be downloaded to a temporary directory and then uncompressed to any desired directory. After the download step, the process differs depending on whether you've downloaded the binary distribution or the source distribution.

Windows users should avoid directories with spaces such as "Program Files," as this can cause problems with the provided batch files.

The Ant documentation warns against installing Ant's JAR files in Java's *lib/ext* directory.* If you do, you are likely to encounter class-loading problems with some Ant tasks. Instead, you should leave Ant's JAR files in the Ant distribution directory.

Ant does not provide an installation program; it runs from wherever you choose to copy the files and directories. Table 2-1 lists the directories that ultimately get created under your main Ant directory.

Table 2-1. Directories provided with Ant

Directory	Description
bin	Batch files, Perl scripts, and shell scripts for running Ant.
docs	Ant documentation.
lib	Libraries required by Ant to run.
src	Source code for Ant. Provided only in the source distribution.[a]

[a] Prior to Ant 1.3, source code was included with the binary distribution.

* Java's *lib/ext* directory is intended for Java "Optional Packages," which extend the functionality of the core Java platform. The documentation included with Sun's JDK explains this in detail.

Binary Installation

We will cover the binary installation first, which should suffice for most users. The term "binary" just means that everything is compiled and packaged into JAR files for easy execution—you don't need to compile Ant from source. The source distribution, covered later in this chapter, must be compiled before it is usable.

Installation of the binary distribution is broken down into the following quick steps:

1. Unzip (or untar) the distribution to the desired directory.
2. Set the `ANT_HOME` environment variable to point to this location.
3. Set the `JAVA_HOME` environment variable to point to the JDK location.
4. Add `ANT_HOME`*/bin* to your system's `PATH` environment variable.

Because of filename limitations, the Unix distribution must be expanded using a GNU-compatible version of *tar*; the *tar* utility included with Solaris and Mac OS/X will not work. GNU tar is available at *http://www.gnu.org/software/tar/tar.html*. Under OS X, you can use the *gnutar* command. The command to expand the Ant 1.4.1 distribution is:

```
tar xzvf jakarta-ant-1.4.1-bin.tar.gz
```

Once installed, type **ant -version** to verify that Ant is located in the path. If this works, it is a good indication that Ant is installed properly. You should see output like this:

```
Ant version 1.4.1 compiled on October 11 2001
```

Like other Apache Java tools, Ant depends on a few key environment variables. When you run the *ant* command, you are actually running a shell script or batch file found in the `ANT_HOME`*/bin* directory. This is why the PATH environment variable must include that directory.

The *ant* script uses the `ANT_HOME` and `JAVA_HOME` environment variables to configure the `CLASSPATH` used by the JVM running Ant. If these variables are not set, the startup script attempts to infer the correct values, subject to operating system limitations. On Windows NT/2000/XP, for example, *ant.bat* uses the `%~dp0` batch file variable to determine its containing directory. It then defaults `ANT_HOME` to the parent directory if necessary. This trick does not work on Windows 9x because `%~dp0` is not supported. Properly setting `ANT_HOME` and `JAVA_HOME` is the best way to avoid problems. (Along with the `CLASSPATH` considerations, which are discussed later in this chapter.)

The binary distributions of Ant Versions 1.1 and 1.2 (but not later) include source code, which is useful for tracking down bugs and learning how to write tasks. Those binary distributions do not, however, include the buildfiles and scripts that are necessary to build Ant. For those, you must download the source distribution as described shortly. However, before we go on to that, optional tasks deserve mention.

Optional Tasks Installation

When downloading Ant, be sure to also download and install the *optional tasks* JAR file. This is found in the binary distribution directory on the Ant web site. In Versions 1.1 and 1.2, it is named *optional.jar*. For Versions 1.3 and 1.4.1, it has been renamed to *jakarta-ant-1.3-optional.jar* and *jakarta-ant-1.4.1-optional.jar*, respectively. To install, download the appropriate optional tasks JAR file and copy it to your `ANT_HOME/lib` directory.

In many cases, optional tasks require additional libraries and programs to function. For instance, the `junit` task requires *junit.jar*,* which you must copy to `ANT_HOME/lib` or add to your `CLASSPATH` environment variable prior to running Ant. In some cases, Apache cannot distribute these libraries due to licensing restrictions. Other tasks may be marked as optional because they deal with specialized tools that fewer numbers of people use or are proprietary. There are numerous helpful optional tasks that most development teams end up using, however, so installing the optional tasks JAR file is a good step to follow.†

Source Installation

Installing the Ant source distribution requires a little more work than installing the binary distribution. As expected, downloading and uncompressing the distribution is the first step. You generally want to place the source files in a directory separate from any existing Ant installations. Next, ensure that `JAVA_HOME` points to the JDK distribution. As with the binary installation, you should also set `ANT_HOME` and update your `PATH`.

Preparing optional tasks

You must now decide which optional tasks you care to compile. Ant will try to compile all of the optional tasks, but omits those that do not compile. In order for an optional task to compile successfully, you must add required JAR files to the `CLASSPATH` or copy them to Ant's *lib* directory. Once you've done that, you can proceed with the build. Again, the Ant documentation for each optional task indicates which libraries are required.

* The Ant optional tasks JAR file contains `org.apache.tools.ant.taskdefs.optional.junit.JUnitTask` in this particular case, which implements the task itself. `JUnitTask`, in turn, has dependencies on files found in *`junit.jar`*, which is distributed separately from Ant.

† For an up-to-date list of optional task JAR file requirements, refer to the user manual included with the Ant distribution. Search for the "Installing Ant" section, then search for the "Library Dependencies" heading.

Building the Ant binaries

You're now ready to compile Ant. If you are using Ant 1.3 or 1.4.1, type the following command from the source distribution directory:

```
build -Ddist.dir=destination_directory dist (Windows)
build.sh -Ddist.dir=destination_directory dist (Unix)
```

The *build* script creates a complete binary distribution of Ant in the specified destination directory. When omitted, `dist.dir` defaults to `build`.

Unless you have installed all of the optional task JAR files, you will probably see a lot of warnings about missing imports and classes. These can be safely ignored unless, of course, you need to build and use those optional tasks. Here is an example error message, shown when *bsf.jar* (required by the `script` task) is not included in the `CLASSPATH`:

```
C:\ant1.4.1src\src\main\org\apache\tools\ant\taskdefs\optional\Script.java:56:
Package com.ibm.bsf not found in import.
import com.ibm.bsf.*;
```

If you don't want to use the `script` task, then you don't need to build it, and this warning is nothing to worry about. However, if you do wish to build and use the `script` task, you'll need to place the JAR file for the *com.ibm.bsf* package into your `CLASSPATH` (or into Ant's *lib* directory) and redo the build.

If you wish to install directly to `ANT_HOME`, the following alternate command line is available:

```
build install (Windows)
build.sh install (Unix)
```

This approach works only when `ANT_HOME` is set, and should be used with caution. When using the *install* option, `ANT_HOME` is always used as the destination, even if you specify *-Ddist.dir*. Using the *install* option is not a particularly safe approach if `ANT_HOME` points to your existing Ant installation, because your existing installation will then be overwritten by the new build. If you overwrite your current build, you won't be able to easily fall back if the new build doesn't work.

Avoiding JavaDoc generation

Generating JavaDoc documentation is quite time-consuming. You can avoid JavaDoc generation by using either the *dist-lite* or *install-lite* options in place of the *dist* or *install* options, respectively. Other than avoiding the JavaDoc generation, these operate identically to their counterparts. Avoiding JavaDoc results in a faster build, and is useful if you are making changes to Ant and do not wish to wait for the JavaDoc generation.

Building Ant 1.2

Under Ant 1.3 and 1.4.1, the *build* script automatically "bootstraps" Ant, meaning that it first creates a minimal build of Ant. It then uses this minimal Ant build in order to finish the remainder of the build process. Parameters passed to the *build* script are passed to the Ant buildfile. For Ant 1.2, you must manually bootstrap Ant by typing the following command first:

```
bootstrap (Windows)
bootstrap.sh (Unix)
```

Once this is complete, you may proceed with the *build* script using a slightly different system property name:

```
build -Dant.dist.dir=destination_directory dist (Windows)
build.sh -Dant.dist.dir=destination_directory dist (Unix)
```

Unlike Ant 1.3 and 1.4.1, the destination directory defaults to *../build* instead of *build*. You can also use the *install* option to copy the build results to ANT_HOME, with the same caveat that any existing installation will be overwritten. Once Ant is built, it behaves the same as if you had downloaded the binary distribution.

Windows Installation Issues

Ant is a relatively nonintrusive application. It does not alter the Windows registry in any way, relying instead on environment variables and batch files as described earlier.

Setting environment variables

If you have administrative rights to your machine, you can set the ANT_HOME, JAVA_HOME, and PATH environment variables using the System Properties applet, found under the System icon on the Control Panel. Otherwise, you can create a simple batch file that sets these variables. One such file is shown in Example 2-1.

Example 2-1. Batch file to configure Ant environment

```
@echo off
REM This batch file configures the environment to use Ant 1.4.1

set ANT_HOME=C:\ant\ant_1.4.1
set JAVA_HOME=C:\java\jdk1.4
set PATH=%ANT_HOME%\bin;%PATH%
```

While a batch file like this works, you can improve on this approach. Its main drawback is the fact that you must manually execute the file before executing Ant. While we could add code to the end of our batch file that directly executes Ant, it is probably a lot easier to directly edit *ant.bat*, which is included with the Ant distribution. As an added bonus, *ant.bat* already accounts for many differences between Windows 9x and Windows NT/2000/XP.

Editing *ant.bat* is rarely required unless you do not have sufficient access rights to set environment variables using the Windows Control Panel.

If you choose to modify *ant.bat*, simply hardcode the three environment variables at the beginning of the batch file. You may also wish to copy the batch file to a new location that is already on the system path, making it possible to type *ant* from any command prompt. This avoids the need to have `%ANT_HOME%/bin` in your system path.

Avoiding CLASSPATH problems

You may want to edit *ant.bat* for a totally different reason. By default, this batch file builds an environment variable called `LOCALCLASSPATH` containing all the JAR files in the `ANT_HOME/lib` directory. It then appends the current system `CLASSPATH` to the `LOCALCLASSPATH`, and passes the resulting path to the Java process running Ant. The command that invokes Java looks something like this:

```
java -classpath %LOCALCLASSPATH% ...
```

Ant's use of the current system `CLASSPATH` is particularly troublesome for multiperson development projects, because each individual may have a different system `CLASSPATH`. A build that works successfully for one developer may fail for another, simply because his `CLASSPATH` is different. If this is an issue for your project, you can edit the following line in *ant.bat*:*

```
set LOCALCLASSPATH=%CLASSPATH%
```

Simply change it to this:

```
set LOCALCLASSPATH=
```

This way, the system `CLASSPATH` of the current user is not visible to Ant. This is fine, because Ant finds its own JAR files by looking in the `ANT_HOME/lib` directory. If your project requires additional JAR files and directories in its `CLASSPATH`, you should list those in your buildfiles rather than relying on users to set up the `CLASSPATH` before running Ant. See the `<path>` portion of Example 4-1 for an example of this technique.

Under Ant 1.2, Windows NT/2000/XP users may also wish to add *setlocal* and *endlocal* commands to the beginning and end of *ant.bat*. This ensures that any environment variables set in the batch file are only scoped within the context of the batch file.

Customizing Ant 1.3 and 1.4.1

Beginning with Ant 1.3, *ant.bat* includes the *setlocal* and *endlocal* commands if running on Windows NT, 2000, or XP. It also adds a new capability that allows you to

* Ant 1.1 and 1.2 scripts include quotes around `%CLASSPATH%`.

execute one batch file at the beginning of *ant.bat*, and another at the end. These are useful if you wish to configure some environment variables just before running Ant, and then restore them to old values after Ant runs.

Before running Ant, *ant.bat* searches for a file named `%HOME%\antrc_pre.bat`. If this file exists, it is executed before anything else happens. This is your hook for setting up your environment just before Ant runs. At the end of the build process, *ant.bat* searches for `%HOME%\antrc_post.bat`, executing it if found. This is your hook for restoring everything back to its initial state.

Ant does not ship with either of these batch files, and it is unlikely that the `HOME` environment variable is set. If you want to use these files, you must create them and then configure `HOME` to point to the directory containing them. Once this is done, however, both batch files are automatically executed when *ant.bat* runs.

One environment variable you may wish to set is `ANT_OPTS`. The value of this variable is passed as a JVM argument. Specifying system properties is a common use. In this simple example, we pass the *log.dir* system property to the JVM running Ant:

```
$ set ANT_OPTS=-Dlog.dir=C:\logs
$ ant run
```

Now this property is available within the buildfile, for instance:

```
<echo>Log directory is set to: ${log.dir}</echo>
```

If the buildfile runs a Java application, the property may be retrieved from within it as follows:

```
String logDir = System.getProperty("log.dir");
```

Setting the maximum heap size is another common use of `ANT_OPTS`. Here is how we set the maximum size to 128 MB when using Sun's JDK:

```
set ANT_OPTS=-Xmx128m
```

And finally, you may specify a value for the `JAVACMD` environment variable. This defaults to `%JAVA_HOME%\bin\java`, typically invoking the JVM provided in Sun's Java Development Kit. Ant provides `JAVACMD` for those who wish to specify an alternate JVM.

Unix Installation Issues

Ant provides a Bourne-shell script called *ant* that works very similarly to the Windows *ant.bat* batch file. Just like its Windows counterpart, *ant* utilizes the same set of environment variables: `ANT_HOME`, `JAVA_HOME`, `CLASSPATH`, `ANT_OPTS`, and `JAVACMD`. Each works the same under Unix as under Windows.

Unlike on Windows, Ant does not have a set of pre- and post-execution files on Unix. Under Unix, you have only the option of executing a command file when Ant starts. If *ant* finds a file named *.antrc* in the current user's home directory, that file is executed before any other part of the *ant* shell script. And this is your hook for customizing environment variables used by Ant. Here is an excerpt from the *ant* shell script showing the code used to invoke *.antrc*:

```
#! /bin/sh
if [ -f $HOME/.antrc ] ; then
  . $HOME/.antrc
fi
```

Because Unix is a multiuser operating system, Ant is commonly installed in a shared directory for system-wide use. For instance, the Ant distribution may be installed in */opt*, and the *ant* Bourne-shell script may be installed in */opt/bin*. (Sometimes */usr/local* and */usr/local/bin* are used instead) Such an installation almost certainly requires a system administrator; however, it does make it easy to configure Ant for a group of developers.

As with the Windows batch file, the Unix shell script also passes the current system CLASSPATH to the Ant process. You may wish to remove references to CLASSPATH, thus ensuring that every developer builds with the same configuration. Reiterating the point made earlier in this chapter, your buildfiles should define the CLASSPATH, rather than relying on users to set their own CLASSPATH before running Ant.

In case you prefer to use Perl or Python, Ant also includes *runant.pl* and *runant.py*, which perform the same tasks as the Unix and Windows scripts.

Configuration

Once Ant is installed properly, it requires very little additional configuration. Provided the *ant.bat* batch file (or *ant* shell script) is installed in a directory that is included in your system path, you should be able to run Ant from any command prompt.

You do not technically have to use the provided *ant* or *ant.bat* script to run Ant. You can run Ant manually, as long as the following items are configured:*

- The system CLASSPATH includes *ant.jar* and any JAXP-compliant XML parser.
- For JDK 1.1, *classes.zip* must be added to the CLASSPATH. For Java 2, *tools.jar* must be added. This is necessary for tasks like `javac`.
- Many tasks require that the `ant.home` Java system property be set to the Ant installation directory. This is accomplished by launching the JVM with the *-D* flag, as shown shortly.
- JAR files for optional tasks must be added to the CLASSPATH.

* Setting these items is exactly what *ant.bat* and *ant* do.

Provided that these items are all set properly, you can use the following command to invoke Ant:*

```
java -Dant.home=pathToAnt org.apache.tools.ant.Main
```

Understanding how to set up and run Ant manually might be useful if you are making customizations to Ant and wish to run it using your IDE's debugger.

XML Issues

Early versions of Ant (prior to Version 1.4) include Sun's Java API for XML Parsing (JAXP) Version 1.0. Ant Versions 1.4 and later ship with JAXP 1.1, as described in the next paragraph. JAXP is an API allowing Java programs to use XML parsers from different vendors in a portable way. The JAXP JAR files, *jaxp.jar* and *parser.jar*, are found in `ANT_HOME/lib`. These, along with any other JAR files found in this directory, are automatically added (by *ant* or *ant.bat*) to the `CLASSPATH` used by Ant. *jaxp.jar* contains the JAXP API, while *parser.jar* is an XML parser implementation from Sun.

If you require DOM Level 2† or SAX 2.0‡ XML support, then JAXP 1.0 is insufficient. For this level of XML, you should upgrade Ant to support JAXP 1.1,§ available at *http://java.sun.com/xml/*. This won't affect you if you are using Ant 1.4 or later, since it ships with JAXP 1.1. Since JAXP 1.1 is backwards compatible with JAXP 1.0, you can safely replace the *jaxp.jar* and *parser.jar* files in your `ANT_HOME/lib` directory with *jaxp.jar* and *crimson.jar* from the JAXP 1.1 distribution. If you prefer a different JAXP-compliant XML parser, such as Apache's Xerces (*http://xml.apache.org*), you can substitute its JAR file in place of *crimson.jar*.

Support for XSL Transformations (XSLT) is another feature of JAXP 1.1. Ant supports XSLT via the `style` task, which can utilize any JAXP 1.1-compliant XSLT processor. Just like the XML parser, your XSLT processor's JAR file must be copied to `ANT_HOME/lib` or added to the `CLASSPATH`. The JAXP 1.1 distribution includes Apache's *xalan.jar*, or you can select a different processor.

As a final note, Sun released J2SE 1.4 in February, 2002. This version of Java includes JAXP 1.1, an XML parser, and an XSLT processor. Since these are now a core part of Java, they get loaded by the "bootstrap" class loader. This means that the corresponding XML libraries in `ANT_HOME/lib` are not even used when you are running under J2SE 1.4. To install updated XML support under J2SE 1.4, see the

* Or you can specify the `CLASSPATH` using the *-classpath* command-line option.

† Document Object Model, at *http://www.w3.org/DOM/*

‡ Simple API for XML, at *http://www.saxproject.org/*

§ As of JAXP 1.1, the acronym now stands for "Java API for XML Processing."

"Endorsed Standards" documentation at *http://java.sun.com/j2se/1.4/docs/guide/standards/*.

XML parsers and XSLT processors are rapidly improving. Although installing *jaxp.jar*, *crimson.jar*, and *xalan.jar* from Sun's reference implementation of JAXP 1.1 is the easiest route to XML and XSLT functionality, you should investigate newer XML parsers and XSLT processors for optimal performance.

Proxy Configuration

Ant network tasks, such as `get`, require a network connection in order to operate. For dial-up users, this means the modem must be dialed up and connected before such tasks can run. Many corporate users, however, will run Ant from within a company firewall. If this is the case, you must often configure the JVM to use a proxy server before you can reach remote computers.

This is easily accomplished by setting the `proxySet`, `proxyHost`, and `proxyPort` JVM system properties. You can set these properties by either modifying Ant's startup script, or by using the `ANT_OPTS` environment variable. The following example shows the Windows commands to specify these properties using `ANT_OPTS`, and then to invoke Ant:

```
set ANT_OPTS=-DproxySet=true -DproxyHost=localhost -DproxyPort=80
ant mytarget
```

The same trick works on Unix, although the syntax is slightly different depending on which shell you use:

```
$ export ANT_OPTS="-DproxySet=true -DproxyHost=localhost -DproxyPort=80"
$ ant mytarget
```

You can issue the command to set `ANT_OPTS` from the command line, from *antrc_pre.bat* (Windows), or from *.antrc* (Unix).

CHAPTER 3
The Buildfile

Building projects with Ant requires you to focus on two things: project organization and the Ant buildfile. Rather than distinct focal points, these subjects are two sides of the same coin; they are closely related and any decision made in the design of one affects the design and implementation of the other. In this chapter, we show how to design a project using Ant to manage the build process, and how to write a buildfile for that project. As we go through the sample project, we explain how we arrive at particular design decisions for the layout of the project, as well as for the various parts of the buildfile. Not every project can fit the model we present, but many can; we hope this exercise will prepare you for writing buildfiles in other development projects.

Before we begin, however, you should understand the features of the buildfile itself. The buildfile is the most important aspect of Ant, and many details need explaining. Your understanding of the buildfile's use of XML is essential. With this, you will be better equipped to examine the major parts of a buildfile. To that end, we'll begin our discussion in this chapter with a look at the reasons behind Ant's use of XML. Then we'll take the sample project and its corresponding layout and define our build requirements. These elements come together and create our example buildfile.

With the buildfile written, we can examine how Ant reads the buildfile and executes the steps defined within it. You can see how the flexibility of Ant results in a complex process. We explain the process so you can use this knowledge in not only writing buildfiles, but also when extending Ant—for example, with a user-written task. Last, we cover some of Ant's oddities, talk about what's missing, and discuss how to work around some of the resulting issues. So, let's get on with it!

Why XML?

Rather than being defined in terms of *dependencies*, a model other build tools use, Java projects are best described in terms of *packages* and *components*, thus closely following the package and object model of the Java language. No current build tool did this when Ant was first developed, and the idea comes from the need for something better for Java than the existing build tools of the time. Because Sun provides a Java library for its tools, which gives users programmatic access to the Java compiler, the *jar* tool, and so on, the best language choice for a new Java project build engine is Java. With a plan and a language, the only thing left for Ant's designer, James Duncan Davidson, to do was to choose the buildfile descriptor syntax.

James had several requirements in mind for the buildfile syntax. First, the syntax should be simple so new users could easily pick it up. Next, it should have available (read: free) Java libraries so the new Java-based build engine would be easy to implement and maintain. Of utmost importance was the concept that writing a new engine shouldn't require writing a new syntax parser—an existing library was crucial. Another design goal was the ability to express a build structure that was a hierarchical tree. And the syntax should be capable of simultaneously describing builds in terms of components and packages and as operations. Let's look at why XML satisfies these requirements.

Developers understand XML since they use it in many areas of Java development, such as Enterprise Java Beans (EJB), Java Server Pages (JSP's), and with data transports such as Simple Object Access Protocol (SOAP). Outside of the Java world, XML finds equally great acceptance, giving Ant a wide potential user base. XML's parser and model libraries are freely available as Java libraries. Documentation is not a problem; there are hundreds of books, magazines, and web sites dedicated to XML technology. As a general-purpose description language, XML fits the complex use-case requirements set forth earlier. It can describe operations, data types, data values, and project layout. These attributes of XML map closely to Ant's design requirements. XML is the best choice for Ant.

Ant Building Blocks

With XML elements and tags, we can look at the primary components of an Ant buildfile as components or building blocks. We build the buildfile using these blocks. Some pieces have very specialized uses, while others are more common and used more frequently. Let's look at the primary components of the Ant buildfile.

The Project

We call the set of tags and elements in an XML file from the root element—in this case `<project>`—to the lowest-nested tag, the *document object model* (or DOM). The first or *root element* of any buildfile is always the `<project>` tag. No buildfile can be without one, nor can it have more than one. The DOM lays elements out in a tree-like hierarchy, making the buildfile more of an object model than simply a plain process-description document. The following example shows a valid project tag:

```
<project name="MyProject" default="all" basedir=".">
...
</project>
```

The <project> tag has three attributes: name, default, and basedir. The name attribute gives the project a name. A project name is valuable for purposes of identifying log output (to know what project you're building). For systems that manage buildfiles, such as an IDE that can read buildfiles, the project name acts like an identifier for the buildfile. The default attribute refers to a target name within the buildfile. If you run Ant without specifying a target on the command line, Ant executes the default target. If the default target doesn't exist, Ant returns an error. While we do not recommend it, the value of default does not have to be a valid target name (i.e., a name corresponding to an actual target name in the buildfile). We suggest either making the default target compile everything or display help for using the buildfile. The basedir attribute defines the root directory of a project. Typically, it is ".", the directory in which the buildfile resides, regardless of the directory you're in when you run Ant. However, basedir can also define different points of reference. For example, a buildfile that is part of a hierarchical project structure needs a different reference point, referring to the project's root directory. You can use the basedir to specify this point of reference.

Targets

Targets map directly to the broad goals set forth in a build's requirements specification. For example, compiling the latest source code for the package *org.jarkarta* and placing it into a JAR is a broad goal and, thus, would be a target in a buildfile. Targets consist of tasks that do the actual work of accomplishing the target goal.

The following target compiles a set of files and packages them into a JAR called *finallib.jar*.

```
<target name="build-lib">
    <javac srcdir="${src.ejb.dir}:${src.java.dir}"
           destdir="${build.dir}"
           debug="on"
           deprecation="on"
           includes="**/*.java"
           excludes="${global.exclude}">
       <classpath>
         <pathelement location="."/>
         <pathelement location="${lib.dir}/somelib.jar"/>
       </classpath>
    </javac>
    <jar jarfile="${dist}/lib/finallib.jar" basedir="${build.dir}"/>
</target>
```

If necessary, targets can be more fine-grained, as in the following example, which contains one target to compile the source code, and another to package the JAR file:

```
<target name="build-lib">
    <javac srcdir="${src.ejb.dir}:${src.java.dir}"
           destdir="${build.dir}"
           debug="on"
```

```
                deprecation="on"
                includes="**/*.java"
                excludes="${global.exclude}">
            <classpath path="${classpath.compile}" />
        </javac>
    </target>

    <target name="package-lib">
        <jar jarfile="${dist}/lib/lib.jar" basedir="${build.dir}"/>
    </target>
```

Such granularity may be required, for example, if the failure of one task (e.g., a task that compiles source code) should not stop the execution of another, related task (e.g., a task building the JAR). In this example, the library JAR builds regardless of the compilation target's success.

In general, it is better that targets are coarse-grained operations. Tasks solve fine-grained goals better than targets. While not every attempt at writing a buildfile will follow the model we are showing, if you at least attempt to maintain a consistent granularity in your targets, you will be much better off in the end. Haphazardly writing buildfiles means more work in the future for you, since everyone on your project team will look to you, the original buildfile author, for guidance as new functions and build goals complicate the project. Your goal should be to create something requiring little modification, if any, and this effort begins with target design.

Tasks

Tasks are the smallest building blocks of a buildfile and solve the more granular goals of a build. They perform the actual work, compiling source code, packaging classes, retrieving file revisions from CVS, or copying files and/or directories. Rather than provide a direct conduit to the underlying shell like some other build tools, Ant wraps all operations into task definitions, each correlating to a Java object within Ant's object model. There are no tasks in Ant that do not have a corresponding object. Contrast this to shells that not only can run executable programs (a similar pattern to Ant's task objects), but also have commands that do not correspond to executables—for example, the Win32 shell's *dir* command. The "every task is an object" architecture provides Ant with its flexible extensibility, which we discuss later in Chapters 5 and 6.

The following task example uses the copy task to copy all the files (and subdirectories) from *jsp* in the project's *www* source directory to the *jsp* directory in the system's WebLogic installation. The "/" path separator works in Windows and Unix, which is one of Ant's benefits:

```
<copy todir="${weblogic.dir}/${weblogic.server.home}/public_html/jsp">
  <fileset dir="${src.www.dir}/jsp"/>
</copy>
```

Tasks can do pretty much anything their implementers design them to do. You could even write a task that deleted the buildfile and all the directories in the project. It would not be useful (at least we don't think it would be) but nothing in Ant stops you from doing this.

While tasks, both as Java objects and as XML tags, follow an object hierarchy, these hierarchies are not related. For instance, you cannot look at a `copy` task and imply that, since it has nested `<fileset>` elements, the `Fileset` object is a subclass of the `Copy` object. Conversely, although the `Jar` object extends from the `Zip` object, this does not imply that a `<jar>` tag can nest within a `<zip>` tag.

Data Elements

Data elements are probably the most confusing aspects of Ant. Part variable, part abstract data type, these elements represent data rather than represent a task to be performed. Data elements fall into two categories: properties and DataTypes. To avoid confusion, let's clarify some terminology used in this chapter and throughout the rest of the book:

property
: A name-value pair represented by the `<property/>` tag in a buildfile.

DataType
: A class of elements that represent complex sets of data. Examples include `fileset` and `path`.

data element
: This term encompasses both properties and DataTypes.

In Chapter 4, we go into more detail as to how Ant's DataTypes work and how you can use them in your buildfiles.

Properties

Properties are the simpler of the two data elements. They represent nothing more than name-value pairs of string data. No other data type besides a string can be associated with a property. As a bonus for Java programmers, properties relate, indirectly, to the `Property` object found in the Java SDK. This means that you can dynamically define properties at build time, using such things as property files or JVM command-line property settings.

The following are some examples of properties being set in a buildfile using the `<property>` tag. The first two elements set one property to a given value, and the third `<property>` element loads a properties file. The code looks for the properties file inside the directory designated by the `<project>` element's `basedir` attribute.

```
<property name="my.first.property" value="ignore me"/>
<property name="my.second.property" value="a longer, space-filled string"/>
<property file="user.properties"/>
```

Reference properties, or more precisely, their values, by using the `${<property-name>}` syntax, as in the following example.

```
<property name="property.one" value="one"/>
<property name="property.two" value="${property.one}:two"/>
```

In the section "Project-Level Data Elements and Tasks" later in this chapter, we describe how Ant uses properties and how they fit in the processing scheme.

An upside of properties, as opposed to DataTypes, is that their values are type-agnostic (i.e., they're always strings. What does this mean? Take, for example, a property representing a directory name. The property doesn't know its value is a directory and it doesn't care if the directory actually exists. This is great if you need to represent the names of temporary build directories that exist only during the build process. However, properties are not always the ideal data element for paths; sometimes, you may want more control over defining a path. For this, you can use a DataType.

DataTypes

Paths and file lists are cumbersome and error-prone as property definitions. For example, say your project has a library directory containing 25 JARs. Represent those using a path string, and you'll end up with a very long property definition, such as the following:

```
<property name="classpath" value="${lib.dir}/j2ee.jar:${lib.dir}/activation.jar:
${lib.dir}/servlet.jar:${lib.dir}/jasper.jar:${lib.dir}/crimson.jar:${lib.dir}/jaxp.
jar"/>
```

Adding and removing JARs to and from your library means you have to add and remove them to and from this path string. There is a better way. You can use a `fileset` DataType instead of one long path string in a property. For example:

```
<path id="classpath">
        <fileset dir="${lib.dir}">
            <include name="j2ee.jar"/>
            <include name="activation.jar"/>
            <include name="servlet.jar"/>
            ...
        </fileset>
  </path>
```

Even better, since all your JARs are under the same directory, you can use wildcard characters and specify only one `<include>` pattern. (Properties cannot use patterns.) For example:

```
  <path id="classpath">
        <fileset dir="${lib.dir}">
            <include name="**/*.jar"/>
        </fileset>
  </path>
```

This is much easier! Aside from the obvious typing savings, the use of the `fileset` DataType has another advantage over the use of the `property` tag. Regardless of whether there are 2 or 25 JARs in the project's library directory, the `fileset` DataType (shown in the most recent example) will set the `classpath` to represent them all. On the other hand, you still need to change a path-property value, adding or changing JAR filenames, every time you add or change a JAR.

Some DataTypes, but not all, can be defined at the "project level" of a buildfile DOM, meaning they are nested within the `<project>` element. This capability is inherent to Ant and you cannot change it, unless you want to maintain your own version of Ant. Refer to Chapter 4 for more information on DataTypes, and Chapters 7 and 8 for details as to how particular tasks use DataTypes.

An Example Project and Buildfile

To provide an example buildfile for this book, we need an example project. We use a project that already exists as a GNU Make–based project called irssibot, an IRC bot* written by Matti Dahlbom (the original can be found at *http://dreamland.tky.hut.fi/IrssiBot*). This project requires all the features of a typical build: compiling source code, packaging classes, cleaning directories, and deploying the application. As an exercise, we took this project and converted it to use Ant.

Understanding the Project Structure

Let's begin by looking at how we configure the directories for the irssibot project. Java project organization methods vary—sometimes considerably so—depending on the project (e.g., web applications have very different project structures from GUI tools). Many times, the tools dictate a project's structure. Some IDE's, for example VisualAge versions prior to 3.5, require that all source code is in one file. EJB and CORBA compilers require naming conventions for source files and directories. For all cases, the project model should fit the requirements of your revision control system (you use a revision control system, right?). Because of such varied requirements and dependencies, a perfect project organizational pattern does not exist and we do not propose to suggest one here. The layout and organization we describe, however, is simple enough to work with many projects, and it works especially well with Ant.

Designing and implementing a project structure is not a trivial task, so do not assign and dedicate less than an hour of work to it and think you will do a good job. It's not just hard, it's tedious. Most Java programs have cross-platform capabilities, and you

* IRC, or Internet Relay Chat, consists of a series of servers that allow users to communicate in real-time using IRC clients. People communicate, or "chat," in channels. Frequently, these channels have "bots," or automated IRC clients that manage the channel and keep it open. Otherwise, if no one is in a channel, it goes away. Irssibot is an example of such a bot.

may be thinking of how to organize projects with this goal in mind. Traditionally, this thinking applies to working across operating systems and/or hardware configurations. However, in development teams, a different platform also means changes as small as toolset differences between heterogeneous workstations. Clean separation of functionality, the ability to be self-contained, and the lack of outside requirements should all be goals for Java projects. The benefits of working out such a structure for your project will not be immediately apparent, but as more developers use your build system, and as functionality is added to your project, you'll be glad you thought ahead. It is much easier to change the buildfile than it is to change an established project with 45 directories and 1,000 classes.

The directories in Figure 3-1 illustrate the directory and file structure we devised to meet the goals just discussed for the example project.

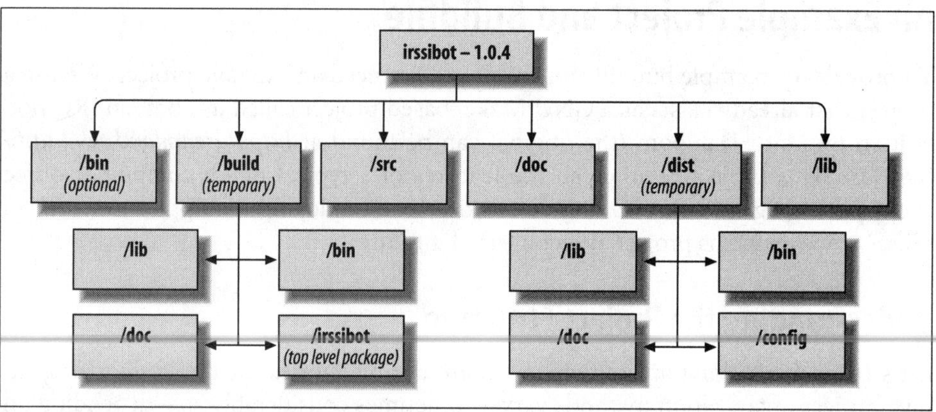

Figure 3-1. irssibot directory structure

Let's begin from the top by talking about *build.xml*, which is the buildfile.* Placing the buildfile in the project's root directory provides us with the ability to use relative paths for project directory definitions in data elements and properties. Avoid the use of absolute paths since it breaks the distributable property of your project. Our Java source package roots begin in the */src* directory. This setup allows us to separate the source from the resulting class files.

The class files are placed in */build*. Sometimes (but not with our project) it is necessary to break the classes apart into groups—for example, into a library and the application. You should make this separation below the */src* and */build* directories, leaving the root directory alone. For one thing, this cuts down on clutter in your project's root directory. On a more technical note, proper segregation makes file manipulation easier on a broad scale. When you delete the */build* directory, for example, you

* Reminder: *build.xml* is the default buildfile name. If you invoke Ant without specifying a buildfile on the command line, Ant will assume the buildfile name is *build.xml*.

delete all of the compiled classes. This method remains valid no matter how much you break down your project. You can always add targets and tasks to handle the more specific details, but you cannot always change the project layout.

JARs and directories of a libraries' classes that are not built as part of the project are in the */lib* directory. Redistributing libraries can be a tricky endeavor, but don't ignore this issue. You may assume that you can explain which libraries are necessary and where to get them in some README file, leaving everything up to the developer. Try to avoid this!* Developers probably have every version of a library known to man stored somewhere on their system because of other projects they work with. You'll never be able to predict what they have. Redistributing the libraries that you *know* work with your project helps these developers. They'll have fewer problems running your application on their machines because you've given them the proper libraries. Redistributing the libraries increases the size of your application package, but the benefits are worth the extra pain.

We put the application's scripts (whether they are installation or execution scripts) in the */bin* directory. The example project provides scripts that run the IRC bot for Windows (*bot.bat*) and Unix (via a Bourne Shell script, *bot.sh*). Sometimes, projects have hard-to-find or custom executables necessary to build the project. These belong in */bin*, also. While relying upon executables may be your easiest option for performing functions not supported by current Ant tasks, consider writing a custom task instead since executables usually eliminate the cross-platform capabilities of Ant.

As for documentation, we place non-JavaDoc documentation in the */doc* directory. This may include READMEs for the project, end-user documentation, and documentation for the included libraries. Basically, any documentation the build cannot generate.

The */dist* directory is where we distribute the finished product. Nonarchive class packages, JARs, WARs, EARs, and TARs, among other files, go here. Under the */dist* directory, we have a *lib* directory (*/dist/lib*) for JARs and other package files needed by the newly built application. There is a *dist/doc* directory for both the distributed documentation and generated javadoc, if necessary. The *dist/bin* directory is for scripts and executables that make running the application easier. A distribution directory facilitates installations since, in most cases, installation is as simple as copying the files from */dist* to some other named location on the filesystem.

Designing and Writing the Example Buildfile

Now that we have our directory structure, let's design and write the buildfile for our example project. To better illustrate the relationship between project goals and parts of the buildfile, we display the resulting buildfile syntax after defining and describing

* This is not a hard and fast rule, but it works more often than not. Even large projects like Tomcat and JBoss ship with libraries normally available elsewhere.

a particular goal. It is almost always better to describe and design your build first before you begin writing the buildfile.

One method to designing and implementing a buildfile for the project is via a set of questions. The answers to these questions make up the various parts of the buildfile, and together constitute the complete solution. Following are the questions, in no particular order:

- How does the buildfile begin?
- What properties and DataTypes should we define for use throughout the build?
- What directories need to be created before any compiling or packaging goals?
- What constitutes the complete program? What about libraries? What about scripts for installation or execution? What about static and generated documentation?
- How do we rebuild the project after changing files? Do we need to delete all of the class files? Do we delete generated JARs?
- What directories need to be created prior to preparing the application for distribution? Do we need to distribute the source as well as the application? What constitutes an application distribution?

In day-to-day work, you are likely to come up with many more questions during your own brainstorming sessions. You should expect this since many questions relate directly to a project's particulars. For instance, you would never ask about building EJBs for this project, but you may for your own. It is much easier to whittle away functionality and scope during the initial project analysis phase than it is to find out that you need to add a particular function or step later on. Therefore, do not be afraid to add questions. You can always combine questions or eliminate them later. Now, let's answer the questions we *did* ask, and get on with writing a properly organized buildfile.

The project descriptor

Our first question is:

- How does the buildfile begin?

All buildfiles begin with a *project descriptor*, which specifies such things as the project name, the default buildfile target, and the project base directory. We call the project "irssibot." The default target is `all`; we'll write that target later in such a way that it compiles the application and bundles it into a JAR file. The current working directory for the project is the base directory of the buildfile, represented by ".". The `<?xml?>` tag is standard for XML files, and is used by the XML parser libraries, not by Ant itself. It should be the first line in the buildfile, and should contain no trailing spaces.

```
<?xml version="1.0"?>

<!-- Comments are just as important in buildfiles, do not -->
<!-- avoid writing them! -->
```

```
<!-- Example build file for "Ant: The Definitive Guide" -->
<!-- and its sample project: irssibot                   -->

  <project name="irssibot" default="all" basedir=".">
```

Global values

The next question we consider is the following:

- What properties and DataTypes should we define for use throughout the build?

The project directories all extend from the root project directory. Thus, all of the directory-related data elements should be relative. We define a property for every major subdirectory and name it accordingly to reflect its use. Doing this provides a single location in the buildfile where changes can be made if directory names change.

```
<!-- Project-wide settings.  All directories are relative to the -->
<!-- project root directory -->

<!-- Project directories -->
<property name="src.dir" value="src"/>
<property name="doc.dir" value="doc"/>
<property name="dist.dir" value="dist"/>
<property name="lib.dir" value="lib"/>
<property name="bin.dir" value="bin"/>

<!-- Temporary build directory names -->
<property name="build.dir" value="build"/>
<property name="build.classes" value="${build.dir}/classes"/>
<property name="build.doc" value="${build.dir}/doc"/>
<property name="build.lib" value="${build.dir}/lib"/>
```

Aside from globally defining directory names, properties are also good for globally defining values for some tasks. Here, we define a global property telling the `javac` task whether to produce bytecode with debug pointers. All instances of the `javac` task use this property.

```
<!-- Global settings -->
<property name="javac.debug" value="on"/>
```

The next property we set is `build.compiler`. The value here, `modern`, means that `javac` uses the latest version of the Sun compiler available in the Java SDK toolkit (i.e., Java SDK Versions 1.3 and higher). This is a "magic property," and some of the negative side effects of these are discussed later in this chapter. Even though it's likely you'll use this value in every buildfile you write, it still makes sense to document its purpose. Many people new to Ant will be understandably confused if they see this property here, but never see it used in the buildfile again.

```
<!-- Global "magic" property for <javac> -->
<property name="build.compiler" value="modern"/>
```

We have one last step before we delve into defining (and meeting) our project's major goals. The irrsibot project ships with a set of libraries, *mysql.jar* and *xerces.jar*. We define a globally available classpath that includes these libraries and any future ones we (or another developer) may add later. The file set and include pattern ('**/*.jar') means that all files in the library directory (*lib/*) and its subdirectories should form a path suitable for use with path-compatible tasks,* such as javac.

```
<path id="classpath">
  <fileset dir="${lib.dir}">
      <include name="**/*.jar"/>
  </fileset>
</path>
```

Directory creation

Now we need to answer the question:

- What directories need to be created before any compiling or packaging goals?

For our project, the compile-related directory (in which Ant saves all compiled classes) is the build directory, build, and its subdirectories, if any. We will define a preparation target to create the build directory.

Furthermore, we add a little bit to this preparation step and timestamp the build, which is most useful with automated, unattended builds.

```
<!-- Target to create the build directories prior to a compile target -->
<!-- We also mark the start time of the build, for the log. -->
<target name="prepare">
   <mkdir dir="${build.dir}"/>
   <mkdir dir="${build.lib}"/>
   <mkdir dir="${build.classes}"/>
   <mkdir dir="${build.classes}/modules"/>

   <tstamp/>

   <echo message="${TSTAMP}"/>
</target>
```

Compiling

To compile our project, we need to answer a number of questions:

- What constitutes the complete program?
- What about libraries?
- What about scripts for installation or execution?
- What about static and generated documentation?

* A *path-compatible task* is capable of operating on a set of directories or files rather than on one directory or file. These tasks typically correspond to tools that exhibit the same behavior, such as javac or rm.

We tackle these questions with one target for each. The term "complete program" can mean many things. For most projects, including ours, the answer is simple. The complete application consists of all the compiled classes, the scripts to execute the application, and the program's configuration file.

First, we compile the application and bundle it neatly into a JAR. In some cases, you may want to separate the compilation and JAR'ing steps. To keep things simple, we made this one target in our example.

```
<!-- Build the IRC bot application -->
<target name="bot" depends="prepare">
    <!-- Compile the application classes, not the module classes -->
    <javac destdir="${build.classes}"
           debug="${debug.flag}"
           deprecation="on">
      <!-- We could have used javac's srcdir attribute -->
      <src path="${src.dir}"/>
      <exclude name="irssibot/modules/**"/>
      <classpath refid="classpath"/>
    </javac>
    <!-- Package the application into a JAR -->
    <jar jarfile="${build.lib}/irssibot.jar"
         basedir="${build.classes}" >
      <exclude name="irssibot/modules/**"/>
    </jar>
</target>
```

The irssibot application also consists of a set of modules that extend the functionality of the bot. Separating the class files between modules and application classes makes updating the application a bit easier. In the future, it is more likely that developers will modify and add modules rather than modify parts of the main application. By separating the packages, we give developers the ability to update only the class files that need updating. We compile and package the modules as a separate JAR.

```
<!-- Build the IRC bot modules -->
<target name="modules" depends="prepare,bot">
    <!-- Compile just the module classes -->
    <javac destdir="${build.classes}/modules"
           debug="${debug.flag}"
           deprecation="on" >
      <!-- We could have used javac's srcdir attribute -->
      <src path="${src.dir}"/>
      <include name="irssibot/modules/**"/>
      <classpath refid="classpath"/>
    </javac>

    <!-- Bundle the modules as a JAR -->
    <jar jarfile="${build.lib}/irssimodules.jar"
         basedir="${build.classes}/modules" >
      <include name="irssibot/modules/**"/>
    </jar>
</target>
```

The irssibot scripts require no processing during a build, so we provide no target to process them. The same goes for the configuration files. Even though we do not write a target for making changes to or packaging the scripts and configuration files, it is still important to consider these files for the future. In your own builds, such consideration may change the implementations of other targets.

When we started all this, we mentioned the default target for the buildfile called `all`. This is simply a target that uses Ant's dependency mechanism to force both the `bot` and `modules` targets to run, building the application. Ant executes the `all` target if you invoke *ant* with no arguments. All we need to write for `all` is the following:

```
<target name="all" depends="bot,modules"/>
```

In your own buildfiles, you don't always need to have a target like `all`. Another option is to provide a default target that does nothing. Our suggestion is to write a help target (you should have one even if it won't be your default). If users invoke *ant* with no arguments, they'll be presented with your buildfile's help documentation. For example, you might display something like the following:

```
Build the foo application with Ant. Targets include:
     full - build the entire application and its libraries
     app - build just the application (no libraries)
     lib - build just the libraries (no application)
     install - install the application. Read README for details
     help - display this information
```

If you're familiar with "usage statements" from console programs, you have some idea of what we're talking about. We show an example of a buildfile target that creates a usage statement in Appendix B.

The last part of our current question, relating to documentation, requires a target that produces JavaDoc for the project. JavaDoc is a tricky concept to manage in a project. The JavaDoc tool cannot process code that cannot compile. In addition, compared to compilation steps, JavaDoc processing is very slow. It is not something you would want your developers to have to wait on for every build. Consider these issues when writing your own JavaDoc targets.

```
<!-- Generate the API documentation irssibot and the -->
<!-- modules -->
<target name="javadoc" depends="bot">
  <mkdir dir="${doc.dir}/api"/>
  <javadoc packagenames="irssibot.*"
           sourcepath="${src.dir}"
           destdir="${doc.dir}/api"
           author="true"
           version="true"
           use="true" >
    <classpath refid="classpath"/>
  </javadoc>
</target>
```

Cleanup

One or more cleanup targets are sometimes necessary as a result of asking the following questions:

- How do we rebuild the project after changing files?
- Do we need to delete all of the class files?
- Do we delete the generated JARs?

Developers sometimes forget to clean up after themselves. This can be a problem since Java compilers' dependency checkers are not the best at determining every dependency between classes. Furthermore, to do its own dependency checking, the `javac` task performs timestamp checks on the compiled class files versus their corresponding source code files. While effective in most cases, timestamp checks are not perfect. Classes with no dependencies,* classes with static finals, and other special cases can result in successful builds (from Ant's standpoint) even though the compilation steps overlook some classes. Because of this, developers should always have the ability to delete everything generated by the build process and start the build fresh. Only then can you guarantee that everything that needed to be compiled was compiled. We call this a *clean build.*

The following example defines two targets that can be used to ensure clean builds:

```
<!-- Delete class files built during previous builds.  Leave directories -->
<target name="clean">
    <delete>
      <fileset dir="${build.classes}" includes="**/*.class"/>
    </delete>

</target>

<!-- Delete any created directories and their contents -->
<target name="cleanall" depends="clean">
    <delete dir="${build.dir}"/>
    <delete dir="${dist.dir}"/>
    <delete dir="${doc.dir}/api"/>
</target>
```

In these targets, we present two different clean build solutions for the irssibot build. The `clean` target deletes the class files, a step that should be sufficient to guarantee a successful dependency check during the compilation step. The `cleanall` target deletes everything generated by previous builds—in effect, returning the project to a state in which no builds seem to have taken place.

* This is a big issue when building Ant itself, since Ant calls most of its classes using introspection; no direct dependencies exist to any of the tasks.

In our example, cleanall doesn't need to depend on clean. However, in practice, the clean target may do more than just delete files. In this case, we want Ant to process it during a cleanall. To be safe, it's good practice to include the dependency by default.

Sometimes, it may be necessary to include a distribution clean target in a project buildfile. A distribution clean deletes all generated files, directories, and all of the source code. While this may sound crazy (in a way, it is), it is most useful for projects under revision control. *Hence, if your project isn't under revision control, don't delete the source code!* Theoretically, it should be possible to distribute a project as just a buildfile with targets to retrieve or update the source code from a revision control system such as CVS.* For our example, we do not provide a distribution clean target because irssibot is not under revision control.

Distribution

The final thing we need to worry about when writing a buildfile for the example project is how to distribute that project. We need to answer the following questions:

- What directories need to be created prior to preparing the application for distribution?
- Do we need to distribute the source as well as the application?
- What constitutes an application distribution?

We can achieve the goals for these questions by defining just one target. Our directory layout for the project provides us with the desired end result. The distribution directories already exist—all that is left is for the build to copy files to those directories. The following target creates the distribution directories and copies the class files, scripts, and other components of the final application:

```
<!-- Deploy the application in a "ready-to-run" state -->
<target name="deploy" depends="bot,javadoc">
    <!-- Create the distribution directory -->
    <mkdir dir="${dist.dir}"/>
    <mkdir dir="${dist.dir}/bin"/>
    <mkdir dir="${dist.dir}/lib"/>
    <mkdir dir="${dist.dir}/doc"/>
    <mkdir dir="${dist.dir}/config"/>

    <!-- Copy the primary program and modules -->
    <copy todir="${dist.dir}/lib">
      <fileset dir="${build.classes}"/>
      <fileset dir="${build.lib}" includes="irssibot.jar"/>
      <fileset dir="${build.lib}" includes="irssimodules.jar"/>
```

* This is *really* convenient if you have stringent bandwidth restrictions on your distribution servers, but not on your CVS servers.

```
        <fileset dir="${lib.dir}" includes="*.jar"/>
      </copy>

      <!-- Copy the documentation -->
      <copy todir="${dist.dir}/doc">
        <fileset dir="${doc.dir}"/>
      </copy>

      <!-- Copy the pre-fab configuration files -->
      <copy todir="${dist.dir}/config">
        <fileset dir="${lib.dir}" includes="*.xml"/>
      </copy>

      <!-- Copy the running scripts -->
      <copy todir="${dist.dir}/bin">
        <fileset dir="${bin.dir}" includes="bot.sh"/>
        <fileset dir="${bin.dir}" includes="bot.bat"/>
      </copy>
    </target>
```

Notice that we place target dependencies on the `bot` and `javadoc` targets. We're simply requiring that the application is up-to-date before we deploy it. Of all the targets, `deploy` makes the most use of Ant's `filesets` since the target's tasks do a lot of file operations. Each `fileset` attempts to group only the files we want to deploy. Look, for example, at the task that copies the configuration files:

```
       <!-- Copy the pre-fab configuration files -->
      <copy todir="${dist.dir}/config">
        <fileset dir="${lib.dir}" includes="*.xml"/>
      </copy>
```

This task copies only XML files. Everything else in the configuration directory (denoted by `${lib.dir}`) is left alone.

Example 3-1 shows the complete buildfile.

Example 3-1. Complete buildfile for the irssibot project

```
<?xml version="1.0"?>

<!-- Comments are just as important in buildfiles, do not -->
<!-- avoid writing them! -->
<!-- Example build file for "Ant: The Definitive Guide" -->

<project name="irssibot" default="all" basedir=".">

    <!-- Project-wide settings.  All directories are relative to the -->
    <!-- project directories -->
    <property name="src.dir" value="src"/>
    <property name="doc.dir" value="doc"/>
    <property name="dist.dir" value="dist"/>
    <property name="lib.dir" value="lib"/>
    <property name="bin.dir" value="bin"/>
```

Example 3-1. Complete buildfile for the irssibot project (continued)

```
<!-- Build directories -->
<property name="build.dir" value="build"/>
<property name="build.classes" value="${build.dir}/classes"/>
<property name="build.doc" value="${build.dir}/doc"/>
<property name="build.lib" value="${build.dir}/lib"/>

<!-- Global settings -->
<property name="debug.flag" value="on"/>
<property name="java.lib" value="${java.home}/jre/lib/rt.jar"/>

<!-- Global property for <javac> -->
<property name="build.compiler" value="modern"/>

<path id="classpath">
    <fileset dir="${lib.dir}">
        <include name="**/*.jar"/>
    </fileset>
</path>

<target name="prepare">
  <mkdir dir="${build.dir}"/>
  <mkdir dir="${build.lib}"/>

  <tstamp/>

   <echo message="${TSTAMP}"/>
</target>

<target name="all" depends="bot,modules"/>

<!-- Build the IRC bot application -->
<target name="bot" depends="prepare">
    <mkdir dir="${build.classes}"/>
    <javac destdir="${build.classes}"
           debug="${debug.flag}"
           deprecation="on">
      <!-- We could have used javac's srcdir attribute -->
      <src path="${src.dir}"/>
      <exclude name="irssibot/modules/**"/>
      <classpath refid="classpath"/>
    </javac>
    <jar jarfile="${build.lib}/irssibot.jar"
         basedir="${build.classes}" >
      <exclude name="irssibot/modules/**"/>
    </jar>
</target>

<!-- Build the IRC bot modules -->
<target name="modules" depends="prepare,bot">
    <mkdir dir="${build.classes}/modules"/>
    <javac destdir="${build.classes}/modules"
           debug="${debug.flag}"
```

Example 3-1. Complete buildfile for the irssibot project (continued)

```
            deprecation="on" >
        <!-- We could have used javac's srcdir attribute -->
        <src path="${src.dir}"/>
        <include name="irssibot/modules/**"/>
        <classpath refid="classpath"/>
      </javac>
      <jar jarfile="${build.lib}/irssimodules.jar"
           basedir="${build.classes}/modules"
            manifest="MANIFEST.MF" >
         <manifest>
            <attribute name="ModuleType" value="irssibot"/>
         </manifest>
        <include name="irssibot/modules/**"/>
      </jar>
    </target>

    <!-- Deploy the application in a "ready-to-run" state -->
    <target name="deploy" depends="bot,javadoc">
      <!-- Create the distribution directory -->
      <mkdir dir="${dist.dir}"/>
      <mkdir dir="${dist.dir}/bin"/>
      <mkdir dir="${dist.dir}/lib"/>
      <mkdir dir="${dist.dir}/doc"/>
      <mkdir dir="${dist.dir}/config"/>

      <!-- Copy the primary program and modules -->
      <copy todir="${dist.dir}/lib">
        <fileset dir="${build.classes}"/>
        <fileset dir="${build.lib}" includes="irssibot.jar"/>
        <fileset dir="${build.lib}" includes="irssimodules.jar"/>
        <fileset dir="${lib.dir}" includes="*.jar"/>
      </copy>

      <!-- Copy the documentation -->
      <copy todir="${dist.dir}/doc">
        <fileset dir="${doc.dir}"/>
      </copy>

      <!-- Copy the pre-fab configuration files -->
      <copy todir="${dist.dir}/config">
        <fileset dir="${lib.dir}" includes="*.xml"/>
      </copy>

      <!-- Copy the running scripts -->
      <copy todir="${dist.dir}/bin">
        <fileset dir="${bin.dir}" includes="bot.sh"/>
        <fileset dir="${bin.dir}" includes="bot.bat"/>
      </copy>
    </target>

    <!-- Generate the API documentation for the IRC library and the -->
    <!-- IRC bot using the library -->
```

Example 3-1. Complete buildfile for the irssibot project (continued)

```
    <target name="javadoc" depends="bot">
      <mkdir dir="${doc.dir}/api"/>
      <javadoc packagenames="irssibot.*"
               sourcepath="${src.dir}"
               destdir="${doc.dir}/api"
               classpath="${lib.dir}/xerces.jar:${lib.dir}/mysql.jar"
               author="true"
               version="true"
               use="true" />
    </target>

    <!-- Delete class files built during previous builds.  Leave directories -->
    <target name="clean">
        <delete>
          <fileset dir="${build.classes}" includes="**/*.class"/>
        </delete>
        <delete dir="${doc.dir}/api"/>

    </target>

    <!-- Delete any created directories and their contents -->
    <target name="cleanall" depends="clean">
        <delete dir="${build.dir}"/>
        <delete dir="${dist.dir}"/>
        <delete dir="${doc.dir}/api"/>
    </target>

</project>
```

The Buildfile Execution Process

We have the buildfile, but what happens when Ant runs? Understanding how Ant parses the buildfile and executes the targets is key to writing good, solid buildfiles.

Error Handling

Ant interprets the buildfile's XML, meaning that it processes the elements as it parses them. The XML library that Ant uses represents a hierarchal tree structure; Ant follows this tree's path during processing. At the *project level*, the level of XML just inside the `<project>` element, Ant does a breadth-first traversal of the XML elements. This means that it loads and processes all of the elements just below the level of the `<project>` element first, and then moves on to the first target. Inside a target, Ant does a depth-first traversal. This means that, starting with a target's first element, Ant processes each element as deep as it can before it moves on to the next element.

Understanding this design is most important when trying to understand how Ant processes its own errors (as opposed to errors from bad compilation or failed file copies). At the project level, Ant does a kind of syntax check before it actually processes any elements. In general, when speaking of Ant processing an element, we mean that Ant goes through the full processing life cycle on that element. Assuming a syntactically correct element declaration, the processing appears to be atomic from the outside; you cannot insert any operations between the time Ant parses the element and when Ant performs the operations that form the basis of the element's definition. Errors, however, occur within two distinct phases during the processing of an element, and understanding these phases alleviates some frustration.

Project-level errors

At the project level, Ant loads all of the elements in the buildfile. It processes every element type except targets. This means any project-level tasks or DataTypes are processed. Processing a target means running the tasks and DataTypes within that target. You do not want Ant to execute all targets when it loads the buildfile. Instead, think of Ant as making a list of targets for future use. The list consists only of target names and attributes, and any invalid values in these particular items cause Ant to fail.

With project-level tasks and DataTypes, errors occur as you might expect. Errors in reading a DataType's element or executing the DataType's operations are build errors, and Ant handles them as such. If Ant discovers a particular element it does not "expect" (e.g., it finds `<notatag/>` as a subelement of `<project>`), this is an error, and the build stops and fails. With all of these errors, keep one very important fact in mind: *by default, Ant breaks at the first error*. There can be 100 attribute and elements errors in the buildfile, and Ant still discovers them one by one (and so do you), with every execution. Furthermore, Ant has no concept of "rollback," so errors break the build immediately with possibly dire consequences. There is nothing to catch, and there is no chance to clean up. You must extend Ant using a listener to have any impact on controlling errors. For these reasons, be careful when you write a buildfile, and be extremely careful editing a *working* buildfile for a stable project. Syntax and processing errors can leave your project in an undefined state, requiring you (or worse, your developers) to do a full rebuild. This can waste valuable time if your build is a long one.

Target-level errors

Errors at the target level have repercussions similar to those at the project level, except that the times at which these errors occur can differ slightly. Rather than load every element nested within a `<target>` element (thus, creating a list like Ant's target list), Ant loads and processes each element one by one. This, of course, makes their order important. If Ant makes it to the second element, Ant considers the operations from the first element successful. Ant considers data, file, or project states associated or created by the completed element to be successful as well. Conversely, when an error occurs in a project-level task or DataType, Ant considers the elements that follow it to be unknown.

Error-handling examples

Let's illustrate the error processing concepts just discussed with a few, invalid buildfiles. We'll look at the following buildfile as a start:

```
<project name="mybad" basedir="." default="all">
    <property naame="oblivion" value="nil"/>
    <notarealtag/>
</project>
```

What will happen if Ant processes this buildfile? Because property is a project-level DataType, the invalid attribute naame causes Ant to fail when it tries to call the setter method associated with the naame attribute and finds none. Ant doesn't display any messages about the <notarealtag/> element because Ant stops when the first failure occurs. Note as well that the buildfile has no all target, even though we set the <project> element's default attribute to all. Once you fix the first two problems (the invalid attribute naame and the invalid <notarealtag/>), a third run results in an error stating there is no all target. Ant (and you) discovers each error *one at a time*.

Following is another erroneous buildfile, based on the earlier example:

```
<project name="mybad" basedir="." default="all">
    <target name="all">
       <notarealtag/>
    </target>
    <property naame="oblivion" value="nil"/>
</project>
```

What happens when Ant process this buildfile? We moved the property DataType to follow the newly added default target, all. Does Ant see the invalid tag before it sees the invalid attribute on the property DataType? No. At the target level, Ant thinks all is well with the all target and moves headlong into the invalid attribute error. Of course, once you fix the attribute error, Ant gladly informs you it cannot process <notarealtag/>.

Modifying the previous examples, we'll correct the attribute and target errors. Additionally, we add a new target, chaos, containing the invalid element, <notarealtag/>. Here is the resulting code snippet:

```
<project name="mybad" basedir="." default="all">
    <property name="oblivion" value="nul"/>
    <target name="all">
        <echo message="Hello there, all you happy people."/>
    </target>
    <target name="chaos">
        <notarealtag/>
    </target>
</project>
```

What does Ant do now? Ant displays the message we instruct it to: "Hello there, all you happy people." There are no errors. Surprised? Unless you make chaos a dependency of the all target, or call the chaos target directly from the command line, Ant misses the error within the chaos target. This is an example of what we call a *festering error*. Errors like this go unnoticed over long periods of time and rear their ugly heads at inopportune moments. Prevent these festering errors by testing early and testing often.

This is how Ant handles and processes nonbuild related errors. Now that you know where errors can come from and how to avoid them, let's take a look at what Ant does when everything is okay.

Project-Level Data Elements and Tasks

Before Ant executes any targets, it takes care of all data elements and tasks defined at the project level. Of course, Ant also makes a list of the targets, as explained in the previous section, but that's not important right now.

There are very few project-level tasks and data elements. Introducing one requires many changes to the core Ant engine, so it's unlikely many will be added in the future. For now, consider the project-level elements to be: `property`, `path`, `taskdef`, `patternset`, `filterset`, `mapper`, and `target`.

In the case of our project example, project-level data elements consist of the properties that define directories, the global property for the `javac` task, and the compilation classpath as a `path` DataType. Ant processes all of these in the order they appear, making them globally available to the rest of the buildfile. Order, as it turns out, is *very* important for related properties.

Let's take a moment to talk about properties. Properties have two prominent characteristics. They are *immutable* and they always have global scope, regardless of where they're defined. Being immutable means a property's value cannot change once Ant processes the property's name-value pair for the first time. This is very important to keep in mind when designing your project and writing your buildfile. Many newcomers to Ant make the mistake of treating properties like variables in a script and expect them to behave as such. To add to the confusion, Ant allows properties to be redeclared, throwing no errors when you try to change the value. Ant defines an order of precedence for declaring properties. Properties declared on Ant's command line always take precedence over properties defined elsewhere. After that, Ant determines precedence based on when it first sees a property declared.

Immutability impacts how property values resolve. Let's use the following code example to illustrate:

```
<property name="property.one" value="${property.two}:one"/>
<property name="property.two" value="two"/>
```

What is the value of `property.one`? Because of Ant's ordered property resolution, the value is *${property.two}:one*, not *two:one*. Usually, you'll rely on this behavior when defining directories with increasing depths. It can be very disconcerting to suddenly discover that you're creating a directory called *${property.two}*. Remember that order counts, and you won't go wrong.

The other prominent property characteristic is properties are always global in scope. A property's global scope means it is a global variable. Look at the following buildfile segment:

```
<property name="prop1" value="one"/>

<target name="target1">
    <property name="prop2" value="two"/>
    <echo message="${prop1}:${prop2}"/>
</target>

<target name="target2" depends="target1">
    <echo message="${prop1}:${prop2}"/>
</target>
```

`target1` defines the property `prop2`. Because all properties are global in scope, `prop2` becomes available to the rest of the buildfile once Ant processes `target1`.

Cascading Buildfiles

Cascading buildfiles can change the rules of property immutability and scope. Developers sometimes use cascading buildfiles in large projects with many subprojects, and each subproject has its own buildfile. A master buildfile at the root of the project executes one or more of the subproject buildfiles to build parts of the project or the whole thing. Developers wanting to build individual subprojects run the buildfile in that subproject's directory and can effectively ignore the other subprojects in their day to day work (hence the reason for the design). A public example of such a project using cascading buildfiles is Jakarta's taglibs. In Appendix B, we provide a section on writing cascading buildfiles, as well as tips on how to manage the problems that the immutability (and possible mutability) of properties may present.

Targets

When you run *ant* with no arguments, Ant reads the `<project>` element and uses the `default` attribute to get the name of the first target to execute. In our example, that target is called `all`. The `all` target in turn has dependencies on the `bot` and `module` targets, meaning that Ant executes these targets before running anything inside of `all` (let's ignore, for the moment, that the `all` target contains no elements); and these targets must complete successfully in order for Ant to start processing `all`. Since there are no elements in our `all` target, the success of `bot` and `module` targets equates to the success of the `all` target.

The bot target

Since it is the first dependency in the list for the `all` target, the `bot` target runs first. The purpose of the `bot` target is to compile the application and then package it up into a JAR file. The `bot` target also has a dependency: the `prepare` target. The `prepare` target creates the temporary build directories needed by the compilation steps. The `mkdir` task it uses is usually successful, even if the directories `mkdir` is trying to create already exist. The `mkdir` task fails only if the I/O system throws an exception because of file permissions, space limitations, or some hardware or operating system error. In addition to creating directories, the `prepare` target also timestamps the build using the `tstamp` task. The `tstamp` task has no attributes and outputs nothing to the console or log. Instead, it sets properties that can be used later, primarily in echo tasks, but also in any other tasks requiring the date and time. See Chapter 7 for details on the `tstamp` task.

The `javac` task compiles the Java source code. Let us take a close look at the `javac` task, as it's defined in the `bot` target:

```
<javac destdir="${build.classes}"
       debug="${debug.flag}"
       deprecation="on">
  <src path="${src.dir}"/>
  <exclude name="irssibot/modules/**"/>
  <classpath refid="classpath"/>
</javac>
```

There are three required settings for every `javac` task:

- The source directory
- The classpath
- The destination directory

We specify the *source directory* (the place in which the Java source files are stored) with the `src` nested DataType.[*] We could have used the `srcdir` attribute, but chose instead to use a DataType for demonstration purposes. In practice, it is probably more common to see the `srcdir` attribute used. We specify the compiler's classpath in a similar manner, using the `classpath` DataType. This time, we use a reference ID to reference an earlier path definition. Earlier in the buildfile, we defined a classpath consisting of all the JARs in the */lib* project directory, and we gave it the reference ID `classpath`. To use that path later, as we do in the `javac` task, we declare a similar DataType having the attribute `refid`. We set `refid` to the reference ID of another DataType, defined earlier (the classpath `path` DataType). Ant manages the values of these DataTypes so that you can define a DataType once and reference it other

[*] Through a slight trick of introspective methods, the `javac` task class hides the fact that `<src>` is just a `<path>` element under a different name. There is no DataType called `src` available to other tasks, although other tasks can duplicate `javac`'s programming trick.

times. It's important to note that DataType references, unlike properties, work only within the same buildfile.*

As for the destination for the compiled classes, we use the `destdir` attribute to specify that information. Since the destination directory is always a single directory and not a collection of files or a directory path, we use an attribute and a property rather than a DataType.

So far, we've discussed the required settings for `javac`, but, if you notice, we also specify a couple of optional attributes and DataTypes. The optional attributes are `debug` and `deprecation`. The optional DataType is `exclude`.

Since we are still developing irssibot, it's likely we will try to run it within a debugger. This requires that the debug flag is on at compile time, and we denote this with the `debug` attribute of `javac`. Since we need this to be a global option, we use a property, set once at the beginning of the buildfile. Note that values of `yes|no` and `true|false` work for Boolean attributes such as `debug`.

By default, the various Java compilers do not provide detailed information concerning deprecated method calls.† Should irssibot use a deprecated method or field, the compiler notifies us only that we use deprecated calls in general. It does not tell us which method or even which class used the deprecated call. To get detailed information, we use `javac's` `deprecation` attribute and set it to "true" (or "yes").

To distinguish between module code and application code, the class package structure is separated into two subpackages, one being *modules*. We do not want these classes becoming part of the application JAR, so we use the `<excludes>` element to tell `javac` not to compile them. Our `<excludes>` element tells `javac` to exclude all files in its `fileset`—in this case, nondependent source code below the *modules* package directory.

All together, we tell `javac` to do the following:

- Compile the source code found in `${src.dir}`, excluding Java files in the *modules* package.
- Send newly built class files to the build directory, as defined by the `${build.dir}` property.
- Include debug information with the class files for use in a debugger.
- Present detailed deprecation error messages stating which classes and calls are deprecated.
- Cause the `bot` target to fail if any operation in `javac` fails.

* Ant 1.5, expected to be released after this book is published, will have a solution for referencing DataTypes across buildfile contexts.

† For more information on deprecated methods and fields, refer to *Java in a Nutshell*, by David Flanagan (O'Reilly).

Sit back and consider that with about 11 lines of XML, we define a step in a build that will always compile the correct Java files with the correct classpath, *no matter how many source files or libraries you add or remove in the future*. Unless the project's requirements (and not just the parameters) change, we will never have to modify this part of the buildfile again. If the requirements do change, then we rework our goals and modify the targets appropriately. This is expected. As an added bonus, XML's verbose and human-readable nature creates an easy-to-maintain build description file. Remember, a new goal means editing the buildfile, but minor project changes require no modifications. If you find yourself modifying your own buildfile frequently, try to take some time and refactor your build's design. The goal is to write the buildfile once and forget about it as much as possible.

Dependency checking

Even though the `javac` task specifies exclusions, you may notice the compiler compiling source code under the module subpackage. From a build perspective, we cannot avoid this if code in the application references code from the modules.* Per the Java compiler specification, the Java compiler is responsible for resolving all dependencies during compile-time. It performs dependency checks on a class-by-class basis as it compiles each class. In other words, if class A is dependent on classes B and C, then, when compiling A, the Java compiler must find compiled versions of B and C. If they do not exist, the compiler must find the source code for classes B and C and compile it before compiling class A.

The job of managing dependencies falls squarely on the shoulders of the developers creating their project's object model. Therefore, Java class dependencies and methods to manage them is a concept that is beyond the scope of this book. As it applies to working with Ant, dependency checking is an automatic behavior.

Packaging the class files

After Ant compiles the source files, which generate the class files, the `bot` target uses the `jar` task to package the class files into a JAR. We do this with only four more lines of XML:

```
<jar jarfile="${build.lib}/irssibot.jar"
     basedir="${build.classes}" >
  <exclude name="irssibot/modules/**"/>
</jar>
```

The `jar` task places all of the files from the *build.classes* directory, excluding those beneath the modules package directory, into a file called *irssibot.jar*.

* We could always write the code to make sure such circular dependencies do not exist. We chose this particular application because it exhibited this codependent behavior, allowing us to discuss it.

The module target

The `module` target is almost identical to the `bot` target. The `javac` and `jar` tasks use nearly the same attributes and DataTypes. The only difference is in what these DataTypes exclude from `javac` and `jar`. For the `bot` target, we explicitly exclude files from below the modules subpackage directory. In the case of the `module` target, we explicitly include files from the modules directories. Indirectly, we exclude all other files.

The result of including the files in the modules subpackage directory, and of our defacto exclusion of the other source files, is that our build produces two JARs with mutually exclusive sets of class files. This result meets our requirements set earlier, which state we need two packages: one for the application and one for the modules.

The `module` and `bot` targets are those that will run by default, because of the `all` target's dependency on them. The `all` target does not include dependencies on distribution, documentation, or cleanup, so Ant doesn't execute these targets unless the user explicitly requests it on the command line at runtime.

The Other Targets

In addition to the `bot` and `modules` targets used for compiling and packaging the irssibot project, our buildfile has targets for generating documentation, post-build cleanup, and for deployment.

The javadoc target

The `javadoc` target compiles the dynamically generated code documentation with the JavaDoc tool. The `javadoc` task operates similarly to the `javac` task. Both perform syntax checking on the Java code: `javac` as a precompile step and `javadoc` to guarantee that the documentation at least represents code that will compile. Most JavaDoc comes from the class, field, and method comments written by the developers, but some of it is dynamically generated; hence the reason why the code must compile.

For our target, we add the dynamic documentation to the existing documentation directory, *doc/*, under a separate directory called *api/*. This way, when the distribution target executes, we need only to package or copy what exists in the *doc/* directory. With the `javadoc` target, we also give the distribution target a dependency. This is helpful for distribution. It will make sure `javadoc` runs, giving us the latest code documentation, and fails if it can't create the most up-to-date documents. Of course, as we mentioned earlier, no other targets should be dependent on the `javadoc` target. The JavaDoc tool can take an extraordinary amount of time to complete—sometimes longer than the compile step itself.

Cleanup

Targets that clean the project directories are the most important targets of any build—even more important than the compilation targets. Why do we say this? Software development is a deterministic operation. Your project, no matter how simple or complex it may be, should run in a deterministic fashion. Your build is no different. At no point should you be unable to explain why a build performed at 8 a.m. is different than one performed at 9 a.m., given no other changes in the project. This deterministic behavior should be the very reason you're creating a build process in the first place.

Clean targets achieve this goal by giving you and your developers a sort of "reset switch." You can and should always be able to return the project to the state prior to compilation. We use two targets for this because there are, technically, two starting points. The first is the *fresh project*. This project state exists after you first download the *zip/tar/jar* or run a checkout from your revision control system. When projects get to be 700+ classes and cover multiple packages and subprojects, tracking all the changes you make can become very cumbersome. Having a build step that effectively resets the project for a developer is very important, almost essential. Without such a step, developers must reverse-engineer the build process to figure out all the changes made on their systems.

Deployment and installation

Deploying and installing Java projects can be a tricky endeavor. In fact, we suggest that, if you're just beginning to manage projects and write buildfiles, you hold off on writing installation targets until the project is in stable condition. If we were writing programs for one platform, say a RedHat distribution of Linux, we have an easy installation goal to solve. We make an RPM (the deploy step) and run some RPM commands (the install step). For Java developers, life is not this easy. Note, we have an entire chapter on installing and configuring Ant, and Ant distributes with an `install` target in its own buildfile. The catch with all installations is that you, the project manager, rarely know how other administrators and developers manage their own servers and workstations. The Ant project actually has it easy. It assumes only a JRE on the workstation and has scripts that should run on many platforms. Installation requires a root installation directory like */usr/local/ant* or *c:\ant* and everything is fine.

For irssibot, we took the tack of creating a distributable package for the `deploy` target, but leaving it up to the individual using the program to decide how to use the package installations. To keep things simple, we do not try to understand the structure of other workstations. You could say irssibot is self-contained; it does not attempt to do anything outside of its own project directory. We create a *dist/* directory, placing in it all of the JARs, documentation, and scripts that constitute the final program. As an exercise, you may consider writing an installation target similar to Ant's. You require some property to be set on the command line (the installation directory), and the target uses it to copy everything from the *dist/* directory to the installation directory.

So far, installation looks somewhat easy and you may be wondering why we omit such a target in our own project. The reason is because of the other portion of Java developers: the server-side developers. Up to the deploy step, our example touches upon all facets of Java development. For web applications or EJB applications, the `deploy` target builds the WARs and EARs. Of course, not all application servers support WARs and EARs (e.g., BEA's WebLogic 5.1 does not support EARs). Installation for these developers is very difficult and we do not want it to appear that it's an easy step. It's better if you make your build create a deployable set of directories and package files, then stop. From there, review how you're installing the application and see if you can move on.

AINASL: Ant Is Not a Scripting Language

After looking at the example project and buildfile, you may begin to look at Ant as a sort of scripting language for builds. With this bit of insight, you may charge forward writing buildfiles with this concept in mind...until the wheels fall off and you're stuck wondering why Ant can't do something you'd expect of any scripting language. Here's why they fell off: XML does not make for a good scripting language.

In a way, you're excused for seeing Ant as a sort of XML scripting language and accompanying parser. The difference is that, viewed as a scripting language, Ant is not very good. In fact, it's horrible. This little oddity of perception can cause a lot of confusion and frustration. Viewing the build as a design and not as a series of steps helps alleviate this confusion. We champion this authoring technique. So where does Ant's XML syntax fail as a scripting language?

Look Ma, No Data Structures!

A more concrete example of an oddity in Ant's syntax is its management of data. Here, the closest analogy to a language variable is the `<property>` tag. This, of course, completely ignores the rich data capabilities of XML, and Ant's developers know this. In addition to the `property`, there is the concept of an Ant data element—for example, the `path` DataType. The limitation is you cannot create DataTypes "in-language," as you can with a scripting language. Instead, you must write a class (or a set of classes) to represent a new data type in Ant; this is probably more effort than you are willing to put in for simply encapsulating groups of data values. If you're looking at Ant as an XML-based build scripting language and want to create your own data elements, you'll run into this dead-end fairly quickly.

So, how to avoid it? You can, of course, fix some of these shortcomings programmatically, but only if you're willing to make the effort of writing extensions and tasks for Ant. Alternatively, if you're not willing or not able to extend Ant programmatically, there's not much else you can do. Consider following the Ant mailing lists and reading the archives to find out more about the efforts Ant's developers are making to refactor this design limitation. The odds are good that refactoring will happen sooner rather than later. For instance, Ant developers introduced the concept of the `path`

DataType between two revisions of Ant, and within a six-month period (Ant 1.1 in April 2000 to Ant 1.2 in October 2000). Being an open source project means Ant's developers can move fast and refactor the project in a matter of months.

Where's the DTD?

If Ant's not a scripting language, and since it uses XML, we should be able to validate the buildfile when Ant parses it. Such validation requires a DTD. There are a few reasons we don't have this luxury.

Didn't you consider the description for runtime and parse-time processing to be very complex? This is because the internal processing design for Ant is complex. It's more out of necessity than from a purposeful design that Ant behaves this way. Because Ant uses a language with well-defined syntax rules, it must obey these rules at all times; it does this using existing XML libraries to load the buildfile. The buildfile is verified as "well-formed" when and as it is loaded. Read that statement again. Rather than validating the file in its entirety, Ant validates XML elements as it reads them. In addition, "syntactically correct" and "well-formed" are not synonyms. To be syntactically correct when loaded, the XML needs to have a corresponding DTD (or schema). It doesn't have one. It can't have one (more on this soon). To compensate for this, Ant iterates across the XML, parsing and executing only the elements it needs to execute, and checking the syntax along the way. This has the side benefit of making Ant faster, because if it attempted to do a full syntax check, especially on a large buildfile, Ant would be slow and, more than likely, a memory hog—well, a greater memory hog than it is now.

Without a DTD or schema, well-formed but syntactically incorrect XML can exist undiscovered for long periods. The problems intensify when the Jakarta team releases a new version of Ant. Consider an infrequently used target. Make a change to the target and test it with Ant 1.4.1. It works fine and everything is good. Usage patterns show that developers use the target once or twice a month, if ever. Three months later, the Jakarta group releases Ant Version 1.5, and now the task that worked in 1.4.1 has a new syntax. Because of its infrequent use, the target goes on without being regression tested. You'll discover that the task is broken only after a build failure far in the future.

Should there be a DTD? Technically, we can't have one. Because of the custom task model, Ant's buildfile DTD would change with each new task. A task to create a DTD exists (`antstructure`), but it only creates a DTD of the core task model. Furthermore, it is unaware of attributes that are required by tasks. As the Ant XML syntax settles down, many users have put in the effort to make their own DTD using `antstructure's` output as a starting point. Unfortunately, due to the earlier point about new tasks, no solution will ever be perfect. To verify your buildfile, test it and test it often.

Flow Control

When you first think of your build design, it's hard not to look at it in terms of a process flow. You may even use a flow chart to describe the various steps. Flow control requires two important features that are (mostly) missing from Ant: conditions and iteration.

Conditions allow us to change the flow of a build depending on values set at or during runtime. For example, you may want the build to run a specific target if another target fails. This level of general conditional control is missing from a normal release of Ant.* If a target fails, any targets that depend on it fail. There's nothing you can do to stop this aside from rewriting or redesigning the task to handle such error events. More likely, you'll need to write a different task that understands the specific conditions and executes the various build steps required under some conditional control. This is okay for simple tasks, but rewriting entire groups of tasks (e.g., two or three Java compilations, some file copying, and JAR'ing) is, understandably, too much effort.

Iteration, as it applies to a build, means to execute a task (such as compiling files), or a group of tasks multiple times, based on some condition or set of conditions. You probably think that without explicit conditionals in the Ant syntax, there can be no iteration. You're right. However, even if there is, we cannot tell Ant to execute a group of tasks across, say, a changing set of DataTypes. A common example of the need for iteration involves recursive file operations. Let's say you have a project with four subprojects. The only difference between each subproject is the name of the subproject's root directory. You want each subproject compiled and packaged, and you've laid the project directories out to do this in a very efficient manner (thanks to this book). As a good designer, you realize that you can re-use the target of one subproject for every subproject, changing only a few properties each time. As you ponder the solution, the wheels begin to fall off. Ant has no way to re-use targets like this. Begrudgingly, you cut and paste the target three times to represent each subproject, and you define each subproject explicitly. If you later remove or add a subproject, you have to edit the buildfile again. The same holds true if you use some form of cascading buildfiles. At some point, you have to define the subprojects explicitly, meaning something (maybe a properties file, an XML data file, or another buildfile) must be edited to make such a change complete.

Without the concept of custom tasks, Ant would be short-lived. You can perhaps solve the condition or iteration problem with an XML file, some XSLT, and some custom tasks, but it's still *your* solution, not Ant's. The buildfile you create is now not portable because you must distribute your Ant modifications with your buildfile. It's a minor annoyance, but an annoyance all the same. Short of extending Ant,

* Conditional tasks do exist, but we consider them experimental. Do not confuse conditonal tasks with flow control.

there's not much else you can do when it comes to these missing features. Your design, therefore, must consider these limitations so that you don't reach a dead-end and wind up seriously refactoring (or more likely, rewriting) your buildfile.

Buildfile Authoring Issues

The example buildfile we present in this chapter is simple compared to the capabilities Ant presents. Our goal is to show how to take a project, organize the files, and write a buildfile that makes life easier for the developers and project managers. The project and the steps we take are exaggerated and expanded to better demonstrate how we came to the decisions we make concerning the design of the project's organization and buildfile.

Beyond these first steps, your best path towards writing better buildfiles is experience. This includes both working with buildfiles and writing new ones. Most major open source Java applications now use Ant, giving you a virtual repository of best (and worst) practices. As an exercise, you may wish to take one of those buildfiles and, using this book as a reference, comment them, making note of what you think is happening and why.

The following issues have not yet been mentioned because they're more workarounds for Ant's shortcomings than buildfile design guidelines. Ideally, Ant's developers will refactor the design to eliminate the need for these workarounds.

Magic properties

Some properties are set but never explicitly used in any target or task. Ant's object model allows any build component to see all of a build's properties. The lack of an in-buildfile reference for these properties has led to their labeling as *magic properties*. A good example of a magic property is the `build.compiler` property for the `javac` task. No attribute exists for specifying the type of compiler the `javac` task uses. Instead, it relies upon the buildfile defining `build.compiler`. If a task uses a magic property, we specify this in the task definition provided in Appendix B.

When writing your own tasks, try to avoid using magic properties, as it makes the buildfile unreadable and hard to maintain.

When failure is success

Consider the following buildfile snippet:

```
<copy todir="newdir">
    <fileset dir="foo">
        <include name="**/*.xml"/>
    </fileset>
</copy>
```

This `copy` task element copies any XML files from *foo* to *newdir*, creating *newdir* if it doesn't exist. But what should happen if *foo* doesn't exist? Or what if there are no XML files?

What *does* happen, in the case of a nonexistent source directory (*foo* in our example), is that `copy` fails. In the case in which there are no files to copy, `copy` succeeds, but doesn't create a target (*newdir* in our case) directory. This behavior leads to an interesting problem: what if your build creates the *foo* directory and generates XML files only in special cases? In instances in which XML is not generated, do you want your entire build to fail when it hits the `copy` task? Yes? No? Maybe? Up until Ant 1.4.1, you couldn't control this. A workaround may be to create the *foo* directory manually in order to keep the task from failing. Beginning in Ant 1.4.1, `copy` has a `failonerror` attribute, allowing you to control its failure state. Using `failonerror`, you can cause Ant to consider a failed copy to still be successful.

The lesson is to be aware of what makes a task fail before you assume its behavior fits in your build's flow. You wouldn't want your 4 a.m. automatic build to fail, causing the loss of a day's worth of testing, because you misunderstood the failure states of a task.

If you get frustrated when designing your build and project layout, remember there is no one correct way to construct a project and write a buildfile. There will always be extenuating circumstances and unique requirements that prevent you from following layouts and patterns we present here and in other chapters. Furthermore, Ant is relatively young and bound to change, requiring you to change with it. Improvements to Ant, together with future custom-tasks, may make some techniques described in this book obsolete; not bad, mind you, just obsolete.

Use the layout of the sample project and the steps we followed as guides to help ensure you're not creating more work for yourself when you design and write your own buildfiles. Our process comes from observation and experience garnered from working with Ant since its first public release. You'll find many project layout and buildfile techniques duplicated in projects such as JBoss, Tomcat, and even Ant itself. This doesn't mean these project designs are the best—it just means that they're popular and have remained popular for quite a while.

CHAPTER 4

Ant DataTypes

In the previous chapter's buildfile example, you saw the `fileset` DataType being used to identify groups of files to copy in order to deploy the irssibot application. DataTypes are important when using Ant, and `fileset` is just one of the many available to you:

argument
: Passes command-line arguments to programs that you invoke from an Ant buildfile.

environment
: Specifies environment variables to pass to an external command or program that you execute from an Ant buildfile.

filelist
: Defines a named list of files that do not necessarily need to actually exist.

fileset
: Defines a named list of files that must actually exist.

patternset
: Groups a set of patterns together.

filterset
: Groups a set of filters together.

path
: Specifies paths (such as a classpath) in a way that is portable between operating systems.

mapper
: Defines a complex relationship between a set of input files and a set of output files.

Let's dig in and learn more about these fundamental Ant DataTypes. They are building blocks used by tasks and are essential to using Ant effectively. In this chapter, we'll talk about each DataType in detail. Before doing that, however, we discuss briefly how DataTypes fit into Ant's overall design, and explain the notation used in this chapter to describe the attributes for the different DataTypes.

DataTypes Defined

Ant DataTypes are found in the `org.apache.tools.ant.types` package, usually extending from the `org.apache.tools.ant.types.DataType` base class. `EnumeratedAttribute`, `Commandline`, `Environment`, and `Reference` are also treated as DataTypes, although they do not extend from `DataType`. Figure 4-1 contains a basic UML class diagram illustrating this aspect of Ant's design.

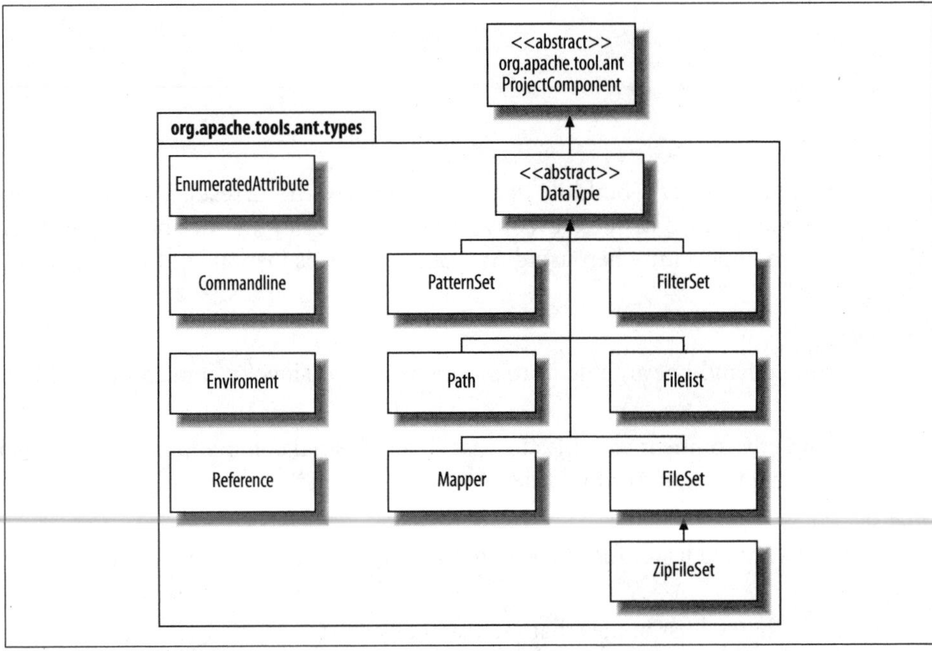

Figure 4-1. Ant DataTypes

The base class, `org.apache.tools.ant.ProjectComponent`, provides logging functionality as well as access to the `Project` object. Not shown here, `ProjectComponent` is also the base class for every Ant task. These tasks are detailed in Chapters 7 and 8.

While the class diagram helps to explain what DataTypes are, understanding the internal structure of Ant is rarely necessary. In most cases you simply want to write buildfiles and use Ant. For this reason, the remainder of this chapter focuses on how these types are used, rather than how their internal implementation works.

XML Attribute Conventions

DataTypes, like tasks, are defined using attributes. As we discuss each DataType in this chapter, we also list all the available attributes for it. These listings describe each attribute, specify which versions of Ant support it, and indicate whether it is required. The attribute listings take on the following form:

attribute_name (version, type, required_flag)
: Is a description of an attribute and its function.

In which:

attribute_name
: Is the name of the attribute. Use this to refer to the attribute when you specify it for a task.

version
: Indicates the version of Ant supporting this attribute. `"all"` means Ant Versions 1.2 and later.

type
: Indicates the type of data that an attribute can hold. For example, `String` indicates that an attribute holds textual data. See Table 4-1.

required_flag
: Indicates whether a given attribute is required when using the task. If this flag is a asterisk (*), then see the notes immediately following the list.

Description of attribute
: Is a description of the attribute and its function.

Table 4-1 summarizes the attribute types frequently referenced throughout this chapter. In all cases, text from XML attributes is converted into one of the basic types listed here. The "Description" column describes how each conversion happens. The "Implemented by" column lists the Java class that Ant uses to represent each of these attribute types.

Table 4-1. XML attribute type summary

Type name	Implemented by	Description
`boolean`	N/A	Performs a case-insensitive string comparison, converting `on`, `true`, and `yes` to `true`. All other values are `false`.
`Enum`	`org.apache.tools.ant.types.EnumeratedAttribute`	Used in cases in which a fixed set of string values are allowed.
`File`	`java.io.File`	Specifies the name of an individual file or directory. Unless stated otherwise, file and directory names are relative to the project base directory. `fileset` and `filelist`, described shortly, allow you to specify multiple files.
`int`, `long`, `etc...`	N/A	The standard Java type wrapper classes like `java.lang.Integer` handle conversion from text in the buildfile to primitive types.
`Path`	`org.apache.tools.ant.types.Path`	Most commonly used by `classpath` and `sourcepath` attributes, representing a list of paths separated by `:` or `;`. This is described in detail under "Path DataType."

Table 4-1. XML attribute type summary (continued)

Type name	Implemented by	Description
`Reference`	`org.apache.tools.ant.types.Reference`	Commonly used in `refid` attributes, and contains a reference to a type defined elsewhere. See the example for the `java` task in Chapter 7, which shows how to reference a classpath defined elsewhere in the buildfile.
`String`	`java.lang.String`	The most commonly used type in Ant. Strings (along with other attributes) are subject to XML attribute limitations. For instance, the < character must be written as `<`.

Argument DataType

The `apply`, `exec`, and `java` tasks accept nested `<arg>` elements, specifying command-line arguments for their respective process calls. The `org.apache.tools.ant.types.Commandline.Argument` class implements this DataType.* If several `<arg>` elements are specified, each is treated as a separate argument to the process call. Following is a list of all `<arg>` attributes:

`file` *(all, File,*)*
: A filename as a single argument. In the buildfile, this filename is relative to the current working directory. The "current working directory" varies depending on the context this type is used in. The name is converted to an absolute path when passed as an argument.

`line` *(all, String,*)*
: A space-delimited list of multiple arguments.

`path` *(all, Path, *)*
: A path, as explained later in the section "Path DataType."

`value` *(all, String, *)*
: A single command-line argument. Use this if your argument has spaces, but you still want to treat it as a single value.

Exactly one of these attributes is required.

Example

Let's look at a complete buildfile to put things into perspective. In Example 4-1, we use the `java` task to invoke Apache's Xalan XSLT processor, transforming an XML file into HTML using XSLT.† As you might expect, the `java` task invokes any Java class with a `main()` method. Use `<arg>` elements to pass arguments to the `java` task.

* `Argument` is treated as a DataType, although it does not extend from the `DataType` base class.

† The `style` task is normally used for XSLT transformations; see Chapter 7.

Example 4-1. <arg> usage

```
<?xml version="1.0"?>
<project name="arg demo" default="xslt" basedir=".">

  <property name="xalan.home" value="C:/java/xalan-j_2_1_0"/>
  <property name="xalan.jar" value="${xalan.home}/bin/xalan.jar"/>
  <property name="xerces.jar" value="${xalan.home}/bin/xerces.jar"/>

  <property name="xmldata" value="familyTree.xml"/>
  <property name="stylesheet" value="familyTree.xslt"/>
  <property name="result" value="Family Tree.html"/>

  <path id="project.class.path">
    <pathelement location="${xalan.jar}"/>
    <pathelement location="${xerces.jar}"/>
  </path>

  <target name="clean">
    <delete file="${result}"/>
  </target>

  <target name="xslt">
    <echo message="Transforming '${xmldata}' using '${stylesheet}'"/>

    <java fork="true" classname="org.apache.xalan.xslt.Process"
          failonerror="true">
      <arg line="-IN"/>
      <arg value="${xmldata}"/>
      <arg line="-XSL"/>
      <arg value="${stylesheet}"/>
      <arg line="-OUT"/>
      <arg value="${result}"/>
      <classpath refid="project.class.path"/>
    </java>

    <echo message="Success! See '${result}' for the output."/>
  </target>
</project>
```

We'll look at other interesting facets of this buildfile later in this chapter. For now, let's focus on the command-line arguments. Here is what the command line looks like if you invoke Xalan directly from a shell:

```
java org.apache.xalan.xslt.Process -IN familyTree.xml
        -XSL familyTree.xslt -OUT "Family Tree.html"
```

You are free to use as many <arg> tags as you want, and the arguments are passed to the command in the order in which they are listed in the buildfile. You can also mix and match usages of the various attributes for each <arg> tag. You might be wondering why we didn't specify all of the arguments at once, like this:

```
<arg line="-IN ${xmldata} -XSL ${stylesheet} -OUT ${result}"/>
```

The answer lies in the final argument, "Family Tree.html". In this example, the filename contains a space. Remember that the line attribute expects several space-delimited arguments, and will treat "Family Tree.html" as two arguments: "Family" and "Tree.html". Since we want to pass the entire filename as a single argument, space included, we must use the value attribute:

```
<arg value="${result}"/>
```

Since we defined each of our filenames as Ant properties, someone might change the XML and XSLT filenames to something else in the future. Since these names may also contain spaces, we chose to use the value attribute for all three filename arguments. We are able to use the line attribute for the "-IN", "-XSL", and "-OUT" arguments because they never contain spaces, although the value attribute would yield the same results in this case.

You may also be wondering why we use the value attribute instead of path for this example. With value, the attribute text is passed unmodified to the process being executed. With the path attribute, text like "familyTree.xml" is converted into a platform-specific path such as *C:\path\to\file\familyTree.xml* before it is passed to the process. Applications that need absolute pathnames require you to use the path attribute. Our Xalan example works regardless of whether you use value or path because it works with both absolute and relative pathnames.*

Additional Examples

This section shows a few additional examples of the argument DataType. argument allows several variations, all of which can be used together to pass several arguments to a process. As we already mentioned, multiple arguments are always passed in the order listed in the buildfile. Here is how you can pass two separate command-line arguments to a process:

```
<arg line="-mode verbose"/>
```

Here is how you pass a single command-line argument containing a space character:

```
<arg value="Eric Burke"/>
```

Finally, here is how you pass a path-like structure as a command-line argument:

```
<arg path="/temp;/tmp"/>
```

This is converted to *C:\temp;C:\tmp*† on Windows systems, and */temp:/tmp* on Unix systems.

* Technically, Xalan expects URLs rather than filenames as arguments. For this reason, the platform-specific filename produced by the path attribute is less desirable than the relative URL possible with the value attribute.

† Or some other drive letter, depending on where your base directory resides.

Environment DataType

The apply and exec tasks, which execute system commands, accept zero or more nested <env> elements. These elements specify which environment variables are passed to the system command being executed, and they are implemented by the org.apache.tools.ant.types.Environment.Variable class. The <env> element accepts the following attributes:

file *(all, File,*)*
: A filename as the value of the environment variable. The name is converted to an absolute path.

key *(all, String,Y)*
: The environment variable name.

path *(all, Path, *)*
: A path as the value of the environment variable. Ant converts this to local conventions, as explained in "Path DataType." For instance, *foo.txt* is converted into *C:\path\to\file\foo.txt* on Windows platforms.

value *(all, String, *)*
: A literal value for the environment variable.

Exactly one of file, path, or value is required.

Example

The following example calls a batch file named *deploy.bat*. Within the batch file, the TOMCAT_HOME environment variable is available because of the <env> element:

```
<property name="tomcat.home" value="/path/to/tomcat"/>

<target name="deploy">
    <!-- Call a deployment script, setting up the TOMCAT_HOME -->
    <!-- environment variable.                                 -->
    <exec executable="deploy.bat">
      <env key="TOMCAT_HOME" value="${tomcat.home}"/>
    </exec>
  </target>
```

Using Environment Variables in Buildfiles

The preceding example shows how you can pass environment variables to system commands using exec and env. Ant also allows you to use environment variables within your own buildfiles. This is an excellent way to avoid hardcoding, although it can limit portability. Because it deals with environment variables, using environment variables in buildfiles is closely related to the environment DataType. However, the environment DataType is not used to access environment variables from within Ant.

Instead, this use of environment variables is implemented as a special feature of the property task, which is described in Chapter 7.

JDK 1.1.x applications can access environment variables using the System.getenv( ) method. As of JDK 1.2, however, System.getenv( ) is no longer supported. It is deprecated and throws an Error when called. Sun made the decision to deprecate this method because environment variables are not available on all platforms supported by Java. The designers of Ant, however, have implemented their own support for reading environment variables—but only on some platforms. Test this feature on platforms you are interested in before relying on it.

As an example, consider a weakness of the buildfile presented in Example 4-1. Look at this line:

```
<property name="xalan.home" value="C:/java/xalan-j_2_1_0"/>
```

While this might work on your PC, it is highly unlikely to work on most other developers' PCs. This is because they probably installed Xalan to a different directory. It is better if your buildfile requires developers to set the XALAN_HOME environment variable before they run it. Here are some changes to Example 4-1 that make this possible:

```
<?xml version="1.0"?>
<project name="arg demo" default="xslt" basedir=".">
  <!-- Set up the 'env' prefix for environment variables -->
  <property environment="env"/>
  <property name="xalan.home" value="${env.XALAN_HOME}"/>

  <!-- Abort the build if XALAN_HOME is not set -->
  <target name="checkXalanHome" unless="env.XALAN_HOME">
    <fail message="XALAN_HOME must be set!"/>
  </target>

  <target name="xslt" depends="checkXalanHome">
    ...
  </target>

</project>
```

The magic happens in this line:

```
<property environment="env"/>
```

Now, you can reference any environment variable by prefixing the variable name with "env.". We also added another target that verifies the environment variable is set. If not, it warns the user and fails the build:

```
<target name="checkXalanHome" unless="env.XALAN_HOME">
  <fail message="XALAN_HOME must be set!"/>
</target>
```

FileList DataType

A filelist is a DataType supporting a named list of files, implemented by org.apache.tools.ant.types.FileList. The files do not have to exist in order to be included in a filelist. Following are the allowable attributes:

dir *(1.4, File, *)*
: The directory used to compute absolute filenames.

files *(1.4, String, *)*
: A comma-separated list of filenames.

refid *(1.4, Reference, N)*
: A reference to a <filelist> defined elsewhere. The <filelist> being referred to defines a list of files. This is useful if you wish to define a list of files once, and then refer to it from several places in your buildfile.

Both dir and files are required, unless refid is specified, in which case neither dir nor files is allowed.

Example

The filelist DataType was introduced in Ant 1.4, along with the dependset task. (Since filelist is only used with dependset, we must talk about the dependset task to explain the filelist DataType). The dependset task compares one or more input files to one or more output files. If any of the input files are newer, then all of the output files are erased. Additionally, if any of the input files are missing, all of the output files are erased. Comparing output files to a set of input files that may not yet exist is why the filelist DataType is necessary.

Let's illustrate why the combination of the filelist DataType and the dependset task is valuable. In this example, we are comparing a list of XML and XSLT files to a single HTML file. The HTML file, *employeeDirectory.html*, should be erased if any input file is missing or newer than it.

```
<?xml version="1.0"?>
<project name="filelist demo" default="xslt" basedir=".">

  <filelist id="stylesheets" dir="." files="header.xslt,footer.xslt,body.xslt"/>
  <filelist id="xmlfiles" dir="." files="employees.xml"/>

  <target name="xslt">
    <!-- erase employeeDirectory.html if any of the XML files or
         XSLT stylesheets are newer -->
    <dependset>
      <srcfilelist refid="stylesheets"/>
      <srcfilelist refid="xmlfiles"/>
      <targetfilelist dir="." files="employeeDirectory.html"/>
    </dependset>
```

```
    <echo message="Transforming Files..."/>
    ...
  </target>
</project>
```

employeeDirectory.html is dependent on four files: *header.xslt*, *footer.xslt*, *body.xslt*, and *employees.xml*. If any of these files are modified, *employeeDirectory.html* is erased by the dependset task. *employeeDirectory.html* is also erased if any of the input files are missing.

We defined two filelists, one for the XSLT files and another for the XML file. We could have just as easily defined a single filelist containing all files, although the buildfile is probably easier to understand if files are logically grouped together by type. We reference both of these filelists within the dependset task:

```
<dependset>
  <srcfilelist refid="stylesheets"/>
  <srcfilelist refid="xmlfiles"/>
  <targetfilelist dir="." files="employeeDirectory.html"/>
</dependset>
```

The <srcfilelist> tags use the refid attribute to refer back to the filelists defined earlier in the buildfile. The <targetfilelist> tag shows an alternate syntax, allowing the filelist to be defined inline. If you plan on referring to a filelist more than once in a buildfile, you should consider the refid approach. Otherwise, it is probably easier to define the filelist inline.

Although we are talking about the filelist DataType, the XML tags are called <srcfilelist> and <targetfilelist>. XML tag names frequently do not match DataType names.

FileSet DataType

The fileset DataType defines a group of files and is commonly represented by the <fileset> element. However, many Ant tasks form *implicit* filesets, which means they support all fileset attributes and nested elements. Unlike the filelist type, files represented by fileset must exist. Filesets may also be specified as target-level buildfile elements (i.e., children of <project>) and referenced by their ids. Following is a list of fileset attributes:

dir *(all, Path, Y)*
: The base directory for the fileset.

casesensitive *(1.4.1, boolean N)*
: If set to false, the fileset is not case-sensitive when matching filenames. Defaults to true. Ant versions prior to 1.4.1 use case-sensitive matching.

defaultexcludes *(all, boolean, N)*
: Determines whether to use default excludes. Defaults to true. Default excludes consists of: ***/*~*, ***/#*#*, ***/.#**, ***/%*%*, ***/CVS*, ***/CVS/***, ***/.cvsignore*, ***/SCCS*, ***/SCCS/***, and ***/vssver.scc*.

excludes *(all, String, N)*
: A comma-separated list of file patterns to exclude. These are in addition to the default excludes.

excludesfile *(all, File, N)*
: The name of a file containing one exclude pattern per line. These are in addition to the default excludes.

includes *(all, String, N)*
: A comma-separated list of file patterns to include.

includesfile *(all, File, N)*
: The name of a file containing one include pattern per line.

In addition to the attributes listed, a fileset may also contain the following:

0..n nested patternset *elements:* <exclude>, <include>, <patternset> *(all);* <excludesfile>, <includesfile>. *(1.4)*
: These define which files are included and/or excluded from the fileset. All are described shortly in the "PatternSet DataType" section. Other than <patternset>, these nested elements are used in place of their corresponding attributes.

Examples

The following examples produce identical results. Since fileset depends heavily on patternset, you should continue on and read the "Patternset DataType" section after studying these examples. The first example uses includes and excludes attributes to select all *.java* files in the *src* directory, excluding any such files underneath any directories named *test*:

```
<fileset id="sources1" dir="src"
         includes="**/*.java"
         excludes="**/test/**/*.java">
</fileset>
```

The next example uses nested <include> and <exclude> tags in place of the includes and excludes attributes:

```
<fileset id="sources2" dir="src">
  <include name="**/*.java"/>
  <exclude name="**/test/**/*.java"/>
</fileset>
```

By using the nested <include> or <exclude> element, you gain the ability to selectively include or exclude files based on properties. For instance, you can selectively include using the following syntax, which is described shortly under "PatternSet DataType":

```
<!-- Skip unit tests unless the includeTests property is set -->
<exclude name="**/test/**/*.java" unless="includeTests"/>
```

You may also use a nested <patternset> element to achieve the same results:

```
<fileset id="sources3" dir="src">
  <patternset>
    <include name="**/*.java"/>
    <exclude name="**/test/**/*.java"/>
  </patternset>
</fileset>
```

And finally, we define a <patternset> in one place and refer to it in two other places. This is more useful than the previous example, because it allows you to reuse a common patternset throughout a buildfile:

```
<patternset id="non.test.source">
  <include name="**/*.java"/>
  <exclude name="**/test/**/*.java"/>
</patternset>

<!-- later in the same buildfile -->
<fileset id="sources4" dir="src">
  <patternset refid="non.test.source"/>
</fileset>
<fileset id="sources5" dir="othersrc">
  <patternset refid="non.test.source"/>
</fileset>
```

Include and Exclude Pattern Syntax

Ant uses patterns to include and exclude files. For instance, ***/*.java* matches all *.java* files in any subdirectory. The syntax is straightforward:

> * matches zero or more characters. **.java* matches *Account.java* and *Person.java*, but not *settings.properties*.
>
> ? matches one character. *File?.java* matches *FileA.java* and *FileB.java*, but not *FileTest.java*.
>
> ** matches zero or more directories. */xml/*** matches all files and directories under */xml/*.

Combinations of patterns are allowed. For instance, a more sophisticated pattern, *com/oreilly/**/*Test.java*, matches any of these files:

com/oreilly/antbook/AccountTest.java
com/oreilly/antbook/util/UnitTest.java
com/oreilly/AllTest.java

PatternSet DataType

While filesets group files together, patternsets group patterns. These are closely related concepts, because filesets rely on patterns to select files. The <patternset> element may appear as a target-level buildfile element (i.e., as a child of <project>), and later be referenced by its id. As shown in the previous examples, it may also appear as a nested element of <fileset>. Tasks that are implicit filesets also support nested <patternset> elements.

The <patternset> element supports four attributes: includes, excludes, includesfile, and excludesfile. These are described in the previous section on filesets. In addition to these attributes, patternsets allow the following nested elements:

0..n nested <include> *and* <exclude> *elements*

These support the following attributes:

name *(all, String, Y)*

The pattern to include or exclude.

if *(all, String, N)*

The name of a property. Ant will only use this pattern if the property is set.

unless *(all, String, N)*

The name of a property. Ant will only use this pattern if the property is not set.

0..n nested <includesfile> *and* <excludesfile> *elements*

These support the following attributes:

name *(all, String, Y)*

Name of a file containing include and exclude patterns, one per line.

if *(all, String, N)*

The name of a property. Ant will only read the file if the property is set.

unless *(all, String, N)*

The name of a property. Ant will only read the file if the property is not set.

Examples

We now present two uses of the patternset DataType. The first shows a patternset being used to copy a related group of files from one directory to another. The second shows a patternset being used to conditionally include files in a compilation.

Copying files

The following is how we can set up a patternset to represent all XML-related filenames in a directory tree:

```
<patternset id="xml.files">
  <include name="**/*.dtd,**/*.xml,**/*.xslt"/>
</patternset>
```

Now we can use the copy task to copy these files from a source directory to a destination directory:

```
<copy todir="${deploy.dir}">
  <!-- select the files to copy -->
  <fileset dir="${src.dir}">
    <patternset refid="${xml.files}"/>
  </fileset>
</copy>
```

Conditionally including files

In this next example, we exclude all unit tests unless the `includetests` property is set:

```
<?xml version="1.0"?>
<project name="patternset_test_project" default="compile" basedir=".">

  <!-- exclude tests unless the 'includetests' property is set -->
  <patternset id="sources">
    <include name="**/*.java"/>
    <exclude name="**/*Test.java" unless="includetests"/>
  </patternset>

  ...remainder of buildfile omitted

  <target name="compile" depends="prepare">
    <javac destdir="build">
      <!-- the directory from which the patternset finds files to compile -->
      <src path="src"/>

      <!-- refer to the patternset which selects the source files -->
      <patternset refid="sources"/>
    </javac>
  </target>

</project>
```

Now, to include unit tests in the build, we can set the `includetests` property when invoking Ant from the command line:

```
$ ant -Dincludetests=true compile
```

FilterSet DataType

The `filterset` DataType was introduced in Ant 1.4, and allows for the definition of groups of filters. These filters (implemented by the `filter` task) perform text substitution in files as they are moved or copied. This is known as *token filtering*. The text substitution occurs when certain tokens are found in the input files. As the files are moved or copied, the tokens are replaced by text defined in the matching filter. Prior to Ant 1.4, the `filter` task always used `@` characters as token delimiters. `filterset` allows you to customize the beginning and ending token delimiters.

The `filterset` DataType is represented by the `<filterset>` element. `<filterset>` elements may appear as nested content within the `copy` and `move` tasks, or as target-level buildfile elements (i.e., children of `<project>`). Following are the allowable `filterset` attributes:

`begintoken` *(1.4, String, N)*
: The string marking the beginning of a token that nested filters search for. Defaults to `@`.

`endtoken` *(1.4, String, N)*
: The string marking the end of a token that nested filters search for. Defaults to `@`.

`id` *(1.4, String, N)*
: A unique identifier for this filter. This is required when the filter is defined as a target-level buildfile element and must be referenced later.

`refid` *(1.4, Reference, N)*
: A reference to a filter defined elsewhere in the buildfile.

A `filterset` may also contain the following:

0..n nested `<filter>` *elements (1.4)*
: Each nested `<filter>` element defines a token and the replacement text. `<filter>` requires the following attributes:

  `token` *(1.4, String, Y)*
  : Specifies the token to replace, not including the delimiter characters. If this filter is intended to replace `@VERSION@`, use `VERSION` as this attribute value.

  `value` *(1.4, String, Y)*
  : Specifies the replacement text whenever the token is encountered.

0..n nested `<filtersfile>` *elements. (1.4)*
: Each specifies a Java properties file from which to load additional filters. Each line of the file contains a token, followed by a colon (:), followed by a value. `<filtersfile>` requires the following attribute:

  `file` *(1.4, File, Y)*
  : The name of the properties file containing filters.

Example

This example target shows how to replace the `%COPYRIGHT!` and `%BUILD_DATE!` tokens as files are copied:

```
<target name="tokenFilterDemo" depends="prepare">
  <!-- set up the timestamp -->
  <tstamp>
    <format property="now" pattern="MMMM d yyyy hh:mm aa"/>
  </tstamp>
```

```
    <copy todir="build" filtering="true">
      <fileset dir="src">
        <include name="**/*.java"/>
      </fileset>

      <!-- search for %COPYRIGHT! and %BUILD_DATE! -->
      <filterset begintoken="%" endtoken="!">
        <filter token="BUILD_DATE" value="${now}"/>
        <filter token="COPYRIGHT" value="Copyright (C) 2002 O'Reilly"/>
      </filterset>
    </copy>
  </target>
```

Notice that filtering="true" must be set on the copy task in order for token filtering to occur. Our filterset consists of two different filters, and we explicitly specify the begintoken and endtoken because we do not want to use the default @ characters.

Here is a source file before it is copied:

```
// %COPYRIGHT!
// Built on %BUILD_DATE!

public class Whatever {
    ...
}
```

And here is what the target file looks like after the copy operation:

```
// Copyright (C) 2002 O'Reilly
// Built on March 12 2002 03:10 PM

public class Whatever {
    ...
}
```

Tokens may appear numerous times in each source file; all are replaced. For another example, see the filter task in Chapter 7.

Path DataType

The path DataType appears frequently, and is sometimes referred to as a *path-like structure*. It may be used as an attribute or a nested element. It is most commonly used to represent a classpath, although it is also used to represent paths for other purposes. When used as an attribute, entries in the path are separated by semicolon (;) or colon (:) characters, which are replaced at build time with whatever path separator character the current platform prefers.

The path DataType, like others, is not always represented by the <path> XML element. For instance, the javac task accepts nested <classpath> elements that are implemented by the path DataType.

The path DataType offers a lot more flexibility when used as an XML element, rather than as an attribute. Following is a list of path attributes:

location *(all, File, *)*
: Represents a single file or directory. Ant expands this into an absolute filename internally.*

path *(all, String, *)*
: A list of file and pathnames, delimited by ; or :.

refid *(all, Reference, *)*
: A reference to a path defined elsewhere in the current buildfile. This is useful if you wish to refer to the same path definition from many places in the buildfile.

Both location and path are optional, unless refid is specified, in which case neither location nor path is allowed. You can't have nested elements when refid is specified.

The path DataType also supports the following nested elements:

0..n nested <pathelement> *elements*†
: Defines one or more files to include in the path. Each nested <pathelement> also supports the location and path attributes, just like the containing path DataType.

0..n nested <fileset> *elements*
: Provides another syntax for including files in the path.

0..n nested <path> *elements*
: Recursively nests paths within other paths.

Here is how a path-like structure represents a path consisting of two JAR files and two directories. The path is built in the order listed in the buildfile:

```
<path>
  <pathelement location="${libdir}/servlet.jar"/>
  <pathelement location="${libdir}/logging.jar"/>
  <pathelement path="${builddir}"/>
  <pathelement path="${utilpath}"/>
</path>
```

The path DataType also supports an abbreviated syntax. For instance, suppose we are using the <classpath> element within a task to define a path:

```
<!-- The classpath element is implemented with the path DataType -->
<classpath>
  <pathelement path="${builddir}"/>
</classpath>
```

* Ant handles the details of converting paths into forms compatible with whatever operating system you are running on.

† <pathelement> is implemented by PathElement, a nested class within org.apache.tools.ant.types.Path. It is a helper class rather than a DataType.

This can be abbreviated as follows:

```
<classpath path="${builddir}"/>
```

The `location` attribute works similarly. As a final variation, one or more `filesets` can be nested inside path-like structures:

```
<classpath>
  <pathelement path="${builddir}"/>
  <fileset dir="${libdir}" includes="**/*.jar"/>
</classpath>
```

In this example, the `fileset` includes all *.jar* files in all directories underneath the directory specified by `${libdir}`.

Mapper DataType

We conclude this chapter with a discussion of `mappers`, which is a feature added in Ant 1.3. `mappers` define how a set of source files relates to a set of target files. `<mapper>`* elements support the following attributes:

`classname` *(1.3, 1.4, String, *)*
: The name of the class implementing the `mapper`. Used for creating custom `mappers` when the built-in `mappers` are not sufficient.

`classpath` *(1.3, 1.4, Path, N)*
: The classpath used when looking up a custom `mapper`.

`classpathref` *(1.3, 1.4, Reference, N)*
: Reference to a classpath defined elsewhere.

`from` *(1.3, 1.4, String, *)*
: The meaning of this attribute depends on which `mapper` it is used with. The upcoming examples show where this is used.

`refid` *(1.3, 1.4, Reference, N)*
: A reference to another `mapper`. If specified, this should be the only attribute listed. This allows you to define a `mapper` once and use it in several places throughout a buildfile. The upcoming examples show where this is of use.

`to` *(1.3, 1.4, String, *)*
: The meaning of this attribute depends on which `mapper` it is used with.

`type` *(1.3, 1.4, Enum, *)*
: One of `identity`, `flatten`, `glob`, `merge`, or `regexp`. Defines the type of built-in `mapper` to use.

* In Ant 1.4.1, the mapper DataType is always represented by a `<mapper>` XML element. Other DataTypes are not so consistent.

Exactly one of the type or classname attributes is required. The from and to attributes may be required, depending on the mapper.

Example

Let's look at a quick example before we talk about the specific types of mappers. Example 4-2 presents a buildfile that creates a backup copy of all *.java* files, appending the *.bak* extension to each filename.

Example 4-2. Backing up files with a glob mapper

```
<?xml version="1.0"?>
<project name="mapper demo" default="backupFiles" basedir=".">

  <!-- define a mapper for backing up files -->
  <mapper id="backupMapper" type="glob" from="*.java" to="*.java.bak"/>

  <target name="clean">
    <delete dir="bak"/>
  </target>

  <target name="prepare">
    <mkdir dir="bak"/>
  </target>

  <target name="backupFiles" depends="prepare">
    <copy todir="bak">
      <!-- select the files to copy with a fileset -->
      <fileset dir="src" includes="**/*.java"/>
      <mapper refid="backupMapper"/>
    </copy>
  </target>
</project>
```

The example also shows another usage of the fileset DataType, used by the copy task to select which files are copied. The copy task is what copies the files. The nested fileset defines the set of files to be copied. The nested mapper references the mapper created earlier in the buildfile, as well as specifies how the files are to be renamed as they are copied. As the files are copied, they are renamed according to the pattern specified by the mapper.

This example used a type of mapper known as a *glob* mapper, which generates a set of target filenames based on a simple wildcard pattern that is applied to a set of input file names. There are several mapper types available. Let's look at each of them.

The Identity Mapper

The *identity* mapper maps source files to target files with the same name. It is the default mapper used by the copy task, so you rarely need to define your own identity mapper. Table 4-2 shows results from the following identity mapper:

```
<mapper type="identity"/>
```

Table 4-2. Identity mapper results

Source file	Target file
Customer.java	*Customer.java*
com/oreilly/data/Account.java	*com/oreilly/data/Account.java*

The Flatten Mapper

The *flatten* mapper removes all path information from filenames. This might be useful if you want to copy a set of files from several different directories into a single target directory. Table 4-3 shows results from the following flatten mapper:

```
<mapper type="flatten"/>
```

Table 4-3. Flatten mapper results

Source file	Target file
Customer.java	*Customer.java*
com/oreilly/data/Account.java	*Account.java*

The Glob Mapper

The *glob* mapper determines target filenames based on simple wildcard patterns. This is useful when you want to rename groups of files that already have consistent filenames, such as all those that end in *Test.java*. The to and from attributes define patterns containing at most one * character. When a source filename matches the from pattern, a target filename is created. The to attribute's * is replaced by matching text from the from attribute's *. Table 4-4 shows results from the following glob mapper:

```
<mapper type="glob" from="*Test.java" to="*UnitTest.java">
```

Table 4-4. Glob mapper results

Source file	Target file
Customer.java	*none*
com/oreilly/data/Account.java	*none*
CustomerTest.java	*CustomerUnitTest.java*
com/oreilly/tests/CustomerTest.java	*com/oreilly/tests/CustomerUnitTest.java*

The "none" text in the first two rows of Table 4-4 indicates that in a copy operation using a glob mapper, the files that do not map are simply not copied.

The Merge Mapper

The *merge* mapper maps any set of source filenames to the same target filename, as specified by the to attribute. The from attribute is ignored. The merge mapper is useful when you want to compare timestamps of a set of source files against a single target file. This is how the uptodate task works, as described in Chapter 7. Table 4-5 shows results from the following merge mapper:

```
<mapper type="merge" to="oreilly.zip">
```

Table 4-5. Merge mapper results

Source file	Target file
Customer.java	*oreilly.zip*
com/oreilly/data/Account.java	*oreilly.zip*

The Regexp Mapper

The *regexp* mapper is similar to the glob mapper, but uses regular expressions instead of simple * characters. The exact syntax of those regular expressions entirely depends on which underlying regular expression library is being used. The mechanism Ant uses for selecting the library is described shortly.

A class implementing the org.apache.tools.ant.util.regexp.RegexpMatcher interface must be provided by the library, regardless of which regular expression library you choose to use in support of the regexp mapper. Ant includes implementation classes for the following libraries:

JDK 1.4
    Included with J2SE 1.4, available at *http://java.sun.com*

jakarta-regexp
    Available at *http://jakarta.apache.org/regexp/*

jakarta-ORO
    Available at *http://jakarta.apache.org/oro/*

To determine which library to use, Ant first looks at the ant.regexp.matcherimpl system property. If this specifies a class implementing the RegexpMatcher interface, then that library is used. Otherwise, it tries searching the classpath for a suitable library in the order just listed, beginning with JDK 1.4. If none is found, the task fails.

CHAPTER 5
User-Written Tasks

The concept of extending Ant through customization has been and still is its most important and acclaimed feature. The creators of Ant provide us with a system robust enough to work with the languages and tools available today and the ability to grow and work with the languages and tools of tomorrow. For example, tasks exist for working with the C# language, which did not exist when Ant first appeared in early 2000. Users have written tasks for working with third-party tools from groupware products, such as StarTeam (a version control system), to application servers such as BEA's WebLogic or the JBoss Group's JBoss. These changes and improvements came about with little or no changes to Ant's core processing engine. Extending Ant without modifying its core engine is very important because it means the core Ant engine can be improved and modified separately from extension development. Development in both areas is done concurrently, resulting in modifications being made faster than had Ant been a monolithic system.

All Ant tasks are Java classes, and any programmer can extend the functionality of Ant by writing a new Java task class. These are *user-written* tasks, and take advantage of the same interface to Ant used by the core tasks shipped with an Ant distribution. The only differences between a user-written task and a core task are the author and the package location of the task (and sometimes that's the same!). Otherwise, they both function on the same level playing field. In this chapter, we'll show you how to extend Ant by writing your own tasks.

The Need for Custom Tasks

Ant has two tasks, java and exec, which are capable of executing any Java class or command-line executable on a system. This ability may make you wonder why there is a need for custom tasks. Technically, you can use these tasks to work with any classes or to run any programs. As it turns out, some custom tasks do, in fact, wind up being nothing more than an execution wrapper, running a Java class or program much in the same way the `java` or exec tasks would. The difference is that custom tasks work more closely with the Ant engine. A custom task can provide more detailed messages and handle errors with greater precision. On the other hand, the `java` and exec tasks are limited in their ability to handle unforeseen errors and make detailed announcements to the user. No matter the nature of an event or error, it's all the same to these tasks, giving you very little control.

A custom task, in most cases, is a better solution to the problem of extending Ant functionality than is the use of the `java` or exec tasks. Build errors, events, and messages are all initiated from tasks and managed by the Ant engine. Ant responds to these events and works with them in a controlled manner, propagating them to its own listeners or to other, user-written listeners (see Chapter 6 for more on user-written listeners). Such fine-grained management of tasks is better for the end users (the software developers who need better information about how their project's build process takes place). It's also better for other developers writing custom tasks as they can extend existing tasks, inheriting their abilities and creating a consistent behavior across a range of related operations. These features alone make custom tasks a good thing. However, there are other benefits to the use of custom tasks.

Tasks are good at abstracting simple operations and making them more powerful with a consistent interface and extra functionality. Some Ant tasks even have the ability to handle the inconsistencies found between some of the commonly used shell functions across platforms. For example, copying and deleting files and directories across platforms is a pain since the names and arguments of the commands change from shell to shell and operating system to operating system. Since it has tasks to abstract the file operations, Ant eliminates this pain and provides a consistent interface to its user. In Ant, there is only one way to copy or delete a file, and it works no matter what platform Ant is running on. This is not the only benefit abstraction provides. Without the limitations of the feature sets in the command-line tools, an abstracted task *increases* the feature set available to you. One Window's *del* command cannot delete all files ending in *.java* and leave alone all the files that begin with *Abstract*. The Ant task `delete` can do this, demonstrating greater flexibility than its command-line cousin can. Even better, it does this on any platform. Task design focuses on a build's needs, never limiting itself to the features of tools whose design focus on a shell and operating system's needs.

With the power available in custom task classes, you can improve upon almost any tool. Don't think of custom tasks as being a Band-Aid™ for fixing Ant's shortcomings. Ant and its task model is more like Lego™. Adding tasks increases and enhances Ant's feature set, but does not increase Ant's bulk. Ant remains modular and extendable the entire time.

Ant's Task Model

Understanding custom tasks means understanding the task model. Ant, being a Java-based program, uses Java's class hierarchy and reflection capabilities to perform its duties. All Ant tasks derive, directly or indirectly, from the abstract class `org.apache.tools.ant.Task`. The Ant engine manages all task objects at this level, manipulating only `Task` objects. For the engine, every task derives from the same class and has the same core methods and properties as every other task. The combination of XML parsing and a method-naming scheme allows Ant to use all of `Task`'s subclasses. Additionally, Ant processes tasks in a fixed manner—in other words, Ant processes every task in a cycle. While understanding this model and process in detail is not a requirement to writing simple tasks, complex tasks may exhibit undesirable behaviors unless you understand the entire task model and execution process.

Writing Custom DataTypes

In addition to tasks, Ant's model handles DataTypes as well. An example of a DataType is the `path` task. The `path` task performs no direct action. Instead, it creates a data set, based on rules and other information given within the XML. As of Ant 1.4, users technically have the ability to write their own DataTypes. However, the method used to declare a DataType (the `typedef` task) is buggy, and does not work. A fix is expected by Release 1.5.

The Parts of a Task

A task has two faces. To an Ant end user, a task is nothing more than the XML in a buildfile. You can dissect this XML and identify the parts of a task for that face. To the task programmer, however, a task looks different. While the XML is still there, it serves only as a guide for the Java code. The Java code is only the tip of the iceberg. Technically speaking, there are many other facets to a task.

The common superclasses

Deriving from a superclass (which, at some point, derives from `Task`) is a requirement for all task classes. The Ant engine strictly operates on `Task` objects and pays no attention to any of the additions developers have made to children of the `Task` class. However, this does not mean you should ignore the `Task` class hierarchy. Understanding it helps you as much as ignoring it hampers your efforts. `Task`'s children not only represent tasks for the buildfile, but they also represent classes containing functionality useful with other tasks. Sometimes, a child class isn't even a task. For example, if your task has requirements to use file sets and patterns, you should extend `org.apache.tools.ant.main.taskdef.MatchingTask`. This class implements many of these file set and pattern operations, alleviating the tedious effort of implementing them yourself. It does you good to stand on the shoulders of powerful giants such as this and other task classes.

You should know the tasks with designs similar to your requirements. A good example of efficient re-use in Ant is the `zip` family of tasks. Since JARs extend the zip-packaging model, the `jar` task derives from `zip`, borrowing most of its functionality and implementing only JAR-specific operations. Taking it a step further, a WAR (Web ARchive) is a JAR with a standard directory structure and an additional, required file: the deployment descriptor *web.xml*. Hence, the `war` task derives from `jar`. In the case of `war`, the implementation for creating the standard directory structure and verifying the descriptor file is in the `War` task class, with the remaining bits of functionality inherited. Later in this chapter, we'll analyze the `jar` task and its hierarchy as an example of a custom task.

Attributes

Attributes are the name-value pairs describing a particular XML tag. Programmatically speaking, Ant parses and loads the attribute name-value pairs from the XML, and passes them on to the individual task objects. Ant redefines the string values to become primitives, `File` objects, or even `Class` objects. Typically, attribute values represent `boolean` primitives, acting as process flags for tasks. For example, the `debug` attribute for `javac` is a `boolean`. With this flag on, `javac` compiles classes with debug information. With the flag off, `javac` compiles classes normally.

Nested elements

Nested elements are, more or less, mutually exclusive alternatives to attributes. They can be tasks or DataTypes. As with attributes, tasks explicitly handle their nested elements. Unfortunately, dealing with nested elements is not as simple and straight forward as the handling of name-value pairs.

The complexity of nested elements can be puzzling because there is no definitive model to which you can design your use of nested elements. Theoretically, your custom task can take any task as a nested element. For example, you could treat `javac` as a nested element. However, such a nested element won't work until you explicitly handle the use of `javac`'s corresponding class, `Javac`. You must be aware of and handle all the quirks of the `javac` implementation; no small feat. Even if you do this, `javac` may perform operations that make it impossible to for you to use it as a nested element. This is because there is no standard way to implement tasks. Since nothing stops you programmatically from using a task such as `javac` as a nested element, you'll only find out it doesn't work when the build breaks.

Tasks use introspective calls to handle nested elements, just as is done to handle attributes. The difference is that a nested element's corresponding class has data and functionality all to itself. Attributes are just name-value pairs. An element needs its class to be instantiated, its own attributes parsed and processed, and its primary functions to be executed. Errors can happen at any time during this process.

The difference between attributes and nested elements is better illustrated by comparing and contrasting a task's use of attributes with its use of nested elements. Consider this copy task:

```
<copy destdir="newdir/subdir">
    <fileset dir="olddir">
        <include name="**/*.java"/>
    </fileset>
</copy>
```

The copy task takes the attribute destdir and the nested element <fileset>. The copy task's handling of destdir is simple. Ant passes the task's class a File object corresponding to the directory. With one call, the attribute is set. Compare this to how Ant must handle the <fileset> element. There are three ways Ant can pass the Fileset object to the task's class. In each case, Ant must put the fileset DataType through the same life cycle as a task (since, at this level, tasks and DataTypes are identical to the Ant engine). Ant's processing of these tasks and DataTypes is a recursive process. The point we're trying to make is that Ant's process for handling DataTypes is much more involved than its process for handling an element's attributes.

While attributes are easier to use and understand than DataTypes, they are less readable and less flexible. Paths, for example, make for ugly and hard-to-maintain attributes. Path values can get long and must change every time the path structure changes. Nested path elements are more readable and easier to maintain. They're certainly more powerful in terms of how they represent paths since they can use complex file patterns (e.g., *.* works in the path DataType but not as a path attribute).

Like everything in life, deciding between implementing a task's attributes and implementing its nested elements has its trade-offs. Although we gain in maintenance and readability when using DataTypes, we lose in initial development time versus using attributes. There are many ways to use nested elements (three method calls, to be exact), and each is prone to mistakes or odd behaviors that can be difficult to debug. For this reason, some task authors support both methods, having, for example, a classpath attribute and a classpath nested DataType.

Remember this can be a confusing solution for users, so document your task accordingly. You'll need to explicitly define what happens if a user specifies both an attribute and a nested element representing the same data. Ant doesn't know how to determine the difference and will attempt to operate on both, with undefined consequences.

Communication Between Ant and Tasks

Now that you have an understanding of the various pieces that can go into the makeup of a task, we can turn our attention towards the mechanisms by which the

Ant build engine communicates with tasks. There are three communication mechanisms that you need to understand when writing custom tasks:

The `Project` *class*
: The `Project` class is available in every task as a public instance variable. The class represents the entire buildfile and everything contained therein, providing you with access to all tasks, targets, properties, and other buildfile parts.

Build Exceptions
: Build exceptions, implemented via the `BuildException` class, provide a mechanism for tasks to signal error conditions to the Ant build engine.

The logging system
: A logging system, accessible via the `Project` class, provides tasks with a way to display progress information for a user to see.

The next three sections describe each of these mechanisms in detail.

The Project class

One class facilitates most of the communication between a task and the Ant engine: the `Project` class. The inclusion of this instance variable for the parent `Task` class* makes this communication possible. Use it as you use any instance variable in any task. A lot of power resides in the `Project` class, so pay close attention to what it can do, and be aware of incidents where you may accidentally abuse this power (you wouldn't purposely abuse power, would you?). Also, keep in mind that some of the clever things you can do with `Project` may go away in the next release of Ant. Have a backup design plan or be prepared to maintain your own version of Ant.

The `Project` class represents the entire buildfile. This class grants access to every one of a buildfile's tasks, targets, properties, and even to some of the core settings defining how the buildfile should execute. Developers rarely use this access, but the functionality and the ability to use it is there. Primarily, task developers use `Project` to provide access to the engine's core auditing system via `log` method calls.

Additionally, `Project` defines system-wide constants and global methods for all tasks. The constants are for system-call parameters, such as for logging. The global methods provide functionality ranging from translating paths to a native form to providing a `boolean` translator for task attributes with `boolean` values.

Within a task, the `Project` class' field name is, appropriately enough, `project`. Here are some common method calls and constants available through `project`:

* Since Ant 1.4, the core component is now the `ProjectComponent`, not `Task`. The `Project` object is now a protected instance variable of the `ProjectComponent` class.

`project.getGlobalFilterSet( )`
: Returns a `FilterSet` object that is global with respect to the build. It is possible to define a global filter set, excluding or including a set of files for every task that makes a file or directory operation. If your task needs to obey this global filter, you can get it with a call to `project.getGlobalFilterSet( )`. See the Ant API JavaDoc for more information on `FilterSet`.

`project.getBaseDir( )`
: Returns the value of the `basedir` attribute in the `<project>` element. If your task needs to perform file operations from or within the project directory, this is the best way to get the path to that directory.

`project.translatePath( )`
: Translates a path to the native format for the operating system being used. Buildfile authors can write paths and filenames in a generic manner, ignoring differences like directory separator characters. When your task needs to perform an actual file operation, you need the native file or directory string to prevent errors. The `translatePath( )` method in the `Project` class translates generic paths into operating system–specific paths. The `Project` class knows the platform in use, and translates the filename or directory to the correct format. For example:

```
File f = new File(dir, project.translatePath(filePath));
```

This example demonstrates creating a file. The task creating the file doesn't require any platform-detection code to generate a valid path for the platform used (e.g., Windows or Unix). Instead, the task's programmer calls `translatePath( )`, knowing that it works no matter what platform is under the JVM.

`project.toBoolean( )`
: Checks a `boolean` value. Tasks with Boolean attributes (e.g., a flag) can take values of `yes|no`, `true|false`, or `on|off`. This is made possible with the method `toBoolean( )`. This eliminates the need to rewrite this simple string-to-Boolean method and provides a consistent interface across all tasks. All tasks with flag-like attributes can use the three combinations of Boolean values. For example, `project.toBoolean("yes")` and `project.toBoolean("on")` both return `true`.

In addition to using the `Project` class to get information *from* the build engine, as we've demonstrated in this section, you can also use it to send information *to* the build engine. But this is a subversive use, and a dangerous one to boot. The `Project` class holds the keys to many of the build engine's operations, meaning you could make changes where you see fit. However, do this only in extreme cases, or, better yet, don't do it at all. We mention this ability only to be complete in our information, not as a recommendation for implementation. The safest and best way to communicate to the build engine is with build exceptions and log messages. This is because the only types of communication a task should make are those of the informative kind, and not anything that can possibly be destructive. This can mean providing status messages for runtime feedback or gracefully failing if an error occurs.

Build exceptions

Build exceptions are thrown using BuildException classes, and provide a mechanism for a task to signal error conditions to the Ant build engine. You can throw BuildExceptions from any point within a task. The engine expects a potential BuildException from every method call it makes on task objects. Look at this example, which shows a BuildException being thrown:

```
        if (!manifestFile.exists( )) {
            throw new BuildException("Manifest file: " + manifestFile + " does not
exist.", getLocation( ));
        }
```

If the specified manifest file doesn't exist at the point the task tries to use it, the task enters into an error state and fails. It informs the Ant engine of this failure by throwing a BuildException containing an error message and a Location object (retrieved using the getLocation( ) method). The Location class contains the name of the buildfile and the line number the engine is currently interpreting. In a way, it's also a class like Project through which a task receives communication from the engine. However, most developers confine the use of information from the Location class to create messages to put in BuildExceptions.

Throwing a BuildException stops a task immediately. A target is not successful unless all of its tasks are. With BuildException, Ant knows when to fail a task, its target, and the build.

One exception to the rule that a target is not successful unless all its tasks is the occasional use of a failOnError attribute within a task. A task using this attribute can avoid throwing a BuildException, thus allowing the build to continue. Of course, nothing like this is automatic, and you, as the task author, are responsible for implementing this feature. Here is some code from the Cvs class showing how to implement failOnError.

The XML:

```
<cvs failOnError="true"
cvsroot=":pserver:anonymous@cvs.phpwiki.sourceforge.net:/usr/phpwiki"
dest="${src.dir}"/>
```

The implementation (an excerpt from the *Cvs.java* source code):

```
/**
 * The task's instance variable, representing the failOnError flag
 * If true it will stop the build if cvs exits with error.
 * Default is false.
 */
private boolean failOnError = false;

...

// Sets the instance variable through the attribute
public void setFailOnError(boolean failOnError) {
```

```
        this.failOnError = failOnError;
    }

    // some method code, blah blah blah

    // Throw a build exception from this method, only
    // if the task is supposed to fail
    public void execute() throws BuildException {
        // more code...

        // Handle an error, but only throw an exception when
        // failOnError is true
        if(failOnError && retCode != 0) {
            throw new BuildException("cvs exited with error code "+ retCode);
        }
        // more code...
    }
```

Simply put, if the failOnError attribute is false, the Cvs class will not throw a BuildException and create an error state for a target containing the cvs task. As an aside, it would be good if, instead of doing nothing, the error condition at least generated some log message so that the end user knows something is going wrong. For example, a better implementation is:

```
    // some method code, blah blah blah
    // Throw a build exception only if the task is supposed to fail
    if(failOnError && retCode != 0) {
        throw new BuildException("cvs exited with error code "+ retCode);
    }

    if (!failOnError && retCode != 0) {
        log("cvs existed with error code " + retCode);
    }
```

The logging system

The Project class allows a task to get system-wide information regarding the buildfile. It also provides methods to access the build engine's auditing system. These methods are log( ) in various forms. All messages display, depending on an engine-wide setting called the message level.

Messages display at one of the following five levels, in order of "verbosity":

- ERROR
- WARNING
- INFO
- VERBOSE
- DEBUG

These levels dictate to Ant at which state a message should appear. For example, if you tell Ant to display only INFO-level messages, all messages sent with ERROR,

WARNING, and INFO settings display in the log. Message-level values are available through the following public, static fields of the `Project` class:

```
Project.MSG_ERR
Project.MSG_WARN
Project.MSG_INFO
Project.MSG_VERBOSE
Project.MSG_DEBUG
```

The VERBOSE and DEBUG levels are special in that they seem identical, but they're really not. When running Ant, you can specify VERBOSE *and* DEBUG-level messages as separate arguments. Specifying DEBUG-level messages does not result in the display of VERBOSE-level messages and vice versa.

The `log( )` method sends messages to the registered log listener of a build. The listener then processes the message strings per its design. The default log listener prints everything to the console. `log( )` is available in three flavors:

`log(`*`message`*`)`
: In tasks, messages make their way to the log via the `Project` class's `log( )` method. By default, a call on `log( )` is an INFO-level (designated by the MSG_INFO variable) message. The following examples send identical, informative messages to the build engine at the default level, MSG_INFO.

```
project.log("This build step has completed successfully with " + numfiles + "
processed");

log("This build step has completed successfully with " + numfiles + "
processed");
```

As the example shows, there is also a default `log( )` method (defined in the `Task` class) so that tasks do not need to even use their `Project` instance variable. It's a good idea to use this default `log( )` method since task-level access to the `Project` class may go away in some future release of Ant.

`log(`*`message, level`*`)`
: Another version of the `log( )` method takes a second, message-level parameter. This is useful sending for DEBUG and VERBOSE-level messages. For example:

```
// Use the project variable's log method to log messages
project.log("For loop to process files begins", Project.MSG_DEBUG);

// Use the log method from Task to log messages
log("For loop to process files begins", Project.MSG_DEBUG);
```

Note there are two ways to call `log( )`. In addition to the `Project` class, the `Task` class has an implementation of a two-parameter version of `log( )`. You should use the two-parameter method, `log(`*`message,level`*`)`, from `Task` whenever you can.

log(message, level, task)
: The third version of the `log()` method from the `Project` object takes a third parameter, a `Task` object. You should not use this call within a user-written task. It is for use within the build engine; we mention it here only for completeness.

The Task Life Cycle

Complex tasks, which perform operations on many files, rely on nested tasks, and use multiple libraries (e.g., the optional `ejbjar` task), require an in-depth understanding of a task's relationship with Ant. Consider this a warning. This section delves into the dark and dirty details involving the life cycle of a task. If you feel that your custom tasks will not meet the complexity level described here, skip this section and move on to our example. You can always come back and read this section later. Understanding the engine and the task life cycle is important for becoming an expert task writer, but it is not a requirement for writing custom tasks that are relatively simple.

Ant processes all tasks identically. Ant sets attributes and processes nested elements at fixed intervals. We can predict how a task operates and design it accordingly. A task's life can be broken down into two primary phases of time: *parse-time* and *runtime*. The parse-time phase begins when Ant reads the task from the XML (think of the engine as interpreting the XML, element by element). The runtime phase begins when the parse-time phase completes successfully.

The Parse Phase

Ant parses a task after its XML parser loads the element. The task's name, attributes, and nested elements are wrapped into a single XML element object and stored in Ant's in-memory DOM.* During parse-time, operations can fail if the task XML is poorly formed or if actions taken within a task's constructor throw exceptions. Here is a detailed list of the actions Ant performs on a task during parse-time:

1. Instantiate the task's class.

   Ant, using the name of the XML element and introspection, instantiates the task's corresponding class. Keep in mind that the attributes are not set and links back to the build system (e.g., the `project` instance variable) are not available at this time.

2. Create references to the `project` and parent target objects.

   Tasks communicate with the task engine using objects made available to them by the engine. At this time, Ant creates these references, making them available for use.

3. Add `id` references.

   Ant stores, in an internal table, a list of tasks that have the `id` attribute. This step, when it occurs, is only important to other tasks and DataTypes. It's especially important to those tasks and DataTypes performing some form of parallel

* If you're confused about programming for elements, DOMs, etc, refer to *Java & XML, 2nd Edition* (O'Reilly) by Brett McLaughlin.

processing. See Chapter 7 for more on the `parallel` task, as this is the only task distributed with Ant that does parallel nested element processing.

4. Call `init()`.

   The `init()` method in the task object is now called. Remember that task attributes are not available at this time. In addition, information your task needs from nested elements is also unavailable. As a side note, many of the distributed tasks don't implement this method.

5. Nested elements are parsed and processed using `addXXX()`, `addConfiguredXXX()`, and `createXXX()` methods.

   This is probably the most important (and most difficult) step to understand in the entire life cycle. Intuitively, you might think that Ant defines and processes task attributes during parse-time, but this is not the case. Ant does not look at task attributes until runtime. This also means that the inclusion of unsupported attributes in the buildfile goes unnoticed until runtime. However, Ant processes nested elements during parse-time. Therefore, it catches the use of unsupported elements before it catches the use of any unsupported attributes.

   So how does Ant process nested elements? It calls `createXXX()`, `addConfiguredXXX()`, or `addXXX()` on your task, where `XXX` is the capitalized name of the nested element. What is the difference between the `createXXX()`, `addConfiguredXXX()`, and `addXXX()` methods? It depends on how you plan to use the nested element and the nature of the element's corresponding object. If your task needs to instantiate the element object itself, or, if the object has no default constructor, then use `create`; think of it as "your task *creates* the nested object." If your task needs a reference to an already instantiated object, then use `add`; think of this as "Ant *adds* the object reference to your object." If you need Ant to fully process the element before it passes the references, use `addConfigured`; think of this as "Ant *adds* the *configured* object reference to your task object." Review existing task implementations if these differences still confuse you. Incidentally, Ant calls `createXXX()` methods first. If you implement more than one method for a particular element type, Ant calls them all. The consequences of doing this can be dire, so try not to do it!

The Runtime Phase

The runtime phase is the moment of reckoning for a task. It begins when the parse-time phase of the task is successfully complete. Other targets and tasks may have already run successfully by the time your task enters the runtime phase. While you may wish to rely upon certain expected behaviors and states set prior to your task's runtime step, resist the temptation! Your task should operate atomically, and be capable of running as the first or last task of a build. Here's a list of what happens at task runtime:

1. All the task's attributes are set.

   Think of attributes as properties for a task. Ant delivers the values to a task object by calling the `setXXX()` method for every attribute, where `XXX` is the capitalized name of the attribute. If a set method is missing, Ant errors out and the task and build fail.

2. Process CDATA text from the XML file.

   XML gives you the ability to place raw text in a file using the `<![CDATA[]]>` construct (i.e., character data). You can send this raw text to your task. Ant calls the method `addText(String msg)`, passing in a `String` object representing the character data from the XML file. Here's an example of a CDATA section:

   ```
   <taskname>
     <![CDATA[Naturalized language to be displayed by an Ant task]]>
   </taskname>
   ```

   When Ant reads the CDATA section, it calls `addText("Naturalized language to be displayed by an Ant task")` on your task. If your task (or its parent) does not implement the `addText()` method and you include a CDATA element, the build fails. There is no default implementation for handling character data.

   Many task authors don't use the CDATA feature. Raw character data typically is useful only in messaging tasks or tasks that must incorporate text that uses no escape codes. For example, the `script` task uses CDATA for the actual script text, since characters like < and [, typical programming language operators, can cause problems in XML if not placed within a CDATA section.

3. All the nested elements' attributes are set.

   Ant parses the attributes of all elements as it reads their XML. However, it doesn't set attributes until runtime. This applies to all elements, including nested elements of a task. You rarely need to worry about the state of attributes with your nested elements. You will likely not use them until your task executes (the next step in this phase), at which time the attributes are available.

4. `execute()` is called.

   Everything up to this point has primarily been data gathering and validation. With `execute()`, your task performs the actions it was designed to do. From this moment onward, you must handle or raise all error conditions. Ant does not expect a return error code and will make no more calls to methods on your task.

Again, you don't need to fully understand the task life cycle in order to write a task. Knowing the life cycle helps you most when you're trying to figure out why a particular thing you're doing in your task is not working. In rare cases, you may find ways to exploit the life cycle to have certain things happen. Avoid this if you can. Certain details of how tasks work will not remain the way they are now and can change with little notice. Unless you plan to maintain your own internal version of Ant, you can find yourself stuck on a release of Ant, as your task will work in one version of Ant but not another.

The life cycle is important because it allows Ant to work with tasks consistently. Borrowing ideas and code from other tasks becomes an easy and common exercise.

An Example Through Analysis: The jar Task

Now that the theoretical stuff is behind us, let's look at what happens when rubber meets the road. To develop your own Ant task, write a Java class that implements your design. The complexity or simplicity of your task is up to you. It's only important that your Java class conform to the conventions set forth in Ant's object model.

As an example of how to write tasks, we present an analysis of an existing task: `jar`. The `jar` task touches upon all of the topics we need to cover. The `Jar` task class is part of a deep hierarchy, demonstrating re-use through inheritance. It derives from `Zip`, which, in turn, derives from `MatchingTask`. The `Jar` task object does not have its own `execute()` method implementation, relying, instead, on that method's implementation in the `Zip` classes. This shows how loose some of the requirements are in regards to your own implementations. The `jar` task also uses a multitude of attributes and nested elements, giving us good examples of how to handle all of these features. Using an existing task as an example reinforces the concept that there is no difference between user-written tasks and those included with the Ant distribution.

Analyzing `jar` gives us some insight into how to design a task. It has unique and easy-to-understand design goals. We have a task design with object re-use that is open for future extension. `War` and `Ear` derive from `Jar`, obtaining the same benefits. However, we will not cover every feature and aspect of the real `jar` task. For further information, take time to look at the code in the source distribution. Learning more about the implementation of not just the `jar` task, but of all tasks, serves to make you a stronger Ant-task developer.

Where to look: The source for `Jar`, `Zip`, and `MatchingTask` is found in the source distribution of Ant (*http://jakarta.apache.org/builds/jakarta-ant/release/v1.4.1/src*). We analyze the `jar` task with code snippets from these source files. If you fail to follow some of our decisions or don't understand how a code snippet fits in with the descriptions, feel free to follow along with the full source code at hand.

Understand, also, that our analysis is not comprehensive in terms of creating a working task. We touch upon and explain the major points of designing and writing the `jar` task, but leave out implementation details like the handling of input streams for JARs. It's an analysis, not a tutorial. If you follow this analysis trying to write and compile the code, you will find that some things won't work. In the conflict between being concise or complete, we chose conciseness, sacrificing, of course, a full-blown user-written task tutorial. However, our analysis accurately describes the effort required to write the jar and other tasks. If you need more detail than we provide, there is no better compliment to learning than the tasks' source code.

To begin, imagine Ant having no jar task. Without it, our example project from Chapter 2 has no task to create JARs of its classes. Using java or exec to run the command-line *jar* tool is too cumbersome and error prone (as discussed in this chapter's introduction).

Design the jar Task

What are the requirements for a task that creates JARs? A good place to start is to the command-line tool, *jar*. At a minimum, our task should replicate the *JAR-creating* features of the tool (as opposed to *all* of the tool's features). This distinction is important. We're not re-implementing the *jar* tool, we're creating an operation for our build, satisfying only our build's requirements. The command-line tool only facilitates reaching that goal. Our build requires that we create JARs, so our task design should focus on JAR creation, nothing more. Should we later define a need, for example, to unpackage JARs, we would need an implementation of those features.

The command-line tool creates a zip-compatible archive with a special directory called *META-INF*. It places a special file called *MANIFEST.MF* into this directory. Without going into too much detail, we describe JARs as *smart zip files*: archives capable of not only packaging a set of files into one file, but also having a type of package-descriptor (the manifest). At a minimum, our task should create JARs and allow the specification of a user-written manifest file, if one exists.

From a build perspective, our design should allow us to create JARs using large sets of files from multiple directories and file types. Since a JAR maintains the directory structure of the classfile locations, we may need to modify how certain groups of files are stored within the JAR file. Experienced Ant users will identify this with file sets and file patterns. (After this chapter, you'll be able to identify this too!) Cursory research across existing tasks reveals some with similar file set designs, such as copy and zip.

Briefly, here are the requirements for our jar task:

Duplicate the command-line tool's JAR creation capabilities
: The command-line tool creates JARs given a name, a manifest filename, and a set of files or directories. Our task should do the same.

Operate across a range of files, directories, and file patterns
: Many tasks have the ability to run user-defined file set information as well as user-defined file patterns. We should be prepared to leverage this functionality.

Add and/or modify the manifest file from XML descriptions.
: This is an example of a task expanding beyond the functionality of its equivalent command-line tool. Rather than maintain a separate manifest file, we allow manifest settings to be made in-buildfile, using, of course, XML elements.

From our requirements analysis, we should have some idea of what the task syntax looks like in XML. When you define this syntax for your own tasks, don't be surprised if the design changes as you go along.

Our task's XML design:

```
<jar jarfile="somefile.jar"
     manifest="somemanifest.mf"
     basedir="somedir">
    <fileset dir="somedir">
        <include name="**/*.class"/>
    </fileset>
    <manifest>
        <attribute name="SomeAttribute" value="SomeValue"/>
    </manifest>
</jar>
```

Leverage Prior Work

Assuming that we have exhausted all other efforts to get the build to work without the `jar` task, we now know we need to write a custom task. There's one more bit of research we must perform: we must make sure that we're the first one to do it! Dozens of custom tasks exist, and Ant distributions contain some, but not all of them. Since Ant 1.4, the Jakarta team has been maintaining a list on the Ant web site so that users have access to some of the more commonly used user-written tasks (see: *http://jakarta.apache.org/ant/external.html*). In addition to the web site, we should search the Ant mailing lists, the Web, or USENET to find existing tasks that might implement the functionality we need. In the future, there may even be a task repository, something similar to Perl's CPAN library system.

We find no existing `jar` task. Next, we look to existing tasks for those whose functionality *resembles* the `jar` task. In practice, you may not have enough experience to see relationships between the task you are writing and existing tasks. Review Chapter 7 and Chapter 8 carefully to determine if a desired task's functionality, or parts of it, exist in some other currently existing task.

As we mentioned earlier, JARs are simply ZIP files with a manifest file and a different file extension. Because of this, we look to the `zip` task for possible reuse. The `zip` task performs a similar operation, creating a single packaged file from a set of patterns and rules. In fact, the operation differs only in the concept of a MANIFEST and in the resulting filename (*.zip* versus *jar*). Decision made! We derive our object from `Zip`.

Here's our `Jar` class signature:

```
package org.oreilly.ant.tasks;

// Need to import it to derive from it
import org.apache.tools.ant.taskdefs.Zip;

/**
 * Implementation class for the <jar> task in Ant.
 *
```

```
 * In your task, be sure to show examples of your task in use
 * here.  Also, if you plan on having others extend your implementation,
 * describe how some of your methods apply and how your task works in
 * general.
 */
public class Jar extends Zip {
// Implementation code
}
```

When we derive from Zip, our derived class automatically becomes part of Ant's task framework. The primary task framework class, org.apache.tools.ant.Task, defines the rudimentary methods needed by a task.* These methods, in addition to those you provide in your task implementation, allow a task to determine the attributes given by the buildfile's XML element, and determine other properties set in the project.

org.apache.tools.ant.taskdefs.MatchingTask extends org.apache.tools.ant.Task and implements file and directory methods needed by tasks with those needs. Tasks such as copy and zip extend from MatchingTask to inherent these methods. Chapter 4 contains a complete explanation of patterns and file sets.

The key here is to look for re-usability. Having a task object model means tasks with common sets of functionality can derive from the same parent task object. Leveraging prior work doesn't just mean looking for code implementations that duplicate effort, but also looking for objects that compliment effort. This object model is very powerful and explains why Ant has expanded so quickly in less than two years. Working hard on the design and initial research pays off in the end. Beneficial changes in the framework benefit all tasks with little or no maintenance.

Implement the Attribute Setter Methods

Ant sets a task's attributes via a group of setter methods defined by the task author. The method names follow a convention similar to JavaBeans property setters: set followed by the capitalized attribute name. The methods must be public visibility and return nothing to the caller. The parameter is usually a String, but can be any object in the list below, any primitive (they are converted from the String object), or any user-defined type with a constructor that takes a String. Valid attribute-setter parameter types are:

String
: The most commonly used parameter. Ant passes the raw value from the XML element's attribute to the setter method.

A File *object*
: If Ant determines the setter method takes a File parameter, it tries to create the File object relative to the directory set in the <project> element's basedir attribute.

* Remember that, as of Ant 1.4, the real framework class is ProjectComponent, from which DataTypes and Tasks derive. However, Tasks always derive from org.apache.tools.ant.Task.

A `Class` *object*

If the attribute value is a fully qualified class name, Ant attempts to load it via the classloader. Within the core and optional Ant 1.4.1 distribution, there is no example of a task using this behavior.*

User-defined objects

If your new class has a constructor taking only a `String`, then you can use your class in any setter-method signatures. As a rule, it's best to make your class a private member of your task object. The class' implementation and visibility remains consistent and restricted to the containing task. This way, you prevent people from trying to use your object as a task if they see it in some class list from a JAR.

Keep in mind that for our `jar` task we're not implementing setters for all of the attributes, just the ones that the `zip` task doesn't handle, or those zip-attributes that need to be processed differently (overriding the parent object's setter method). Table 5-1 lists the attributes for our `jar` task (see the XML sample for `jar` shown earlier).

Table 5-1. JAR-specific attributes of the jar task

Attribute name	Description	Need to implement in Jar task object?
`jarfile`	Name of the resulting JAR file.	Yes, it is not available in the `Zip` task object.
`manifest`	Name of the manifest file to validate and include.	Yes, it is not available in the `Zip` task object.
`basedir`	Root directory from which the JARs files will come from.	No, the `Zip` task object implements the setter method for this attribute.

Following is the implementation of the `setJarfile( )` attribute setter method. It takes a `File` object as a parameter. Ant detects this through introspection and tries to create a `File` object with the attribute value from the XML. Failures in creating a `File` come from within Ant itself; you don't have to worry about handling invalid filenames, etc. Also, since we're borrowing methods from `zip`, we need only to call `zip`'s `setZipFile( )` method, since that method sets the task-instance's `File` object.

```
/**
 * Set the value of the JAR filename
 * The instance variable is zipFile
 */
public void setJarFile(File pValue) {
    log("Using Zip object 'setZipFile' to identify the JAR filename", MSG_DEBUG);
    super.setZipFile(pValue);
}
```

* While theoretical, this technique may have applicable uses. Providing a runtime class instance during the task's execution may be useful with complex operations that can only be given definition at runtime.

For another example, we'll show a setter of an attribute unique to `jar`: `manifest`. Like `setJarFile( )`, the `setManifest( )` method takes a `File` object as its parameter:

```
/**
 * Set the manifest file to be packaged with the JAR
 *  The manifest instance variable can be used to add new
 * manifest attribute entries with nested elements of the
 * jar task.
 */
public void setManifest(File manifestFile) {
   // This attribute is a File

   // Check to make sure the file is where it says it is.
   // If it isn't, throw a BuildException, failing the task
   if (!manifestFile.exists( )) {
      throw new BuildException("Manifest file: " + manifestFile + " does not exist.",
getLocation( ));
   }

   // Set the instance variable of the manifest file object
   this.manifestFile = manifestFile;

   InputStream is = null;
   // load the manifest file.  An object to handle manifest files
   // was written by Conor MacNeil and is available with Ant.  This
   // object guarantees that the manifest file is properly formatted
   // and has the right default values.
   try {
      is = new FileInputStream(manifestFile);
      Manifest newManifest = new Manifest(is);
      if (manifest == null) {
      manifest = getDefaultManifest( );
   }

   manifest.merge(newManifest);
   // Let's log this operation for task developers
   log("Loaded " + manifestFile.toString( ), Project.MSG_DEBUG);
} catch (ManifestException e) {
   //  ManifestException is thrown from the Manifest object

   // Just like the Manifest object, a custom object exists
   // to warn about manifest file errors.
   log("Manifest is invalid: " + e.getMessage( ), Project.MSG_ERR);
   throw new BuildException("Invalid Manifest: " + manifestFile, e,getLocation( ));
} catch (IOException e) {
   // IOException is thrown from any file/stream operation, like FileInputStream's
constructor
   throw new BuildException("Unable to read manifest file: " + manifestFile, e);
} finally {
   // Since we're done reading the file into an object, let's close
   // the stream.
   if (is != null) {
      try {
         is.close( );
```

```
        } catch (IOException e) {
          // do nothing but log this exception
          log("Failed to close manifest input stream", Project.MSG_DEBUG);
        }
          }
        }
    }
```

As noted in the attribute table, we do not need an implementation of the `setBasedir( )` method.

Implement Nested Element Handling

Implementing code to handle nested elements is the most complicated part of writing tasks. Similar to attributes, you handle the processing of nested elements via methods with naming conventions. Ant takes each nested element's corresponding task object and attempts to call one of three methods. In this case, the method naming convention is `addXXX( )`, `addConfiguredXXX( )`, and `createXXX( )`, where `XXX` is the capitalized name of the nested element (e.g., `addFileset( )` handles a task's `<fileset>` nested element). Knowing which method to implement can be difficult and confusing. The subtle differences between the methods lie in how Ant manipulates the individual nested-element objects. The following list provides a loose definition of when to implement an `addXXX( )`, `addConfiguredXXX( )`, or `createXXX( )` method for a nested element. Typically, you will choose the technique that is best for your needs and implement the corresponding method. Even understanding how the definitions apply to your needs can be difficult. However, our analysis of the `jar` task later on should help clear this up.

`addXXX( )`
: When you "add" a nested element, you're telling Ant to instantiate the class before it calls your `addXXX( )` method. If the nested element's corresponding object has no default constructor, Ant cannot do this and an error is thrown. If it does, Ant passes the instantiated nested element object on to your task object where you may deal with the object as you wish (e.g., storing it in a collection, and so on). We suggest waiting until the execute phase of your task to actually *use* nested element objects (i.e., call methods or extract values on), if only to avoid possible problems with the fact that the nested elements' attributes are unset.

`addConfiguredXXX( )`
: So now you're thinking, "I *need* to use that nested element before the execute phase!" Luckily, Ant provides an alternative method for adding objects. The `addConfiguredXXX( )` methods direct Ant to not just instantiate, but to configure the nested element object before passing it to the task object. In other words, Ant guarantees that the attributes and nested elements for the given nested element are set and processed before it reaches the task object. Since this technically

breaks the task life cycle, there is some danger in using this method, although it's minor in its impact. Even though Ant configures this element for you, remember that Ant has not finished configuring the task at hand. You'll find that the parent task's attributes are `null` during an `addConfiguredXXX( )` call. If you try to use these attributes, you'll cause errors, ending the running build. You are limited to which types you can use in your method parameters. Just like with the `addXXX( )` methods, if the object in question does not have a default constructor, you can't use the nested elements' objects as parameters for `addConfiguredXXX( )` methods.

`createXXX( )`
: If Ant calls a `createXXX( )` method, it gives complete control of parsing the nested element to the task object. Instead of passing an object to the task, Ant expects the task to return the nested element's object. This has some side benefits; most notably, it eliminates the requirement that nested element objects have default constructors. The downside is that you are responsible for understanding how the element object works when it's initialized. You may not have the documentation or source code on hand, so this can be a formidable job.

These are loose definitions because there is nothing programmatically forcing you to use them. As long as you have an implementation for one of the three methods corresponding to the nested element, Ant will be able to use your task and its nested elements. However, as you look at Ant's source code distribution—specifically, source code for other user-written tasks—you will notice places where developers defy these definitions, and, in fact, mix them up. Without any hard and fast rules for writing element-handler methods, there will always be alternate uses that defy the definitions set forth here.

The `jar` task requires the ability to specify a set of patterns for including and excluding various files and directories. It also requires a way to add entries to the JAR's manifest file. In our design, we chose to implement this ability with nested elements. The first requirement, pattern handling, is already part of the implementation of the `MatchingTask` object. The second requirement, specifying attributes for the manifest file, needs explicit handling in our implementation of `jar`. Look again at the task's XML, in particular at the nested elements:

```
<jar jarfile="test.jar"
     manifest="manifest.mf"
     basedir="somedir">
    <manifest>
        <attribute name="SomeAttribute" value="SomeValue"/>
    </manifest>

    <fileset dir="somedir">
        <include name="**/*.class"/>
    </fileset>
</jar>
```

From this sample XML, we can make a table (see Table 5-2) of the jar task's nested elements. We specify their description and note whether the class must implement the related functionality. Remember that nested elements each have their own corresponding class. We assume, in this analysis, that those classes are written and working. Their implementations differ little in concept from the implementation of the jar task.

Table 5-2. Nested elements of the jar task

Nested element name	Description	Need to implement in Jar task object?
Manifest	Add entries to the JAR's manifest file.[a]	Yes, it is not available in the Zip object.
Fileset	Create file patterns for inclusion and exclusion to and from the JAR.	No, the MatchingTask object implements these methods. Zip inherits from MatchingTask.

[a] For more information on JARs and their manifests, see Sun's documentation on the JAR specification.

The JAR Manifest File

Manifest files are a traditionally underused part of the JAR specification. With a manifest file, you can add descriptions of what an archive contains. Usually, these descriptions are version numbers or library names. Being able to specify manifest entries in a buildfile can alleviate the need to manage a manifest file within the source code itself. In writing the original jar task, the developers provide a Manifest object that manages manifest information (such as its attributes and their values) and can write it to disk for inclusion with a JAR. Additionally, the Manifest object knows about and can process nested <attribute> elements. For our purposes, we assume this class already exists and is in working order.

Initially, it appears we need Ant to process the <manifest> element during the normal "nested element" phase. That follows the normal task life cycle. However, waiting to process the <manifest> element means that the values and data from the element will not be available until the execute phase of the life cycle. This requires us to actually implement the Jar task object's execute( ) method, which we're trying to avoid. We expect to use the Zip object's execute( ) method. We need Ant to process the <manifest> element before the execute phase. Enter the addConfiguredManifest( ) method (for the Jar class):

```
public void addConfiguredManifest(Manifest newManifest)
            throws BuildException {
    if (manifest == null) {
        throw new BuildException( );
    }
    manifest.merge(newManifest);
}
```

The addConfiguredXXX( ) family of methods tells Ant to process the element when it is parsed rather than waiting for the runtime phase. In our case, the newManifest parameter should be a fully populated Manifest object. The method has nothing left to do but perform some rudimentary error checks and merge the contents with the existing manifest file. The existing manifest file comes from the manifest attribute on the jar task. If no current manifest exists, however, the merge method forces Manifest to create a new one; the method is a feature of the Manifest object.

File pattern matching is common with many Ant tasks, so understanding its implementation is very important. You'll rarely have to implement the code to handle file patterns yourself. To view the full implementation of file pattern matching, review the Zip and MatchingTask source code inside the Ant source distribution. Here is the implementation of the <fileset> nested element processing method, addFileset( ):

```
/**
 * Adds a set of files (nested fileset attribute).
 */
public void addFileset(FileSet set) {
     // Add the FileSet object to the instance variable
     // filesets, a Vector of FileSet objects.
    filesets.addElement(set);
}
```

After all that talk about life cycles and nested elements being complex, you thought things would be more complicated, right? The neat thing about Ant is its heavy reliance on object-oriented designs and introspection. The nature of object programming means that the designs are sometimes complex, with the trade-off being ease of coding and code maintenance. The very concept of the XML tag-to-class relationship is what makes the preceding code segments short. When you write a task like jar, you can assume the FileSet object takes care of everything. You need only worry about the nice, well-designed interface.

Since the Jar class needs to maintain a list of FileSet objects, it also needs something to store them in. Thankfully, Java is rich with collection classes—in this case, we use a Vector.* Of course, what we actually *do* with the Vector of FileSet objects is much more complicated. Luckily, we only have to write that implementation in one place, the execute( ) method; for the jar task, we don't even have to write it ourselves!

Implement the execute( ) Method

The execute( ) method implements the core logic of any task. When writing tasks, implementing the execute( ) portion of a task is the easiest part. The Ant engine calls execute( ) when it reaches the final phase of a task's processing. The execute( )

* You may be thinking, "Why not a List or ArrayList? Why the synchronized Vector?!?" Ant's design requirements call for compatibility with JDK 1.1. The collection classes were not added until Java2; hence the use of Vector.

method neither takes arguments nor returns any value. It is the last method Ant ever calls on a task, so, by this time, your task class should have all the information it needs to do its work.

In an earlier section, we mentioned that Zip implements a perfectly acceptable version of the execute( ) method; we don't need to write one for the Jar class. That's not a cop-out on our part, it's just a good example of efficient code re-use. To explain why we don't have to write our own execute( ) method, we'll go ahead and analyze Zip's execute( )method. We won't cover ZIP/JAR-specific operations in our analysis, since we're concentrating on learning how to write Ant tasks, not how to programmatically build and manage JARs.

We divide the analysis of execute( ) into three parts: validation, performing the actual work, and error handling. These are simple and generic ways to describe how to implement a task's core operations. Keep these parts in mind when writing your own tasks, as it could help you design a better task. Before getting into the individual parts of the execute( ) method, however, let's look at the method signature:

```
public void execute( ) throws BuildException {
```

There is nothing special here. No parameters or return values to worry about. Errors propagate via BuildExceptions, just as in all of the other task-interface methods.

Validation

The first part of our analysis concerns validation. We need to validate the values of the jar task's attributes. Additionally, we must test to see if the task needs to run at all, based on the attributes' values. Valid attributes are non-null, and represent values within the parameters of how the task uses the attribute. For the most part, this validation takes place within the setter methods. However, since there is no order in how Ant calls the setter methods (e.g., given six attributes, it's technically impossible to specify which will get set first), any relational validation between two or more attributes must be made in execute( ). All runtime validation must also take place within execute( ).

In the following code segment, we check the "required" attributes and elements of the task. In our case, we need only the basedir attribute and the <fileset> elements.

```
if (baseDir == null && filesets.size( ) == 0) {
    throw new BuildException( "basedir attribute must be set, " +
       "or at least one fileset must be given!" );
}
```

Here, we check to make sure that the name is valid (not null) for the ZIP file—or, in our case, the JAR file.

```
if (zipFile == null) {
    throw new BuildException("You must specify the " + \
      archiveType + " file to create!");
}
```

That's all for validation. Not much to it, actually, but these little snippets are great at preventing future errors. Hours of effort are saved when good validation is part of a task's implementation.

Doing the actual work

The second part of our execute( ) method analysis concerns the creation of the JAR file using Ant-provided objects for creating collections of files. Here, we introduce two helper objects, FileSet and FileScanner. Both represent different ways to store collections of files and directories, but they are not identical in function. The FileSet object relates directly to the <fileset> element and its subelements. A FileScanner is an object capable of doing platform-agnostic analysis of the underlying filesystem. It can compare file sets or other scanners to itself to determine if files have changed or are missing. Once Ant processes the <fileset> element, the FileSet object has many powerful methods that extract information from the populated object.

The following segment uses the base-directory attribute (basedir) and the file sets to create a list of scanners. In this case, we create a list of scanners to compare against the archive file, if it exists (e.g., from a previous build). It's an up-to-date check, eliminating unnecessary effort, if possible. The getDirectoryScanner method comes from MatchingTask.

```
// Create the scanners to pass to isUpToDate( ).
Vector dss = new Vector ();

// Create a "checkable" list of the files/directories under the base
// directory.
if (baseDir != null) {
   // getDirectoryScanner is available from the MatchingTask object
   dss.addElement(getDirectoryScanner(baseDir));
}

// Create a "checkable" list of the files/directories
// from the FileSet, using the FileSet's characteristics
// We pass the project object in so the list can include
// global filters set in the project's properties.
for (int i=0; i<filesets.size(); i++) {
   FileSet fs = (FileSet) filesets.elementAt(i);
   dss.addElement (fs.getDirectoryScanner(project));
}

// Create the FileScanner array for the isUpToDate method
int dssSize = dss.size();
FileScanner[] scanners = new FileScanner[dssSize];
dss.copyInto(scanners);

// quick exit if the target is up to date
// can also handle empty archives
if (isUpToDate(scanners, zipFile)) {
   return;
}
```

The next code segment takes place within a try-catch block, which catches an IOException and has a finally clause that closes the ZIP archive's file stream. (We analyze the catch block in the next part our analysis.) This segment adds the files from the file sets and under the base directory to the input stream that is the ZIP/JAR archive. The implementation of addFiles isn't that important. It uses the FileSet object to get individual file names and place them into an InputStream.

```
try {
// Add the implicit fileset to the archive.
// The base direcory is set via the basedir attribute
if (baseDir != null) {
    addFiles(getDirectoryScanner(baseDir), zOut, "", "");
}

// Add the explicit filesets to the archive.
// addFiles is made available with the Zip object
addFiles(filesets, zOut);
}
```

The part of the try block providing the actual functionality for creating archive files and streams is not shown in this chapter. Briefly, it uses its helper objects to create explicit file lists for the archive file. It cleans up any temporary files and closes the streams and file objects. If there are any errors, the Zip object must throw a BuildException, causing the build to fail. That's why the file and stream-related cleanup and closing routines are in the finally clause. Those files and streams must close, regardless of the error state of the build. Let's look at that a little more closely in the next section.

Error handling

The third part of our analysis concerns error handling. You might assume that our earlier validation handles all errors, but that's not the case. Since we're dealing with files and filesystems, the threat of an IOException looms. We communicate errors back to Ant with BuildException, so everything that represents an error, null objects, and IOException eventually turns into a BuildException. For accuracy and better communication to the user, analyze your errors and create descriptive error messages. These are messages that show up in the build log, so they should be human-readable while providing a consistent text layout at the same time so you and other users can run text searches on your logs.

The following snippet is the catch block for the try block shown in the previous section. Should an IOException occur when manipulating streams or files, the code creates a descriptive message. This includes showing the results of some tests on the archive file before it's deleted. The BuildException consists of the message, the original error exception, and the location. Recall that Ant maintains an object named location as a kind of execution pointer. It has the line number of the XML and name of the buildfile from which the error comes from.

```
} catch (IOException ioe) {
// Some IO (probably file) has failed.  Let's check it out.

// Create a descriptive message
   String msg = "Problem creating " + archiveType + ": " + ioe.getMessage( );

// delete a bogus ZIP file
// This essentially rids us of the partially created zip/jar
   if (!zipFile.delete( )) {
      msg += " (and the archive is probably corrupt but I could not delete it)";
   }

// This functionality deals with updating jars
   if (reallyDoUpdate) {
      if (!renamedFile.renameTo(zipFile)) {
         msg+=" (and I couldn't rename the temporary file "+
         renamedFile.getName( )+" back)";
      }
   }

// the message has been built.  Send it back to Ant.
   throw new BuildException(msg, ioe, location);
 }
```

Compile the Task

Compiling a task involves using the current Ant library file, *ant.jar*, and some rudimentary package structure for your task. Many people put their custom tasks in the `org.apache.tools.ant.taskdefs.optional` package, although there is no requirement by Ant to do this. Pick a package and project organization that's best for you. Unless you're writing many tasks, changing the packages later should be an easy operation anyway.

You can always write an Ant buildfile to build your tasks. Here's a small one to get you started.

```
<!-- Build the custom tasks in this project directory.  We'll
     assume that all the custom task classes are packaged under
     the 'src' directory and that the results will wind up in
     'dist'.  Users must change the value for the Ant directory
     and include any further libraries they choose to use with their
     tasks.
-->
<project name="customtasks" basedir="." default="all">
    <property name="src.dir" value="./src"/>
    <!-- Note the absolute directory.  CHANGE THIS BEFORE BUILDING -->
    <!-- It would be possible to use environment variables, but we do
         not assume they are set -->
    <property name="ant.dir" value="/opt/ant"/>
    <property name="ant.lib" value="${ant.dir}/lib"/>

    <proptery name="build.dir" value="./build"/>
```

```
    <property name="dist.dir" value="./dist"/>

    <!-- Compile all of the task object classes -->
    <target name="all">
        <mkdir name="${build.dir}"/>
            <javac srcdir="${src.dir}"
                    destdir="${build.dir}">
                <classpath>
                    <fileset dir="${ant.lib}">
                        <include name="**/*.jar"/>
                    </fileset>
                </classpath>
            </javac>
        <copy todir="${dist.dir}">
            <fileset dir="${build.dir}"/>
        </copy>
    </target>
</project>
```

This buildfile compiles your custom task objects, found in the subdirectory *src* and the corresponding package directories. It then copies the resulting classes into the right package structure under the *dist* directory. Once we have the classes, we only need to deploy and define the task, making it visible to Ant. We use the `<taskdef>` element for this (see more on this element in the subsequent section "Deploy and Declare the Task").

For this chapter's version of `jar`, a project setup like the following should work:

```
mytasks/
build.xml
dist/
build/ (temp build directory)
src/org/myorg/tasks/*.java
```

Keep it simple. If you're only writing one task, there's no point in going overboard in managing your task project beyond this directory structure. Once we build the `jar` task, we put it into a JAR inside the *dist* directory.

Between the directory and the buildfile, creating a new JAR with your task(s) should be a piece of cake. All that's left to do now is deploy the task and make it available for your buildfiles.

Deploy and Declare the Task

User-written tasks deploy in two ways as open classes or as JARs, the difference being nothing more than a maintenance preference. To give some comparison, all of the built-in tasks deploy as a JAR; they are part of the Ant JAR (*ant.jar*). Within that archive is a file, *defaults.properties*. In this, the maintainers declare each task available for Ant by default. Being a properties file, it's a list of name-value pairs. We can extend that property list to declare our own custom task.

If you add a task in Ant's source tree, in theory you can modify the *default.properties* file, adding your new task. In this case, rather than compile your task separately, you must rebuild Ant entirely, creating a new Ant JAR. This method is best for system-wide distributions of Ant, where you need all developers in a team to maintain and use a homogenous development environment. Your team must maintain its own internal version of Ant, but it's probably already maintaining other sets of tools, so one more will not be much of a change.

Here is an example. If you want to add the task `foo` (with the corresponding object `org.apache.tools.ant.taskdefs.optional.Foo`) to the core task collection in Ant, open the file *defaults.properties*, in *src/main/org/apache/tools/ant/taskdefs*, and add the line:

```
foo=org.apache.tools.ant.taskdefs.optional.Foo
```

As a result, the next time you build Ant, your task's class and its declaration will become part of the core task list. If you are interested in more details on building Ant, see `docs/manual/install.html#buildingant` in Ant's source distribution.

If you do not use the aforementioned method, you must declare a user-written task to Ant with a `<taskdef>` element in every buildfile that uses the new task. You may place these elements at the project level or target level of your buildfile, depending on the functional scope you desire for each custom task you are declaring. Project-level tasks are available throughout a buildfile in every target, while target-level tasks are available only within that particular target. In the case of target-level declarations, the position of the declaration is important. You cannot use a custom target-level task before you declare it.

Following is an example of a `<taskdef>` element that defines the task `jar` and specifies `Jar` as the implementation class:

```
<taskdef name="jar" classname="org.apache.tools.ant.taskdefs.Jar"/>
```

The `<taskdef>` element has a set of attributes from which it determines which property set(s) to use. Typically, you use the `name` and `classname` attributes to define the name of the task (the element name) and its class implementation. You can also specify a resource of, say, a property file where a list of task names and task classes reside. See the documentation for `taskdef` in Chapter 7 for complete details on all of its attributes.

Miscellaneous Task Topics

Being something that changes every six months, Ant is by no means in a perfect state. Some of its behaviors are not always immediately obvious. There are quirks, open issues (read: bugs), and hidden features not in the distributed documentation. The following sections describe items you need to be aware of when writing your own tasks. If you want to live dangerously, implement your task, deploy it, and see what happens. When you have a problem you can't explain, jump back to this section and see if one of these items help. Some issues, such as `System.exit()`, will never go away unless the JVM specification changes. Other problems, such as magic properties, may go away after some new task model implementation finds its way to release in the future. Of course, you can try to avoid all issues in the future by implementing a task test.

Magic Properties

Many moons ago, the `javac` task came to be. Many people said it was good and many others nodded in agreement. At the time, at least three different compilers were available for the primary Java platforms (Solaris, Linux, and Windows). These compilers were *javac* (and its different compile modes), IBM's *jikes*, and Symantec's *sj*. Rather than have the compiler type defined as an attribute of the `<javac>` element, the developers decided that there should be a global setting, affecting *all uses of the* `javac` *task*. This global setting applies to every occurrence of `javac` or any related task that derives from the `Javac` class. For example, with one line change, an Ant user could switch from *jikes* to *javac*. This is good, right? Yes and no.

A global compiler flag is good in that it guarantees consistency in the generated bytecode. On average, you don't compile one part of your project with *jikes* and another part with *javac*. In practice, a flag such as the compiler flag is a good idea. However, the downside is that it is all-encompassing. What if you actually want some `<javac>` elements in the buildfile to use *jikes* and others to use *javac*? Ant's answer would be "tough, you can't." It would not be good for your task's design to take on the same attitude. So why do we have to worry about magic properties now, even after we know the consequences?

The implementation that makes magic properties possible depends on what some consider a design hole in Ant's task model. All tasks have references to the `Project` object. Simply put, the `Project` object is *the* all-powerful object in the Ant engine. It holds references to all properties, targets, tasks, DataTypes, etc. With the `Project` object, any task can see any property (including magic properties), even if a task is not explicitly stated in the task element's markup. As long as you use this power in a reasonable, read-only manner, everything should be fine, programmatically speaking.

To illustrate our point that magic properties are not a good idea, let's look at the problem from the eyes of a buildfile writer—specifically, in terms of the buildfile's XML markup. In the XML, tasks are self-contained elements. A task's "scope" begins at its opening tag and ends at its closing tag. When you introduce properties that affect a task's operation but are defined outside of the task's opening and closing tags, you break the readability of the XML and eliminate any visual and intuitive concept of scope.

It is possible to argue that everyday property substitution (for example, `attribute="${some.predefined.property}"`) is part of the problem we're describing, but we're talking about something different. Even though you may define a property outside of a task's scope, or even outside of the buildfile's scope, the place where you *use* that property is very apparent in the task's XML markup. Use the property as the value for a task's attribute or for an attribute of a task's nested elements. In either case, an attribute is a clear indication in the buildfile of what the property value is for. In contrast, you declare a magic property once and never mention it again. Nothing forces you to connect the declaration of a magic property to the task that uses it. Of course, you could always add some XML comments to the buildfile, but Ant does not force you to write comments. Ant forces you to set an attribute if a task requires it.

With small buildfiles, you probably won't notice a problem with magic properties. In these buildfiles, scope is rarely an issue. In large projects, especially those using cascading project directories and buildfiles, magic properties can cause problems. It's possible to declare a magic property in the master buildfile, having its value cascade down to the other buildfiles. In other words, a build's behavior can change because of a not-so-obvious declaration of properties. This creates confusion and can cause errors that are hard to trace.

With `javac`, there's nothing you can do short of making changes to the source code and maintaining your own version of Ant, which is something you probably want to avoid. When you use `javac`'s magic property, document it well and let your users know why the buildfile must use one compiler instead of another. When writing your own tasks, avoid referring to project-level properties at all costs.

The Problem with System.exit( )

As with many good things, there are dark linings around the silver clouds. One of these dark linings is the common misuse of the `System.exit( )` call in Java programs. Copying the C programming model, Java developers implement many of their programs using `System.exit( )` to stop execution, either when an unhandled error occurs or when the program is ordered to stop by the user. The `System.exit( )` call returns an error code back to the system (more precisely, back to the JVM). Tradition dictates that 0 means success or no error, and any nonzero value means failure (some programs attach meaning to various nonzero values). The problem lies in the fact that `System.exit( )` talks to the JVM directly, regardless of how a class is instantiated or how deep into the call stack a program might be. People mistakenly think Java programs can handle the exit calls, when, in fact, they cannot. The JVM handles the exit call, period. So how does this seemingly unrelated problem affect Ant in general, and you, specifically?

If a task or the classes used by a task call `System.exit( )`, the Ant engine dies because its JVM dies. Since the effect is similar to turning off a computer (you're "turning off" a virtual machine, after all), the build stops with no error messages. The build just *stops*. With regards to you as a task writer, you should not write a task using a class that you know calls `System.exit()`.* If you can't avoid the call, you need to use the exec or `java` tasks, or borrow these tasks' implementations for your own task. exec and `java` fork the JVM process from Ant's JVM, meaning the `System.exit()` call is never made inside Ant's JVM. If think you need to implement something like this, read about the `java` task and forking in Chapter 7 and in Appendix B. You can always look at the source code for the `java` task's class, `Java`.

Calls to `System.exit()` may be responsible for odd, unexpected behaviors during a build. For instance, if you use `java` to call that new XSLT program you found on the Internet and the build dies unexpectedly during the program's execution, it's likely that a call to `System.exit()` within the new XSLT program is your culprit. Just remember, for future reference, that `System.exit()` is not your friend. It should exist only in the `main()` method of any class, if anywhere.

* Unless you're absolutely certain you can avoid the method call completely.

CHAPTER 6

User-Written Listeners

Writing a log is intrinsic to Ant. As you might expect, this functionality is built-in, and always on by default. What you might not expect is that you can modify the way Ant writes its logs. In fact, you're not limited to just changing the logging mechanism. You can change the way Ant behaves during certain steps of a build. Ant provides this wonderful bit of flexibility in the form of an event model. Those familiar with GUI development have heard this term before, as GUI programming libraries are the most common libraries to put event models into practice. The concept of the event model is simple. The Ant engine maintains a list of objects that have requested to "listen" to the build's various "events." During processing, Ant announces these events, in the form of `BuildEvent` objects, to each of its listeners. The listeners, incidentally, are called `BuildListeners`. The `BuildListener` is a Java interface. Any time you want to write a new listener, implement the `BuildListener` interface in your new class and fill in the logic for each of the interface methods.

Writing your own class implementing the `BuildListener` interface is a straightforward undertaking, especially if you compare the effort to the effort required for writing an Ant task. The typical user-written listener turns out to be some form of specialized logger, replacing Ant's built-in logging mechanism. Knowing this, Ant's developers provide a `BuildLogger` class, extending from `BuildListener` and adding the privilege of being able to write directly to Ant's log. This is important because users can control Ant's output at build time. By default, Ant directs its log output to `stdout`, but it can also direct log output to a log file using the command-line option *-logfile <filename>*. If you're writing a `BuildLogger` instead of just a `BuildListener`, your class inherits this ability to use Ant's output, making it easier for developers to use your new class with their builds. Otherwise, you would force them to manage Ant's output as well as your class' own output.

Keep in mind that listeners aren't just limited to being replacements for Ant's logging system. With a listener, you may incorporate Ant-functionality within a bug tracking system such as Bugzilla, for example. To do this, write a listener to act as a bridge between Ant and Bugzilla. On one side of this bridge, Ant's build events arrive for processing. The bridge translates the events and propagates them to Bugzilla, making the appropriate HTTP requests with the appropriate parameters. Rather than changing the log output, this listener makes changes to Ant, or, more appropriately, increases its processing abilities. The neat part is neither Ant nor Bugzilla have designs explicitly meant to integrate one with the other. It's all done using Ant's listener-producer event system, and it's easy to use.

To provide an example of a `BuildListener`, we borrow (again) from the Ant source distribution, taking a close look at the `XmlLogger` class. As its name implies, this listener writes logging output, just like the default logger, except it writes the output as XML markup.

The BuildEvent Class

Ant and all its listeners, including their cousins the loggers, use the `BuildEvent` class to communicate. Ant dispatches seven types of events, representing various stages Ant goes through to process a buildfile. We describe these events in the next section. Note that the seven types of events are in no way related to the task life cycle.

The `BuildEvent` class acts as an information container for events passed between Ant and its listeners. The Ant engine places vital information into a `BuildEvent` object and passes it on to its listeners so that they have more information about the build. Sometimes, due to constraints in implementation and design, Ant might restrict the amount of information in these objects. There's no pattern to where or why these restrictions occur. Just be aware that these restrictions exist, so that when you write your own listener, you don't get too frustrated wondering why, for example, you're not getting a task's name.*

Here are the globally available property methods on the `BuildEvent` object:

`getProject( )`
: Returns the `Project` object for the running build. This object controls all aspects of the build, so be careful when using it.

`getTarget( )`
: Returns the `Target` object corresponding to the active target at the time the event is sent.

`getTask( )`
: Returns the `Task` object corresponding to the active task at the time the event is sent.

The next method is available only when a task, target, or the build has finished:

* You could always dig down into Ant and figure out why you're not getting the information. If it's a case of someone lazily forgetting to add it to the `BuildEvent` object, you're more than welcome to fix this problem and submit the change to Ant's maintainers. That's the community development process!

`getException()`
: Returns the active `BuildException` thrown at the time of the event. Especially useful for stack traces.

The next methods are available only when Ant is logging a message:

`getPriority()`
: Returns the priority level for the message. Levels correspond to the logging message levels stored as `public static` fields in the `Project` object. See Chapter 3 for a summary of the logging levels.

`getMessage()`
: Returns the content of the message for logging. Never assume the code logging the message has formatted the text in any way.

A listener that you write can use these methods on the `BuildEvent` objects that Ant passes to perform all sorts of powerful operations. The `Project`, `Target`, and `Task` objects give your listener access to detailed information about the build. Tasks are especially good to write combined with listeners if you need more control over your build process than XML elements provide. You can always add more public methods to your task class. Your listener class can then use these additional methods for added functionality.

The BuildListener Interface

Ant, via its event framework, tracks a variety of build-processing events using listener classes implementing the `BuildListener` interface. The design of the `BuildListener` interface and its implementation follows a pattern similar to the AWT* concept of listeners. In both models, an engine propagates events, whether the events are system or user-driven. Classes that wish to receive these events register themselves as listeners (in this case to the Ant engine), usually making restrictions through interface types on the kinds of events they wish to receive. When an event occurs, the engine tells all of the listeners that have registered for the event type in question. Using `BuildEvent` objects, the Ant engine passes detailed information to the listeners. This communication model makes Ant the most flexible build system available, because it doesn't force the user to rely on complicated parsing of Ant's output.

Below are the event types and their corresponding interface methods:

`buildStarted(BuildEvent event)`
: Ant fires the `buildStarted` event when it begins processing the buildfile. Listeners implementing this method can perform actions when the build starts.

* Abstract Windowing Toolkit, Java's cross-platform GUI library. Modern GUI's are written using a methodology called event-driven programming. Rather than continuously processing information, event-driven programs perform actions only when a particular event tells them to.

`buildFinished(BuildEvent event)`
: Ant fires the `buildFinished` event when it has finished processing. Nothing happens in the Ant engine after this event. Consider this the final message for any given build.

`targetStarted(BuildEvent event)`
: Ant fires the `targetStarted` event just before processing a target's first task.

`targetFinished(BuildEvent event)`
: Ant fires the `targetFinished` event after it has processed the last task of a target. Ant fires the event regardless of the error state.

`taskStarted(BuildEvent event)`
: Ant fires the `taskStarted` event just before starting a task's or a DataType's life cycle.

`taskFinished(BuildEvent event)`
: Ant fires the `taskFinished` event immediately after completing a task's or a DataType's life cycle. Ant fires the event regardless of the task's or DataType's error state.

`messageLogged(BuildEvent event)`
: Ant fires the `messageLogged` event after any part of Ant calls one of the log methods. The event parameter contains the message from the method call as well as its priority.

Please take note of the descriptions for `taskFinished()` and `taskStarted()`. The names of these events are a bit misleading since they refer to tasks. This harks back to the early days of Ant when every element in the buildfile was considered a task. It would be better to think of these events as "elementStarted" and "elementFinished," meaning that Ant calls these events when it processes any element in the buildfile, not just tasks.

Whenever you write a class implementing the `BuildListener` interface, you must, of course, write implementations for every interface method. This holds true even if you do not plan on doing anything with a given event. When you don't want to handle an event, leave its interface method's implementation empty. Ant still calls the method, but nothing happens. The design of Ant's event model does not require you to resend each event in case you run across an error or can't handle the event.* Theoretically, if any errors occur during your listener's processing, you throw a `BuildException`. However, if your object happens to be a logger, you handle things a bit differently. Throwing `BuildExceptions` from a logger is not good practice. You cannot make a call to the logging system from the `messageLogged()` method. Your

* As opposed to some event models, such as the original Java GUI library, which require event handlers to propagate messages instead of consuming them.

logger class would be, in effect, calling itself, resulting in a circular operation and possibly an infinite loop (assuming the error keeps happening). In order to avoid any possibility of circular calls and infinite loops, your `messageLogged( )` method needs to display error and debugging messages directly to the console (e.g., with calls to `System.err.println( )`) or to some other mechanism that does not involve Ant.

Probably the simplest and most common use of the listener model is for augmenting or replacing Ant's own logging system. Ant's own default log module is technically a listener, the class `org.apache.tools.ant.DefaultLogger`. Through this, Ant takes build events and sends messages to an output stream; this is, by default, standard output. Barring the occasional "direct-to-console" messages using `System.out.println( )` calls (used by poorly written tasks), Ant generates all logging messages via build events. User-written loggers typically redirect the messages to either different message formats, such as XML, or to different auditing systems, like Log4J.

In the next section's example, we take a closer look at one such user-written logger: the `XmlLogger`. This class augments, rather than replaces the default logger in Ant. The design is simple. Take all of the build events and use the information available during each event to create some XML markup. The XML output follows no schema or design. The implementation is more of a proof-of-concept rather than a useful tool.*

An Example: XmlLogger

The `XmlLogger` source code is included with every source distribution of Ant. If you wish to follow along with the code, you'll need to download the source distribution.† The `XmlLogger` redirects the normal logging output from Ant and writes it to a file in XML markup. Its simplicity and wide availability in source form make it a good example for learning how to write build listeners.

If you're interested in seeing how `XmlLogger` works, test it with your standard Ant installation. There's no need to download the source distribution as the `XmlLogger` class comes with all binary distributions. Unlike the case when adding tasks, there's no need for you to declare a listener using markup in the buildfile like `<taskdef>`. Instead, declare it on the command line. First, insure the class is visible to Ant. You can do this by adding it to your system's classpath or by packaging it into a JAR and placing the JAR in `ANT_HOME/lib`. Then, specify the listener class as an argument to the *ant* command. The *-listener listenerClass* argument notifies the Ant engine that it must add the specified listener class to the internally managed list of build listeners. You may specify more than one listener argument, with no limit on the total number.

* However, the source distribution ships with a stylesheet that the XML logger references in its output. With this stylesheet, it is possible to transform the XML output into HTML, SVG, or whatever format you can imagine (and implement).

† In the source distribution, the source file is located at *src/main/org/apache/tools/ant/XmlLogger.java*.

Well, there's *almost* no limit. Any command-line byte-length limitations inherent to your shell still apply. To use the XmlLogger listener, you call *ant* like so:

```
ant -listener org.apache.tools.ant.XmlLogger
```

Running this command and its argument against a buildfile results in Ant writing the build messages to the console and to an XML markup file called *log.xml*. The logger writes the XML file to the current working directory.

The following code examples show the implementation for three of XmlLogger's interface methods: taskStarted( ), taskFinished( ), and messageLogged( ). The examples represent only a portion of the source for the XmlLogger class. Most of the XML-specific method calls and classes are missing, saving print space, and, hopefully, avoiding any confusion you might have about what constitutes a logger and what constitutes code for building XML files. Because some of the code is missing, the example does not compile. The XML-specific classes and method calls are unimportant for our demonstration purposes.

The TimedElement class, used to manage XML data (and which you'll see in the following code example), is a private, static class encapsulating an absolute time value (a long class) and an XML element object (an Element class). Without going into too much detail, think of the Element class as an object representing an XML element, its attributes, and its nested elements, if applicable. The following example shows the code for the XmlLogger's taskStarted( ) method (ellipses denote places where code has been omitted for clarity):

```
package org.apache.tools.ant;

import java.io.*;
import java.util.*;
import javax.xml.parsers.*;
import org.w3c.dom.*;
import org.apache.tools.ant.util.DOMElementWriter;

/**
 * Generates a "log.xml" file in the current directory with
 * an XML description of what happened during a build.
 *
 * @see Project#addBuildListener(BuildListener)
 */
public class XmlLogger implements BuildListener {

...

    static private class TimedElement {
        long startTime;
        Element element;
    }

...
```

```
    public void taskStarted(BuildEvent event) {
        // Get the task object from the BuildEvent
        Task task = event.getTask( );

        // Create a new <task> XML element with the
        // current time as the start time and the
        // label "task" from TASK_TAG
        TimedElement taskElement = new TimedElement( );
        taskElement.startTime = System.currentTimeMillis( );
        taskElement.element = doc.createElement(TASK_TAG);

        // Derive the name of the task from the task's class
        // name
        String name = task.getClass().getName( );
        int pos = name.lastIndexOf(".");
        if (pos != -1) {
            name = name.substring(pos + 1);
        }

        // Set the attributes of the <task> element and
        // place it into the element stack.
        taskElement.element.setAttribute(NAME_ATTR, name);
        taskElement.element.setAttribute(LOCATION_ATTR,\
            event.getTask().getLocation().toString( ));
...
    }
```

When Ant calls `XmlLogger`'s `taskStarted( )` method, `XmlLogger` takes the `BuildEvent` object and uses its information to populate the element's logging XML markup (with a `TimedElement`). From the system time, `XmlLogger` populates the `TimedElement`'s start time. This is used later in `taskFinished( )` to calculate a total processing time for the element in question. `XmlLogger` retrieves the name of the currently executing task and the physical location (i.e., line number) of the task in the buildfile from the `BuildEvent` object (`event`).

In `taskFinished( )`, `XmlLogger` uses the event object to get the name of the element Ant just finished processing. It uses this name to retrieve the already created `TimedElement` from a list of elements maintained by the class. Once this object is found, the logger takes this opportunity to calculate the processing time of the element and set the appropriate attribute. Following is the code for `XmlLogger`'s `taskFinished( )` method. Again, some code has been omitted, which is denoted by ellipses:

```
    public void taskFinished(BuildEvent event) {
        Task task = event.getTask( );
        TimedElement taskElement = (TimedElement)tasks.get(task);
        if (taskElement != null) {
            long totalTime = System.currentTimeMillis( ) - taskElement.startTime;
            taskElement.element.setAttribute(TIME_ATTR, DefaultLogger.
formatTime(totalTime));
...
    }
```

Next is the messageLogged( ) method for XmlLogger. Before calling messageLogged( ), Ant has already made a decision about the logging level. It is not up to your loggers to decide when to display certain messages. XmlLogger's messageLogged( ) method uses the level value from the event object to set the proper attribute in the markup. The method then retrieves the message from the event object and places it into a CDATA field. Therefore, the resulting XML from the logger presents strings from the build messages in their raw character format.

```
    public void messageLogged(BuildEvent event) {
        Element messageElement = doc.createElement(MESSAGE_TAG);

        String name = "debug";
        switch(event.getPriority( )) {
            case Project.MSG_ERR: name = "error"; break;
            case Project.MSG_WARN: name = "warn"; break;
            case Project.MSG_INFO: name = "info"; break;
            default: name = "debug"; break;
        }
        messageElement.setAttribute(PRIORITY_ATTR, name);

        Text messageText = doc.createCDATASection(event.getMessage( ));
        messageElement.appendChild(messageText);

...

}
```

Message events are slightly different from the other events in that the Ant engine is not the exclusive originator (as it is with the other build events). The nonmessage events all come from the Project object as it enters and leaves the elements of a buildfile. Log messages can come from classes other than Project. These messages still travel through the Ant engine, making their way out as events passed to messageLogged( ).

The Parallel Problem

Ant versions since 1.4 include a task that runs other tasks in parallel. Before 1.4, tasks within a target ran sequentially—in most cases, this was okay and to be expected. However, targets that, for example, compile mutually exclusive sets of code or create unrelated directories can benefit from threading these operations so that they are run simultaneously. Users with multiple-CPU systems see performance benefits from parallelizing such tasks. Another benefit of parallelization is for those people who wish to run unit tests against application servers. Their application servers and tests must run simultaneously, which was not easily done in Ant before Version 1.4. Unfortunately, for those who write or have written custom build listeners, parallelization can break their previously working code.

Some build event listeners rely upon certain events occurring in a particular order. For example, if a listener expects to see a `taskFinished()` event after the `taskStarted()` event for the `javac` task, the listener would fail or act strangely if two `javac` tasks were run in parallel. The second `javac` may end before the first. Listener code, while watching for the event saying Ant is finished with the second `javac` task, may prematurely trigger operations intended for the first `javac` task, or vice versa. Consequently, the output from, or operations of, the listener would be wrong, possibly leading to further problems. If you're ever given a buildfile using the `parallel` task, it's best to test your custom listeners to see whether nonsequential behavior is okay.

`XmlLogger` is a good example of a listener that handles tasks run in parallel. Let's look at an execution flow in which `XmlLogger` listens to the following set of operations from a buildfile:

```
<parallel>
  <copy todir="test">
    <fileset dir=".\irssibot-1.0.4" includes="**/*.java"/>
  </copy>
  <mkdir dir="testxml"/>
  <mkdir dir="testxml2"/>
  <copy todir="test">
    <fileset dir=".\oak-0.99.17" includes="**/*.java"/>
  </copy>
  <mkdir dir="testxml3"/>
</parallel>
```

Let's assume that the engine, being multithreaded, executes the tasks such that they complete in the following order:

1. MKDIR(TESTXML)
2. MKDIR(TESTXML2)
3. MKDIR(TESTXML3)
4. COPY(irssibot)
5. COPY(oak)

Because it was written to handle out-of-order events, `XmlLogger`'s resulting XML markup does not output any elements out of order. The tasks' markup appears in the order listed above, with their nested elements intact. While there is no "right" way to write a multithreaded aware listener, `XmlLogger` shows that some clever foresight in design can thwart future catastrophes. This foresight makes a listener long-lived, even with the possibility of future dramatic changes in the task library.

CHAPTER 7
Core Tasks

This chapter lists core tasks and attributes from Ant Versions 1.2, 1.3, 1.4, and 1.4.1. Whenever the word "all" appears in reference to a version, it means that all of these versions of Ant support a given feature. Ant 1.1 is not considered; tasks and attributes that work only in Ant 1.1 are not described in this chapter.

This chapter is comprised of the following major sections:

Task Summary
: Provides a quick summary of Ant tasks

Common Types and Attributes
: Describes attribute types, followed by a list of attributes used by all Ant tasks

Project and Target
: Describes the syntax of the `<project>` and `<target>` elements

Core Task Reference
: Describes each of the core Ant tasks

Each task description includes the following information:

- A brief summary of the task
- A list of Ant versions supporting the task
- The name of the Java class implementing the task
- A list of XML attributes for the task
- A description of the allowable content, which is either nested XML elements or text
- Example usage

Task Summary

Table 7-1 summarizes all of Ant's core tasks. The remainder of this chapter describes each task in detail.

Table 7-1. Core task summary

Task name	Ant versions	Synopsis
`ant`	all	Invokes Ant on another buildfile.
`antcall`	all	Calls a target in the current buildfile.
`antstructure`	all	Creates an XML Document Type Definition (DTD) for Ant buildfiles.
`apply`	1.3, 1.4	Executes a system command on a set of files.
`available`	all	Sets a property if a resource is available.
`chmod`	all	Changes permissions on files and directories (Unix platforms only).
`condition`	1.4	Sets a property if a condition is true.
`copy`	all	Copies files and directories.
`copydir`	all	Deprecated in Ant 1.2; use the `copy` task instead.
`copyfile`	all	Deprecated in Ant 1.2; use the `copy` task instead.
`cvs`	all	Executes Concurrent Versions System (CVS) commands.
`cvspass`	1.4	Adds passwords to a *.cvspass* file; equivalent to the CVS *login* command.
`delete`	all	Deletes files and directories.
`deltree`	all	Deprecated in Ant 1.2; use the `delete` task instead.
`dependset`	1.4	Manages dependencies between files, removing all target files if any are out-of-date with respect to their source files.
`ear`	1.4	Builds Enterprise Application Archive (EAR) files.
`echo`	all	Writes a message to the Ant log or a file.
`exec`	all	Executes a native system command.
`execon`	all	Deprecated in Ant 1.4; use the `apply` task instead.
`fail`	all	Throws a `BuildException`, causing the current build to terminate.
`filter`	all	Sets token filters for the current project.
`fixcrlf`	all	Cleans up special characters in source files, such as tabs, carriage returns, linefeeds, and EOF characters.
`genkey`	all	Generates a key in a keystore.
`get`	all	Gets a file from a URL.
`gunzip`	all	Unzips a GZip file.
`gzip`	all	Creates a GZip file.
`jar`	all	Creates a JAR file.
`java`	all	Executes a Java class.
`javac`	all	Compiles Java source code.
`javadoc`	all	Runs the JavaDoc utility to generate source code documentation.
`mail`	all	Sends email using SMTP.
`mkdir`	all	Creates a directory.
`move`	all	Moves files and directories.
`parallel`	1.4	Executes multiple tasks in concurrent threads.
`patch`	all	Applies a diff file to originals.

Table 7-1. Core task summary (continued)

Task name	Ant versions	Synopsis
pathconvert	1.4	Converts Ant paths into platform-specific paths.
property	all	Sets properties in the project.
record	1.4	Logs output from the current build process.
rename	all	Deprecated in Ant 1.2; use the move task instead.
replace	all	Performs string replacement in one or more files.
rmic	all	Runs the *rmic* compiler.
sequential	1.4	Executes multiple tasks sequentially; designed for use with the parallel task.
signjar	all	Executes the *javasign* command-line tool.
sleep	1.4	Pauses the build for a specified interval.
sql	all	Executes SQL commands using JDBC.
style	all	Performs XSLT transformations.
tar	all	Creates a tar archive.
taskdef	all	Adds custom tasks to the current project.
touch	all	Updates the timestamp of one or more files.
tstamp	all	Sets the DSTAMP, TSTAMP, and TODAY properties.
typedef	1.4	Adds a DataType to the current project.
unjar	1.3, 1.4	Expands a ZIP file, WAR file, or JAR file.
untar	all	Expands a tar file.
unwar	1.3, 1.4	Expands a ZIP file, WAR file, or JAR file.
unzip	1.3, 1.4	Expands a ZIP file, WAR file, or JAR file.
uptodate	all	Sets a property if one or more target files are up-to-date with respect to corresponding source files.
war	all	Creates a Web Application Archive (WAR) file.
zip	all	Creates a ZIP file.

Common Types and Attributes

All Ant tasks are written using XML—for instance:

```
<copy file="logo.gif" todir="${builddir}"/>
```

In this example, file and todir are attributes. The attribute values, "logo.gif" and "${builddir}", have specific data types. This section summarizes the allowable data types for task attributes, followed by a list of attributes common to all tasks.

XML Attribute Conventions

There are many XML attribute listings in this chapter. They take the following form:

attribute_name (version, type, required_flag)
Is a description of the attribute and its function.

In which:

attribute_name
: Is the name of the attribute. Use this to refer to the attribute when you specify it for a task.

version
: Indicates the version of Ant supporting this attribute. `all` means Ant Versions 1.2 and later.

type
: Indicates the type of data that an attribute can hold. For example, `String` indicates that an attribute holds textual data. See Table 7-2.

required_flag
: Indicates whether a given attribute is required when using the task. If this flag is an asterisk (*), then see the notes immediately following the list.

Description of attribute
: Is a description of the attribute and its function.

Table 7-2 summarizes the attribute types frequently referenced throughout this chapter. In all cases, text from XML attributes is converted into one of the basic types listed here. The "Description" column describes how each conversion happens. The "Implemented by" column lists the Java class that Ant uses to represent each of these attribute types.

Table 7-2. XML attribute type summary

Type name	Implemented by	Description
`boolean`	N/A	Performs a case-insensitive string comparison, converting on, `true`, and yes to `true`. All other values are `false`.
`Enum`	`org.apache.tools.ant.types.EnumeratedAttribute`	Used in cases in which a fixed set of string values are allowed.
`File`	`java.io.File`	Specifies the name of an individual file or directory. Unless stated otherwise, file and directory names are relative to the project base directory. `Fileset` and `filelist`, described shortly, allow you to specify multiple files.
`int, long, etc.`	N/A	Standard Java type wrapper classes, such as `java.lang.Integer`, handle conversion from text in the buildfile to primitive types.
`Path`	`org.apache.tools.ant.types.Path`	Most commonly used by `classpath` and `sourcepath` attributes, representing a list of paths separated by `:` or `;`. This is described in detail under "Path DataType," in Chapter 4.

Table 7-2. XML attribute type summary (continued)

Type name	Implemented by	Description
`Reference`	`org.apache.tools.ant.types.Reference`	Commonly used in `refid` attributes, and contains a reference to a type `id` defined elsewhere. See the example for the `java` task, which shows how to reference a classpath defined elsewhere in the buildfile.
`String`	`java.lang.String`	This is the most commonly used type in Ant. Strings (along with other attributes) are subject to XML attribute limitations. For instance, the < character must be written as `<`.

To understand what this table means, consider the following task:

```
<copy file="src/com/oreilly/ejb/manifest.mf"
      tofile="build/META-INF/manifest.mf"/>
```

For the copy task, both the `file` and `tofile` attributes are of type `File`. Ant converts the XML attribute values, which are always character data, into `java.io.File` objects. This is useful to know because you need to list valid filenames for these arguments. If you do not, the build fails. Now, let's look at three attributes available to all of the Ant tasks.

Common Attributes

The following list describes attributes supported by every Ant task. Since these attributes are available for every task, they are listed once here rather than once for each task.

`id` *(all, String, N)*
: Unique identifier for a task instance; used with the `Reference` type.

`taskname` *(all, String, N)*
: A name for the task instance that shows up in logging output.

`description` *(all, String, N)*
: Comments about the task.

Project and Target

The `<project>` and `<target>` elements are not tasks; however, they are found in every buildfile. Each buildfile must contain one `<project>` element, which in turn contains one or more `<target>` elements.

project

The `<project>` element is found in every buildfile, and is always the root XML element. It specifies a descriptive name for the buildfile, the default target, and the base directory. It also contains all of the `<target>` in the buildfile.

Attributes

`basedir` *(all, File, N)*
: The base directory from which all relative paths in the project are computed. Defaults to the directory containing the buildfile. And if this attribute is not specified, then you can set the `basedir` property when you invoke Ant as follows: **ant** `-Dbasedir=`***`mydirectory target`***

`default` *(all, String, Y)*
: Specifies the target to execute when no target is specified on the *ant* command line.

`name` *(all, String, N)*
: A descriptive name for the Ant project. This name is used for documentation purposes and is displayed when you type **`ant -projecthelp`**.

Content

0..n nested `<description>` *elements (1.4)*
: Defines a description of the project for documentation purposes. Each `<description>` element contains text content. Multiple descriptions are appended and displayed when you type **`ant -projecthelp`**.

0..n nested `<filelist>` *elements (all)*
: Defines project-wide `filelists` that can be referenced throughout the buildfile. See Chapter 4 for a description of the `filelist` DataType.

0..n nested `<fileset>` *elements (all)*
: Defines project-wide `filesets` that can be referenced throughout the buildfile. See Chapter 4 for a description of the `fileset` DataType.

0..n nested `<filterset>` *elements (1.4)*
: Defines project-wide `filtersets` that can be referenced throughout the buildfile. See Chapter 4 for a description of the `filterset` DataType.

0..n nested `<mapper>` *elements (1.3, 1.4)*
: Defines project-wide `mappers` that can be referenced throughout the buildfile. See Chapter 4 for a description of the `mapper` DataType.

0..n nested `<path>` *elements. (all)*
: Defines project-wide `paths` that can be referenced throughout the buildfile. See Chapter 4 for a description of the `path` DataType.

0..n nested `<property>` *elements (all)*
: Defines project-wide property name-value pairs. See the `property` task for more information.

1..n nested `<target>` *elements (all)*
: Defines named groups of tasks, and dependencies between targets.

0..n nested `<taskdef>` *elements (all)*
: Adds custom task definitions to the project. See the `taskdef` task for more information.

target

Every buildfile contains one or more `<target>` elements, which in turn contain tasks. The tasks do the actual work of the build, while the targets define dependencies. This is fully explained in Chapter 3.

Attributes

`depends` *(all, String, N)*
: A comma-separated list of other targets on which this target depends. Each listed target is executed in order before this target is executed.

`description` *(all, String, N)*
: A descriptive name for this target. The description is used for documentation purposes and is displayed when you type **`ant -projecthelp`**.

`if` *(all, String, N)*
: Specifies the name of a property. This target executes only if the named property is set.

`name` *(all, String, Y)*
: The name of this target. The name is how the user executes targets from the command line, and is used for listing dependencies between targets.

`unless` *(all, String, N)*
: Specifies the name of a property. This target executes unless the named property is set.

Content

Targets may contain nested DataTypes and tasks. DataTypes are described in Chapter 4. Now, let's look at all of Ant's core tasks.

Core Task Reference

The remainder of this chapter provides detailed information on Ant's core tasks.

ant

all

Invokes Ant on a target in another buildfile **org.apache.tools.ant.taskdefs.Ant**

Invokes Ant on a specific target in another buildfile. This is particularly useful for large projects that break up the build process into multiple Ant buildfiles, each of which builds a smaller portion of the overall application.

It instantiates a new Ant project (as an instance of the `org.apache.tools.ant.Project` class). The way that properties propagate from the calling project to the new project has evolved with different versions of Ant. In Ant 1.1, the properties of the calling project are visible in the new project. If both projects define the same property, the calling project takes precedence. Ant 1.2 added the ability to specify nested `<property>` elements as shown later in this section, and Ant 1.4 added the `inheritall` attribute.

This task sets the `ant.file` property in the newly created `Project` object to the same value as the calling project, which is the name of the buildfile.

Attributes

`antfile` *(all, String, N)*
: The name of the buildfile to invoke. Defaults to `build.xml`.

`dir` *(all, File, N)*
: The base directory used by the new project; the `antfile` attribute is relative to the directory specified by `dir`. Defaults to the current working directory.

`inheritall` *(1.4, boolean, N)*
: Controls how properties are passed from the current project to the new project. Defaults to `true`, meaning that all properties in the current project are available in the new project. This is how Ant versions prior to 1.4 work. If set to `false`, properties defined in the current project are not passed to the new project unless they are defined on the *ant* command line (i.e., exist as "user properties"). Properties explicitly passed by nested `<property>` elements are not affected by this attribute, meaning that they always take precedence over properties in the callee.

`output` *(all, String, N)*
: The filename to write output to.

`target` *(all, String, N)*
: The name of the target to invoke in the new project. If omitted, the new project's default target is invoked.

Content

0..n nested `<property>` *elements (all)*
: Passes a property to the new build process.

Example Usage

Invoke the default target on *util_buildfile.xml* in the current directory:

```
<ant antfile="util_buildfile.xml"/>
```

Invoke the `clean` target on *build.xml* in the *gui* directory:

```
<ant dir="gui" target="clean"/>
```

Invoke another buildfile, passing a new value for the builddir property. The value is explicitly set to utiloutput even if the property was defined elsewhere in the calling buildfile:

```
<ant antfile="util_buildfile.xml">
  <property name="builddir" value="utiloutput"/>
</ant>
```

See Also

See the property task for allowable attributes on nested <property> elements.

antcall

all

Invokes a target in the current buildfile — **org.apache.tools.ant.taskdefs.CallTarget**

Invokes a target in the current buildfile. Properties are passed to the new target using nested <param> elements. An investigation of the Ant source code reveals that antcall instantiates and calls the ant task using the current buildfile. This means that a new project instance is created and properties work the same as they do for ant.

Attributes

inheritall *(1.4, boolean, N)*

Defines how properties are propagated to the new target. Defaults to true, meaning all properties in the current build process are inherited by the new target. Prior to Ant 1.4, this was the only behavior. When false, properties set by users on the command line are the only ones passed to the new target.

target *(all, String, Y)*

The name of the target to call.

Content

0..n nested <param> *elements (all)*

Passes a property to the new build process. Each <param> element is implemented using the same class as the property task; all property attributes are applicable.

Example Usage

Call the cleandir target and specify the dir-to-clean property:

```
<target name="clean">
  <antcall target="cleandir">
    <param name="dir-to-clean" value="javadocs"/>
  </antcall>
</target>
```

Delete a directory specified by the dir-to-clean property:

```
<target name="cleandir">
  <delete dir="${dir-to-clean}"/>
</target>
```

See Also

See the property task for allowable attributes on nested <param> elements.

antstructure

all

Creates a DTD for Ant buildfiles — org.apache.tools.ant.taskdefs.AntStructure

Creates an XML Document Type Definition (DTD) for Ant buildfiles. This uses Java reflection to determine allowable attributes and content for all tasks. Since the underlying Ant task API does not indicate which attributes are required, the DTD marks all attributes as `#IMPLIED`.*

Attributes

`output` *(all, File, Y)*
: The name of the DTD file to generate.

Content

None.

Example Usage

Create *project.dtd* in the current directory:

```
<target name="createdtd">
  <antstructure output="project.dtd"/>
</target>
```

apply

1.3, 1.4

Executes a system command — org.apache.tools.ant.taskdefs.Transform

Executes a system command. As of Ant 1.4, the deprecated execon task is merely an alias for `apply`. Unlike the exec task, this task requires a nested `<fileset>` specifying one or more files and directories as arguments to the command.

Attributes

`dest` *(1.3, 1.4, File, *)*
: The destination directory for any target files generated by the command.

`dir` *(1.3, 1.4, File, N)*
: The working directory for the command.

`executable` *(1.3, 1.4, String, Y)*
: The name of the command to execute. Does not include command-line arguments.

`failonerror` *(1.3, 1.4, boolean, N)*
: If `true`, the build fails when the command returns anything other than 0. Defaults to `false`.

`newenvironment` *(1.3, 1.4, boolean, N)*
: If `true`, do not propagate existing environment variables to the new process. Defaults to `false`.

* In DTDs, `#IMPLIED` means optional.

`os` *(1.3, 1.4, String, N)*
: A list of operating systems this task applies to. Executes only if the list contains a string matching the return value from `System.getProperty("os.name")`.

`output` *(1.3, 1.4, File, N)*
: A file to redirect the command output to.

`outputproperty` *(1.4, String, N)*
: The name of a property that stores the command output.

`parallel` *(1.3, 1.4, boolean, N)*
: If `true`, the command is executed once, passing all files as arguments. If `false`, the command is executed once for each file. Defaults to `false`.

`skipemptyfilesets` *(1.4, boolean, N)*
: If `true`, do not execute the command if no source files are found, or if source files are up-to-date with respect to destination files. Defaults to `false`.

`timeout` *(1.3, 1.4, int, N)*
: The number of milliseconds to wait before stopping the command. Waits infinitely if not specified.

`type` *(1.3, 1.4, Enum, N)*
: Determines if names of plain files or directories are sent to the command. Allowable values are `file`, `dir`, or `both`. Defaults to `file`.

`vmlauncher` *(1.4, boolean, N)*
: Specifies whether to attempt using the JVM's built-in command launcher, rather than an *antRun* script. Defaults to `true`.

`dest` is required if you specify a nested `<mapper>`.

Content

0..n nested `<arg>` *elements (1.3, 1.4)*
: Defines command-line arguments.

0..n nested `<env>` *elements (1.3, 1.4)*
: Specifies environment variables to pass to the command.

1..n nested `<fileset>` *elements (1.3, 1.4)*
: Specifies which files and directories are passed as arguments to the command. Unless the `<srcfile>` element is specified, files are appended to the end of the command line.

0,1 nested `<mapper>` *elements (1.3, 1.4)*
: When defined, compares timestamps of target files to timestamps of source files.

0,1 nested `<srcfile>` *elements (1.3, 1.4)*
: When present, controls where files specified by the `<fileset>` elements are placed on the command line. The `<srcfile>` element does not have any attributes, and is placed between the appropriate `<arg>` elements.

0,1 nested `<targetfile>` *elements (1.3, 1.4)*
: This element is only allowed when a `<mapper>` element and the `destdir` attribute are specified. It has no attributes, and is used to mark the position of target filenames on the command line. It works the same as the `<srcfile>` element.

Example Usage

Show the contents of *build.xml* using the *type* command—only if running Windows 2000:

```
<!-- Set vmlauncher="false", otherwise this fails when using
     JDK 1.4beta1 on Windows 2000 -->
<apply executable="type" vmlauncher="false" os="Windows 2000">
  <fileset dir=".">
    <include name="build.xml"/>
  </fileset>
</apply>
```

See Also

See the exec task for another way to execute system commands, particularly when you do not want to pass a list of filenames to the command. See Chapter 4 for more information on `<arg>`, `<env>`, `<fileset>`, and `<mapper>`.

available **all**

Conditionally sets a property if a resource is available **org.apache.tools.ant.taskdefs.Available**

Conditionally sets a property if a *resource* is available at runtime. The resource can be a class, file, directory, or Java system resource. If the resource is present, the property is set to `true`, or whatever the optional `value` attribute is set to. Otherwise, the property is not set.

Attributes

`classname` *(all, String, *)*
: A Java class name to look for, such as `com.oreilly.book.Author`.

`classpath` *(all, Path, N)*
: The classpath to use when looking up a class name or resource.

`classpathref` *(all, Reference, N)*
: A reference to a classpath defined elsewhere in the buildfile.

`file` *(all, File, *)*
: The name of a file to look for.

`filepath` *(1.4, Path, N)*
: The path of the file.

`property` *(all, String, Y)*
: The name of the property this task sets if the resource is found.

`resource` *(all, String, *)*
: A Java resource to look for. For more information on what constitutes a resource, see the various `getResource( )` methods in `java.lang.ClassLoader`.

`type` *(1.4, String, N)*
: Specifies what the `file` attribute represents. In Ant 1.4, legal values are `"file"` or `"dir"`. If not specified, the `file` attribute represents either a file or directory.

`value` *(all, String, N)*
: The value assigned to the property if the resource is found. Defaults to `"true"`.

One of `classname`, `file`, or `resource` is required.

Content

0,1 nested `<classpath>` *elements (all)*

Path element used in place of the classpath attribute.

0,1 nested `<filepath>` *elements (1.4)*

Path element used in place of the filepath attribute.

Example Usage

The following example sets the Servlet23.present property to true if Version 2.3 or later of the Java servlet API is available on the classpath:

```
<available classname="javax.servlet.ServletRequestWrapper"
           property="Servlet23.present"/>
```

This works because the javax.servlet.ServletRequestWrapper class was not included in earlier versions of the servlet API.

chmod

all

Changes file permissions — org.apache.tools.ant.taskdefs.Chmod

Changes permissions on one or more files, just like the Unix *chmod* command. This task only works on Unix platforms.

Attributes

defaultexcludes *(all, boolean, N)*

Determines whether to use *default excludes*, as described in Chapter 4 under "FileSet DataType." Defaults to true.

dir *(all, File, *)*

The directory holding files whose permissions will be changed.

excludes *(all, String, N)*

A comma-separated list of file patterns to exclude. These are in addition to the default excludes.

excludesfile *(all, File, N)*

The name of a file containing one exclude pattern per line.

file *(all, File, *)*

The name of a file or directory to change permissions on.

includes *(all, String, N)*

A comma-separated list of file patterns to include.

includesfile *(all, File, N)*

The name of a file containing one include pattern per line.

parallel *(all, boolean, N)*

If true, change permissions of all files using a single *chmod* command. Defaults to true.

perm *(all, String, Y)*

The new permissions to apply, such as g+w.

type *(all, Enum, N)*

Determines if names of plain files or directories are sent to the command. Allowable values are file, dir, or both. Defaults to file.

Exactly one of dir or file must be specified, or at least one nested <fileset> element.

Content

0..n nested patternset *elements:* <exclude>, <include>, <patternset> *(all);* <excludesfile>, <includesfile> *(1.4)*

Used in place of their corresponding attributes, these specify the set of included and excluded source files.

0..n nested <fileset> *elements (all)*

Specifies which files and directories are passed as arguments to the command.

Example Usage

Change the permissions to read-only (444) for all HTML files in the JavaDoc output tree:

```
<chmod perm="444">
  <fileset dir="${javadocs}">
    <include name="**/*.html"/>
  </fileset>
</chmod>
```

condition 1.4

Sets a property if condition is true **org.apache.tools.ant.taskdefs.ConditionTask**

Sets a property if a condition is true. This task combines basic Boolean expressions with the available and uptodate tasks.

Attributes

property *(1.4, String, Y)*

The name of a property to set if the condition is true. If the condition is false, the property is not set.

value *(1.4, String, N)*

The value assigned to the property if the condition is true. Defaults to true.

Content

The following elements are considered to be conditions. Exactly one condition must be nested directly within this task. These, in turn, may contain other nested conditions as outlined here.

<not>

Contains exactly one nested condition, negating its result. Does not have any attributes.

<and>

Contains any number of nested conditions, evaluating to true if all nested conditions are true. Conditions are evaluated left-to-right, and evaluation stops if a condition evaluates to false.* Does not have any attributes.

* This is the same behavior as Java's && operator.

<or>
: Contains any number of nested conditions, evaluating to true if any nested condition is true. Conditions are evaluated left-to-right, and evaluation stops when a condition evaluates to true.* Does not have any attributes.

<available>
: Identical to the available task, except its property and value attributes are ignored.

<uptodate>
: Identical to the uptodate task, except its property and value attributes are ignored.

<os>
: Evaluates to true if the current operating system is of a given type. This element has an optional family attribute of type String. Legal values are windows, dos, mac, and unix. The dos attribute includes OS/2 as well as Windows systems. When family is not specified, this condition evaluates to false.

<equals>
: Evaluates to true if two Strings are equal. Does not allow nested conditions. The two Strings are specified using the arg1 and arg2 required attributes.

Example Usage

This example sets the Environment.configured property to true if Version 2.3 of the servlet API and Version 1.1 of JAXP are on the classpath, and if the version of Java is any one of those listed.

```
<condition property="Environment.configured">
  <and>
    <!-- test for servlet version 2.3 -->
    <available classname="javax.servlet.ServletRequestWrapper"/>
    <!-- test for JAXP 1.1 -->
    <available classname="javax.xml.transform.TransformerFactory"/>
    <or>
      <equals arg1="${java.version}" arg2="1.3.0"/>
      <equals arg1="${java.version}" arg2="1.4.0-beta"/>
      <equals arg1="${java.version}" arg2="1.4.0"/>
    </or>
  </and>
</condition>
```

The entire example is equivalent to: (servlet 2.3 is available) AND (JAXP 1.1 is available) AND ((Java=1.3.0) OR (Java=1.4.0-beta) OR (Java=1.4.0)).

copy **all**

Copies files and directories **org.apache.tools.ant.taskdefs.Copy**

Copies files and directories to new locations. A file is copied when the destination file does not exist or when the source file is newer than the destination.

* This is the same behavior as Java's || operator.

Attributes

`file` *(all, File, *)*
: Specifies a single file to copy. Use nested `<fileset>`s to copy multiple files.

`filtering` *(all, boolean, N)*
: If `true`, token filtering (see the `filter` task) using any global buildfile filters takes place. Nested filters that are specified using `<filterset>` are always applied, regardless of this attribute. Defaults to `false`.

`flatten` *(all, boolean, N)*
: If `true`, the directory structure of the source files is not preserved, and all files are copied to a single destination directory. You can achieve the same results using a nested `<mapper>`. Defaults to `false`.

`includeemptydirs` *(all, boolean, N)*
: If `true`, empty directories are also copied. Defaults to `true`.

`overwrite` *(all, boolean, N)*
: If `true`, files are copied even when destination files are newer. Defaults to `false`.

`preservelastmodified` *(1.3, 1.4, String, N)*
: If `true`, destination files are given the same last modified timestamp as source files. Defaults to `false`.

`todir` *(all, File, *)*
: The destination directory to which files are copied.

`tofile` *(all, File, *)*
: The destination file, applicable only when a single file is copied using the `file` attribute.

Either the `file` attribute must be set, or at least one nested `<fileset>` must be specified. When the `file` attribute is set, either the `todir` or `tofile` attribute is required. When nested `<fileset>` elements are used, only `todir` is allowed.

Content

0..n nested `<fileset>` *elements (all)*
: Selects files to copy. The `todir` attribute is required when `<fileset>`s are present.

0..n nested `<filterset>` *elements (1.4)*
: Defines token filters for text substitution as files are copied. See the `filter` task for more info.

0,1 nested `<mapper>` *elements (1.3, 1.4)*
: Defines how filenames are transformed when copied. By default, an identity transformation is performed, meaning that filenames are not modified.

Example Usage

This example copies all Java source files to a new directory, replacing all occurrences of `@VERSION@` with the value of `app.version`.

```
<copy todir="${builddir}/srccopy">
  <fileset dir="${srcdir}">
    <include name="**/*.java"/>
  </fileset>
```

```
    <filterset>
      <filter token="VERSION" value="${app.version}"/>
    </filterset>
  </copy>
```

See Also

See Chapter 4 for more information on `<fileset>` and `<mapper>`. See the `filter` task for information on the `<filterset>` element and token filtering.

copydir

This task was deprecated in Ant 1.2. Use the copy task instead.

copyfile

This task was deprecated in Ant 1.2. Use the copy task instead.

cvs — all

Executes CVS commands — org.apache.tools.ant.taskdefs.Cvs

Executes CVS commands. CVS is an open source version control system, available at *http://www.cvshome.org*.

For information about CVS, see the *CVS Pocket Reference* by Gregor N. Purdy (O'Reilly).

Attributes

`command` *(all, String, N)*
: The name of the CVS command. Defaults to `checkout`.

`cvsroot` *(all, String, N)*
: Specifies where the repository is located. Equivalent to the `CVSROOT` environment variable.

`date` *(all, String, N)*
: Specifies that this command applies to files up to and including the specified date. Equivalent to the `-D` CVS option.

`dest` *(all, File, N)*
: Specifies where to put checked-out files. Defaults to the project base directory.

`error` *(all, File, N)*
: A file for logging standard error output from the CVS command. Defaults to the Ant log using the `MSG_WARN` log level.

`noexec` *(all, boolean, N)*
: When `true`, do not do anything that modifies the filesystem. Equivalent to the `-n` CVS option. Defaults to `false`.

`output` *(all, File, N)*
: A file for logging standard output from the CVS command. Defaults to the Ant log using the `MSG_INFO` log level.

`package` *(all, String, N)*
: Specifies the CVS module to retrieve.

`passfile` *(1.4, File, N)*
: The name of a CVS password file. Defaults to `~/.cvspass`.

`port` *(1.4, int, N)*
: The port number CVS uses to communicate with a server. Defaults to 2401.

`quiet` *(all, boolean, N)*
: When `true`, CVS output is less verbose. This is equivalent to the `-q` CVS option. Defaults to `false`.

`tag` *(all, String, N)*
: Specifies a CVS tag name. Equivalent to the `-tag` CVS option.

Content

None.

Example Usage

This simple example displays the version of CVS:

```
<cvs command="-version"/>
```

This next example checks out all files in the *antbook* module with the `release1.1` tag, placing the checked-out files in the directory specified by `${builddir}`. This hints at how CVS makes it possible to rebuild previous versions of software packages:

```
<cvs dest="${builddir}"
     cvsroot=":local:C:\cvsrepository\cvsroot"
     tag="release1.1"
     package="antbook"/>
```

See Also

The cvspass task.

cvspass 1.4

Updates .cvspass file org.apache.tools.ant.taskdefs.CVSPass

Updates the *.cvspass* file. This is equivalent to executing the *cvs login* command.

Attributes

`cvsroot` *(1.4, String, Y)*
: Specifies where the repository is located. Equivalent to the `CVSROOT` environment variable.

`passfile` *(1.4, File, N)*
: Specifies the name of the password file. Defaults to the *.cvspass* file in the *user.home* directory.

`password` *(1.4, String, Y)*
: The password to add.

Content

None.

Example Usage

This example adds the `anttester` password to the *.cvspass* file in the current user's home directory:

```
<cvspass cvsroot=":local:C:\cvsrepository\cvsroot" password="anttester"/>
```

See Also

The cvs task.

delete

all

Deletes files and directories **org.apache.tools.ant.taskdefs.Delete**

Deletes one or more files and directories.

> This is the most dangerous task in Ant. You can very easily erase your entire project with a single tag: `<delete dir="."/>`.

Attributes

`defaultexcludes` *(all, boolean, N)*
: Determines whether to use default excludes, as described in Chapter 4 under "FileSet DataType." Defaults to `true`.

`dir` *(all, File, *)*
: The directory to delete, including all its files and subdirectories. Somewhat surprisingly, this attribute has nothing to do with the `file` attribute or nested `<fileset>`. Specifically, it does not specify the directory where a file given in the `file` attribute is found. Instead, this attribute tells the task to "brutally" delete an entire directory tree.

`excludes` *(all, String, N)*
: A comma-separated list of file patterns to exclude. These are in addition to the default excludes.

`excludesfile` *(all, File, N)*
: The name of a file containing one exclude pattern per line.

`failonerror` *(1.4, boolean, N)*
: If `true`, the build process fails when this task fails. Defaults to `true`.

`file` *(all, File, *)*
: The name of a file to delete.

`includeemptydirs` *(1.3, 1.4, boolean, N)*
: If `true`, directories are deleted even if they are empty. Relevant only when using nested `<fileset>`s. Defaults to `false`.

`includes` *(all, String, N)*
: A comma-separated list of file patterns to include.

`includesfile` *(all, File, N)*
: The name of a file containing one include pattern per line.

`quiet` *(1.3, 1.4, boolean, N)*
: If `true`, do not fail if a file or directory cannot be deleted. Defaults to `false`.

`verbose` *(all, boolean, N)*
: When `true`, show the names of files as they are deleted. Defaults to `false`.

At least one of either `dir` or `file` is required, or a nested `<fileset>`.

Content

0..n nested `patternset` *elements:* `<exclude>`, `<include>`, `<patternset>` *(all);* `<excludesfile>`, `<includesfile>` *(1.4)*
: Used in place of their corresponding attributes, these specify the set of included and excluded source files.

0..n nested `<fileset>` *elements (all)*
: Selects files to delete. Deletes only empty directories when `includeemptydirs=true`.

Example Usage

Here is a common target found in just about every Ant buildfile. It deletes the build directory and all of its contents:

```
<target name="clean" description="Remove all generated code">
  <delete dir="${builddir}"/>
</target>
```

deltree

This task was deprecated in Ant 1.2. Use the `delete` task instead.

dependset 1.4

Manages dependencies **org.apache.tools.ant.taskdefs.DependSet**

Manages dependencies between files, removing all target files if any are out-of-date with respect to a group of source files. This task does not perform a positional, file-by-file timestamp comparison. Instead, it compares the most recent timestamp from the group of source files to the most recent timestamp from the group of all target files.

Attributes

None.

Content

Requires at least one of either `<srcfileset>` or `<srcfilelist>`, as well as at least one `<targetfileset>` or `<targetfilelist>`. The `fileset` elements are used when missing files are not important. When using `filelists`, on the other hand, any missing files cause *all* target files to be removed.

0..n nested <srcfileset> *elements (1.4)*
: All files in this fileset are compared against all files specified by the <targetfileset> and <targetfilelist> elements.

0..n nested <srcfilelist> *elements (1.4)*
: All files in this filelist are compared against all files specified by the <targetfileset> and <targetfilelist> elements.

0..n nested <targetfileset> *elements (1.4)*
: All files in this fileset are compared against all files specified by the <srcfileset> and <srcfilelist> elements. If any are older, all are deleted.

0..n nested <targetfilelist> *elements (1.4)*
: All files in this filelist are compared against all files specified by the <srcfileset> and <srcfilelist> elements. If any are older, all are deleted.

Example Usage

This example erases all *.class* files in the build directory if the Ant buildfile or any one of the *.java* files are newer than any of the *.class* files.

```
<dependset>
  <srcfileset dir="${basedir}" includes="build.xml"/>
  <srcfileset dir="${srcdir}" includes="**/*.java"/>
  <targetfileset dir="${builddir}" includes="**/*.class"/>
</dependset>
```

See Also

The fileset and filelist types are described in Chapter 4.

ear — 1.4

Creates EAR files — org.apache.tools.ant.taskdefs.Ear

Creates Enterprise Application Archive (EAR) files. Although the jar task is also capable of creating EAR files, the ear task simplifies the process. EAR files are the deployment mechanism for J2EE applications, and are little more than JARs consisting of well-defined directories and files.

Attributes

appxml *(1.4, File, Y)*
: Specifies the location of the deployment descriptor, which is always renamed to *META-INF/application.xml* in the generated EAR file. The source file does not have to be named *application.xml*.

basedir *(1.4, File, N)*
: Specifies the base directory from which to add files to the EAR file.

compress *(1.4, boolean, N)*
: If true, compress the EAR file. Defaults to true.

defaultexcludes *(1.4, boolean, N)*
: Determines whether to use default excludes, as described in Chapter 4 under "FileSet DataType." Defaults to true.

earfile *(1.4, File, Y)*
: Specifies the name of the EAR file to create.

encoding *(1.4, String, N)*
: Specifies the character encoding for filenames inside the EAR file. Defaults to UTF-8. The Ant specification warns that changing this attribute probably renders the EAR file unusable by Java.

excludes *(1.4, String, N)*
: A comma-separated list of file patterns to exclude. These are in addition to the default excludes.

excludesfile *(1.4, File, N)*
: The name of a file containing one exclude pattern per line.

filesonly *(1.4, boolean, N)*
: If true, do not create empty directories. Defaults to false.

includes *(1.4, String, N)*
: A comma-separated list of file patterns to include.

includesfile *(1.4, File, N)*
: The name of a file containing one include pattern per line.

manifest *(1.4, File, N)*
: The name of the manifest file to use.

update *(1.4, boolean, N)*
: If true, update the existing EAR file when changes are made, rather than erasing and creating it from scratch. Defaults to false.

whenempty *(1.4, Enum, N)*
: The behavior used when no files match. Legal values are fail (abort the build), skip (don't create the EAR file), or create. Defaults to create, meaning create an empty EAR file when no files are present.

Content

0..n nested patternset *elements:* <exclude>, <include>, <patternset> *(all);* <excludesfile>, <includesfile> *(1.4)*
: Used in place of their corresponding attributes, these specify the set of included and excluded source files.

0,1 nested <metainf> *elements (1.4)*
: Defines a fileset containing all files placed in the *META-INF* directory of the EAR file. If a file named *MANIFEST.MF* is found, it is ignored and a warning is issued.

0..n nested <fileset> *elements (1.4)*
: Specifies the files and directories to include in the EAR file.

0..n nested <zipfileset> *elements (1.4)*
: See the documentation for the zip task for more information.

Example Usage

These two examples produce identical results. This first example uses attributes:

```
<ear earfile="${builddir}/myapp.ear"
     appxml="ear_deploy_descriptor/application.xml"
```

```
        basedir="${builddir}"
        includes="*.jar,*.war"/>
```

This example uses a nested <fileset> in place of the basedir and includes attributes:

```
<ear earfile="${builddir}/myapp2.ear"
     appxml="ear_deploy_descriptor/application.xml">
  <fileset dir="${builddir}" includes="*.jar,*.war"/>
</ear>
```

See Also

See the jar task. The implementation class for ear extends from jar's implementation class.

echo

all

Writes to a log or file **org.apache.tools.ant.taskdefs.Echo**

Writes a message to the Ant log or a file. The verbosity defaults to Project.MSG_WARN, which means that messages appear on the console.

Attributes

append *(all, boolean, N)*
  If true, append to an existing file. Defaults to false.

file *(all, File, N)*
  The file to write the message to.

message *(all, String, *)*
  The text to write.

The message attribute is required unless text is included as content of the XML tag, as shown in the example that follows.

Content

Text content (all)
  Text content is allowed when the message attribute is not specified. Property references such as ${builddir} are allowed.

Example Usage

The first of the following examples specifies the text to write using the message attribute. The second example specifies the text to write by enclosing it within <echo>...</echo> tags.

```
<echo message="Building to ${builddir}"/>

<echo>You are using version ${java.version}
of Java! This message spans two lines.</echo>
```

exec

all

Executes a system command **org.apache.tools.ant.taskdefs.ExecTask**

Executes a system command. Like the `apply` task, this provides a way to access native functionality outside of the Java and Ant build environment.

The `apply` task requires a nested `<fileset>`, specifying a list of files and directories passed as arguments to the system command. The exec task differs in that it does not allow this nested `<fileset>`.

Attributes

`command` *(1.1, CommandLine, *)*
: The command to execute, including arguments. Deprecated as of Ant 1.2.

`dir` *(all, File, N)*
: The working directory for the command.

`executable` *(all, String, *)*
: The name of the command to execute. Does not include command-line arguments.

`failonerror` *(all, boolean, N)*
: If `true`, the build fails when the command returns anything other than 0. Defaults to `false`.

`newenvironment` *(1.3, 1.4, boolean, N)*
: If `true`, do not propagate existing environment variables to the new process. Defaults to `false`.

`os` *(all, String, N)*
: A list of operating systems this task applies to. Executes only if the list contains a string matching the return value from `System.getProperty("os.name")`.

`output` *(all, File, N)*
: A file to redirect the command output to.

`outputproperty` *(1.4, String, N)*
: The name of a property that stores the command output.

`timeout` *(all, int, N)*
: The number of milliseconds to wait before stopping the command. Waits infinitely if not specified.

`vmlauncher` *(1.4, boolean, N)*
: Specifies whether to attempt using the JVM's built-in command launcher, rather than an *antRun* script. Defaults to `true`.

Technically, exactly one of `command` or `executable` must be set. Since `command` has been deprecated since Ant 1.2, `executable` is recommended.

Content

0..n nested `<arg>` *elements (all)*
: Each specifies command-line arguments, as described in Chapter 4.

0..n nested `<env>` *elements (all)*
: Each specifies an environment variable.

Example Usage

Executes *dir /b* in the build directory on Windows 2000:

```
<exec executable="dir" dir="${builddir}"
      vmlauncher="false" os="Windows 2000">
  <arg line="/b" />
</exec>
```

See Also

See the `apply` task. The syntax for command-line arguments and environment variables is described in Chapter 4.

execon

1.2, 1.3 (deprecated in 1.4)

Executes a system command — **org.apache.tools.ant.taskdefs.ExecuteOn**

Executes a system command. This task was deprecated in Ant 1.4; use the `apply` task instead.

Attributes

`dir` *(1.2, 1.3, File, N)*
: The working directory for the command.

`executable` *(1.2, 1.3, String, Y)*
: The name of the command to execute. Does not include command-line arguments.

`failonerror` *(1.2, 1.3, boolean, N)*
: If `true`, the build fails when the command returns anything other than 0. Defaults to `false`.

`newenvironment` *(1.3, boolean, N)*
: If `true`, do not propagate existing environment variables to the new process. Defaults to `false`.

`os` *(1.2, 1.3, String, N)*
: A list of operating systems this task applies to. Executes only if the list contains a string matching the return value from `System.getProperty("os.name")`.

`output` *(1.2, 1.3, File, N)*
: A file to redirect the command output to.

`parallel` *(1.2, 1.3, boolean, N)*
: If `true`, the command is executed once, passing all files as arguments. If `false`, the command is executed once for each file. Defaults to `false`.

`timeout` *(1.2, 1.3, int, N)*
: The number of milliseconds to wait before stopping the command. Waits infinitely if not specified.

`type` *(1.2, 1.3, Enum, N)*
: Determines if names of plain files or directories are sent to the command. Allowable values are `file`, `dir`, or `both`. Defaults to `file`.

Content

See the apply task.

Example Usage

See the apply task.

fail

all

Throws an exception and ends current build **org.apache.tools.ant.taskdefs.Exit**

Throws a `BuildException`, causing the current build to fail.

Attributes

`message` *(all, String, N)*
: Specifies the message displayed when this task executes.

Content

Text content. (1.4)
: Ant 1.4 adds the ability to specify nested text. This is useful when the message spans multiple lines.

Example Usage

The following example aborts the build without any descriptive message:

```
<fail/>
```

In this case, Ant displays the following message, where 104 is the line number in the buildfile of the line invoking `fail`:

```
BUILD FAILED
C:\cvsdata\ant\mysamples\build.xml:104: No message
```

The following call to `fail` results in a message being displayed. The message is specified between the `<fail>` and `</fail>` tags.

```
<fail>Java version ${java.version} is not allowed!</fail>
```

The next example produces the same results as the previous one; the only difference is that the message is specified using the `message` attribute.

```
<fail message="Java version ${java.version} is not allowed!"/>
```

See Also

Use the echo task to write messages without aborting the build.

filter

all

Defines token filters **org.apache.tools.ant.taskdefs.Filter**

Defines token filters. These are used to perform text substitution, known as token filtering, when copying files. In Ant 1.2 and 1.3, tokens are always of the form `@`*`token`*`@`. Ant 1.4 adds the ability to use a character other than @ with the <filterset> element. Filters should not be used with binary files.

The <filter> element can appear inside of targets, or as a nested element in various tasks that copy files.

Attributes

filtersfile *(all, File, *)*
: A file containing token/value pairs, formatted as a Java properties file.

token *(all, String, *)*
: The text to replace in the source file, not including the @ characters.

value *(all, String, *)*
: The text to substitute in place of @*token*@. The @ characters are not preserved.

You must specify either the filtersfile attribute, or both token and value.

Content

None.

Example Usage

Let's start with the following source file:

```
// %COPYRIGHT!

/**
 * @version @VERSION@
 */
public class Hello {
  ...
}
```

We want to replace %COPYRIGHT! with a copyright notice, and @VERSION@ with the correct version number. Here is a target within a buildfile that does this:

```
<target name="tokenFilterDemo" depends="prepare">
  <filter token="VERSION" value="1.0"/>

  <copy todir="build" filtering="true">
    <!-- select files to copy -->
    <fileset dir="src">
      <include name="**/*.java"/>
    </fileset>
    <filterset begintoken="%" endtoken="!">
      <filter token="COPYRIGHT"
              value="Copyright (C) 2002 O'Reilly"/>
    </filterset>
  </copy>
</target>
```

The first <filter> element takes care of replacing @VERSION@ with 1.0 as the files are copied. In order for this to work, the filtering attribute of the copy task must be set to true.

The <filterset> element, new to Ant 1.4, is required for the %COPYRIGHT! token because it does not use @ characters as delimiters. With <filterset>, we can use whatever tokens we desire. <filterset> elements may contain one or more <filter> elements, so we could have listed both <filter>s as content.

Here is what the file looks like after copying:

```
// Copyright (C) 2002 O'Reilly

/**
 * @version 1.0
 */
public class Hello {
    ...
}
```

See Also

See the copy task.

fixcrlf all

Cleans up special characters org.apache.tools.ant.taskdefs.FixCRLF

Cleans up special characters in source files, such as tabs, carriage returns, linefeeds, and EOF characters.

Attributes

`cr` *(all, Enum, N)*
: Deprecated in Ant 1.4. Specifies how CR characters are modified. Legal values are `add`, `asis`, and `remove`. On Unix platforms, defaults to `remove`, converting Windows-style CRLF to LF. On Windows platforms, defaults to `add`, converting Unix-style LF characters to CRLF.

`defaultexcludes` *(all, boolean, N)*
: Determines whether to use default excludes, as described in Chapter 4 under "FileSet DataType." Defaults to `true`.

`destdir` *(all, File, N)*
: Specifies where "fixed" files are placed. If unspecified, source files are overwritten.

`eof` *(all, Enum, N)*
: Specifies how DOS-style EOF characters (Ctrl-Z) are handled. Supports the same attributes and default values as the `cr` attribute. When the default `remove`, remove the EOF character if present. When it is `add`, add an EOF character if necessary. When it is `asis`, do nothing.

`eol` *(1.4, Enum, N)*
: Replaces the deprecated `cr` attribute, adding better support for Macintosh. Legal values are `asis`, `cr`, `lf`, and `crlf`. Each of these values specifies what EOL characters are placed in the "fixed" files. Defaults to `lf` on Unix, `cr` on Macintosh, and `crlf` on Windows.

`excludes` *(all, String, N)*
: A comma-separated list of file patterns to exclude. These patterns are in addition to the default excludes.

`excludesfile` *(all, File, N)*
: The name of a file containing one exclude pattern per line.

`includes` *(all, String, N)*
: A comma-separated list of file patterns to include.

`includesfile` *(all, File, N)*
: The name of a file containing one include pattern per line.

`javafiles` *(1.4, boolean, N)*
: If `true`, indicates the nested `<fileset>` specifies a set of Java files. This ensures that tab characters are not modified inside of Java string and character constants. Defaults to `false`.

`srcdir` *(all, File, Y)*
: The directory containing files to fix.

`tab` *(all, Enum, N)*
: Controls how tab characters are modified. Legal values are `add`, `asis`, and `remove`. Defaults to `asis`, meaning tab characters are preserved. When `add`, consecutive spaces are converted to tabs. `remove` converts tabs to spaces.

`tablength` *(all, int, N)*
: The number of spaces that a tab character represents. Legal values are 2–80, inclusive. Defaults to 8.

Content

0..n nested `patternset` *elements:* `<exclude>`, `<include>`, `<patternset>` *(all);* `<excludesfile>`, `<includesfile>` *(1.4)*
: Used in place of their corresponding attributes, these specify the set of included and excluded source files.

Example Usage

The following example converts tab characters into sequences of four spaces in Java source files. It preserves existing EOL and EOF characters:

```
<fixcrlf srcdir="${srcdir}"
         destdir="${builddir}"
         eol="asis"
         tab="remove"
         tablength="4"
         eof="asis"
         includes="**/*.java"
         javafiles="true"/>
```

genkey — all

Generates a key-pair — **org.apache.tools.ant.taskdefs.GenerateKey**

Generates a key-pair, adding them to a keystore file. This is essentially a wrapper around the *keytool -genkey* command. The *keytool* application is included with the JDK, and manages private keys and public certificates.

Attributes

alias *(all, String, Y)*
: The identity of the new keystore entry.

dname *(all, String, *)*
: The X.500 distinguished name associated with the alias.

keyalg *(all, String, N)*
: The algorithm used to generate the entry.

keypass *(all, String, *)*
: The password used to protect the private key.

keysize *(all, String, N)*
: The size of the generated key.

keystore *(all, String, N)*
: The name of the keystore file. Defaults to *.keystore* in the user's home directory.

sigalg *(all, String, N)*
: The algorithm used to sign the certificate.

storepass *(all, String, Y)*
: The password used to protect the keystore.

storetype *(all, String, N)*
: The keystore type.

validity *(all, String, N)*
: Number of days the generated certificate is valid.

verbose *(all, boolean, N)*
: Verbose mode. Defaults to false.

The dname attribute is only required if the <dname> content is not specified. keypass is required if the private key password is different than the keystore password.

Content

0,1 nested <dname> *elements (all)*
: Optionally used in place of the dname attribute. Contains 0–n nested <param> elements as shown in the example.

Example Usage

The following example generates a new keystore entry:

```
<genkey dname="CN=Eric Burke, OU=Authors, O=O'Reilly,
               L=Sebastopol, S=California, C=US"
   alias="ericb"
   storepass="aidansdaddy" />
```

This next example accomplishes the same task using a nested <dname> element:

```
<genkey alias="ericb" storepass="aidansdaddy">
  <dname>
    <param name="CN" value="Eric Burke"/>
    <param name="OU" value="Authors"/>
    <param name="O" value="O'Reilly"/>
    <param name="L" value="Sebastopol"/>
```

```
    <param name="S" value="California"/>
    <param name="C" value="US"/>
  </dname>
</genkey>
```

See Also

See the documentation included with Sun's Java Development Kit for the *keystore* command-line program.

get

all

Retrieves a file from a URL **org.apache.tools.ant.taskdefs.Get**

Retrieves a file from a URL.

Attributes

`dest` *(all, File, Y)*
: The local name to store the file as.

`ignoreerrors` *(all, boolean, N)*
: If `true`, log errors but do not abort the build. Defaults to `false`.

`src` *(all, URL, Y)*
: The URL of the remote file to retrieve.

`usetimestamp` *(all, boolean, N)*
: If true, download only the file if the remote timestamp is newer than the local file. Works only with the HTTP protocol. When the file is downloaded, its timestamp is set to the timestamp on the remote machine. Defaults to `false`.

`verbose` *(all, boolean, N)*
: When `true`, display a "." for every 100 KB of data retrieved. Defaults to `false`.

Content

None.

Example Usage

Get the O'Reilly home page:

```
<get src="http://www.oreilly.com/" dest="${builddir}/oreilly_home.html"/>
```

If behind a firewall, specify proxy server configuration using the `ANT_OPTS` environment variable (as explained in Chapter 2) before running Ant.

gunzip

all

Unzips a GZip file **org.apache.tools.ant.taskdefs.GUnzip**

Expands a GZip file. The file is only expanded if the destination file does not exist or is older than the source file.

Attributes

`dest` *(all, String, N)*
: The destination file or directory name. If omitted, `dest` defaults to the directory containing the source file. When `dest` is a directory, the destination filename is the `src` name, minus any *.gz* filename extension.

`src` *(all, String, Y)*
: The name of the file to unzip.

Content

None.

Example Usage

Expand *manuscript.tar.gz* to *manuscript.tar* in the same directory:

```
<gunzip src="manuscript.tar.gz"/>
```

Expand *manuscript.tar.gz* to *${builddir}/manuscript.tar*:

```
<gunzip src="manuscript.tar.gz" dest="${builddir}"/>
```

Use the `untar` task to expand the tar file after unzipping it.

See Also

The `gzip` task, and the `untar` task.

gzip

all

Creates a GZip file **org.apache.tools.ant.taskdefs.GZip**

Creates a GZip archive.

Attributes

`src` *(all, File, Y)*
: The name of the file to compress.

`zipfile` *(all, File, Y)*
: The name of the file to create.

Content

None.

Example Usage

Compresses *manuscript.tar* to *manuscript.tar.gz*:

```
<gzip src="manuscript.tar" dest="manuscript.tar.gz"/>
```

See Also

The `gunzip` task.

jar

all

Creates a JAR file

org.apache.tools.ant.taskdefs.Jar

Creates a JAR file from one or more source files and directories.

Attributes

`basedir` *(all, File, N)*
: Specifies the base directory containing files to be added to the JAR file.

`compress` *(all, boolean, N)*
: If `true`, compress the JAR file. Defaults to `true`.

`defaultexcludes` *(all, boolean, N)*
: Determines whether to use default excludes, as described in Chapter 4 under "FileSet DataType." Defaults to `true`.

`encoding` *(1.4, String,N)*
: Specifies the character encoding for filenames inside the JAR file. Defaults to UTF-8. The Ant specification warns that changing this attribute probably renders the JAR file unusable by Java.

`excludes` *(all, String, N)*
: A comma-separated list of file patterns to exclude. These are in addition to the default excludes.

`excludesfile` *(all, File, N)*
: The name of a file containing one exclude pattern per line.

`filesonly` *(1.4, boolean, N)*
: If `true`, do not create empty directories. Defaults to `false`.

`includes` *(all, String, N)*
: A comma-separated list of file patterns to include.

`includesfile` *(all, File, N)*
: The name of a file containing one include pattern per line.

`jarfile` *(all, File, Y)*
: The name of the JAR file to create.

`manifest` *(all, File, N)*
: The name of an existing manifest file to place in the JAR file. If not specified, Ant generates a new manifest file containing the version of Ant used.

`update` *(1.4, boolean, N)*
: If `true`, update the existing JAR file when changes are made, rather than erasing and creating it from scratch. Defaults to `false`.

`whenempty` *(all, Enum, N)*
: The behavior used when no input files are found. Defaults to `create`. Legal values are:

    `fail`
    : Abort the build.

    `skip`
    : Don't create the JAR file.

    `create`
    : Create an empty JAR file when there are no files present.

Content

0..n nested `<attribute>` *elements (1.4)*

Each specifies a name-value pair to place in the "unnamed" section of the JAR file's manifest. Manifest sections are separated by blank lines, and may optionally have names. Use the `<section>` element to create named manifest sections. Following are the allowable attributes for the `<attribute>` nested element.

`name` *(1.4, String, Y)*

The attribute name.

`value` *(1.4, String, Y)*

The attribute value.

0..n nested `patternset` *elements:* `<exclude>`, `<include>`, `<patternset>` *(all);* `<excludesfile>`, `<includesfile>` *(1.4)*

Used in place of their corresponding attributes, these specify the set of included and excluded source files.

0..n nested `<fileset>` *elements (all)*

Specifies the files and directories to include in the JAR file.

0,1 nested `<metainf>` *elements (1.4)*

Defines a `fileset` containing all files placed in the *META-INF* directory of the JAR file. If a file named *MANIFEST.MF* is found in this `fileset`, its content is merged with the *MANIFEST.MF* placed in the generated JAR file.

0..n nested `<section>` *elements (1.4)*

Each defines a named manifest section. Each `<section>` can contain zero or more nested `<attribute>` elements. The `<section>` element requires the following attribute:

`name` *(1.4, String, Y)*

The section name.

0..n nested `<zipfileset>` *elements (1.3, 1.4)*

See the documentation for the `zip` task for more information.

Example Usage

Create *sample.jar* containing all *.class* files in the build directory tree:

```
<jar jarfile="${builddir}/sample.jar"
     basedir="${builddir}"
     includes="**/*.class"/>
```

This example does the same thing, but uses a nested `<fileset>` element instead of the `includes` attribute:

```
<jar jarfile="${builddir}/sample2.jar">
  <fileset dir="${builddir}" includes="**/*.class"/>
</jar>
```

This last example shows how to use Ant 1.4's `<section>` and `<attribute>` elements to create the JAR file's manifest:

```
<jar jarfile="build/sample.jar" basedir="src" includes="**/*.java">
  <manifest>
    <attribute name="Version" value="3.2"/>
    <attribute name="Release-Date" value="20 Mar 2002"/>
```

```
        <section name="drinks">
          <attribute name="favoriteSoda" value="Coca Cola"/>
          <attribute name="favoriteBeer" value="Amber Bock"/>
        </section>

        <section name="snacks">
          <attribute name="cookie" value="chocolateChip"/>
          <attribute name="iceCream" value="mooseTracks"/>
        </section>

      </manifest>
    </jar>
```

Here is the resulting *META-INF/MANIFEST.MF* file:

```
Manifest-Version: 1.0
Release-Date: 20 Mar 2002
Version: 3.2
Created-By: Ant 1.4.1

Name: snacks
cookie: chocolateChip
iceCream: mooseTracks

Name: drinks
favoriteBeer: Amber Bock
favoriteSoda: Coca Cola
```

See Also

The unzip task.

java

all

Executes a Java class | **org.apache.tools.ant.taskdefs.Java**

Executes a Java class using Ant's VM instance or by forking a new VM process. If the executed application calls `System.exit()`, be sure to set `fork="true"` or Ant will exit.

Attributes

`args` *(all, String, N)*
: Deprecated in Ant 1.2; use nested `<arg>` elements instead.

`classname` *(all, String, *)*
: The name of the Java class to execute.

`classpath` *(all, Path, N)*
: The classpath to use. This is added to Ant's classpath unless `fork="true"`.

`classpathref` *(all, Reference, N)*
: A reference to a classpath defined elsewhere in the buildfile.

`dir` *(all, File, N)*
: The working directory for the VM. Ignored unless `fork="true"`.

failonerror *(all, boolean, N)*
: If true, the build fails when the command returns anything other than 0. Defaults to false. Ignored unless fork="true".

fork *(all, boolean, N)*
: If true, the class is executed in a new VM instance. Defaults to false.

jar *(1.4, File, *)*
: The name of an executable JAR file to execute. The JAR file must contain a Main-Class manifest entry, and fork must be true.

jvm *(all, String, N)*
: The command name of the Java interpreter (may be a full pathname to the command). Defaults to java. Ignored unless fork="true".

jvmargs *(all, String, N)*
: Deprecated in Ant 1.2; use nested <jvmarg> elements instead.

maxmemory *(all, String, N)*
: Maximum amount of memory allocated for the forked VM. Ignored unless fork="true". Equivalent to -mx or -Xmx Java command-line options, depending on which version of Java is in use.

output *(1.3, 1.4, File, N)*
: A filename to write output to.

Either classname or jar is required.

Content

0..n nested <arg> *and* <jvmarg> *elements (all)*
: Specifies command-line arguments to the application and to the JVM, respectively. See "Argument DataType" in Chapter 4.

0..n nested <sysproperty> *elements (all)*
: Each specifies a system property.

0,1 nested <classpath> *elements (all)*
: Uses path element in place of the classpath or classpathref attributes.

Example Usage

This example shows how various command-line arguments are passed to an application:

```
<java classname="com.oreilly.antbook.JavaTest">
  <sysproperty key="oreilly.home" value="${builddir}"/>
  <arg value="Eric Burke"/>
  <arg line="-verbose -debug"/>
  <arg path="/home;/index.html"/>
  <classpath>
    <pathelement path="${builddir}"/>
  </classpath>
</java>
```

First, the oreilly.home system property is specified. This is equivalent to invoking the following command:

```
java -Doreilly.home=build etc...
```

Additionally, the following four command-line arguments are specified:

- `Eric Burke`
- `-verbose`
- `-debug`
- `C:\home;C:\index.html`*

This next example shows how to reference a classpath defined elsewhere in the Ant buildfile:

```
<!-- this is defined at the "target level", parallel to <target>s -->
<path id="thirdparty.class.path">
  <pathelement path="lib/crimson.jar"/>
  <pathelement path="lib/jaxp.jar"/>
  <pathelement path="lib/xalan.jar"/>
</path>

<target name="rundemo">
   <java classname="com.oreilly.antbook.JavaTest">
      <classpath refid="thirdparty.class.path"/>
   </java>
</target>
```

javac

all

Compiles Java source code — org.apache.tools.ant.taskdefs.Javac

Compiles Java source code. This task compares *.java* files with *.class* files. Affected source files are compiled when the class files do not exist, or when the source files are newer than their respective class files.

This task makes no effort to analyze source code or to perform logical dependency analysis. For example, Ant does not know if subclasses need compiling after the source code for a base class is modified.

Numerous compilers are supported. For JDK 1.1/1.2, the default compiler is `classic`. For JDK 1.3/1.4, it defaults to `modern`. To choose a different compiler, set the `build.compiler` property as shown in Table 7-3. The "Alias" column lists alternate property values having the same effect as the value in the "Property" column.

Table 7-3. Compiler selection properties

Property	Alias	Description
`classic`	`javac1.1` or `javac1.2`	The standard JDK 1.1 or 1.2 compiler.
`modern`	`javac1.3` or `javac1.4`	The standard JDK 1.3 or 1.4 compiler.
`jikes`		IBM's Jikes compiler.
`jvc`	`Microsoft`	Microsoft's Java SDK compiler.

* Notice how the command line is converted into platform-specific pathnames. This was discussed in Chapter 4.

Table 7-3. Compiler selection properties (continued)

Property	Alias	Description
kjc		The kopi compiler.
gcj		The gcj compiler from gcc.
sj	Symantec	The Symantec compiler.
extJavac		Run either modern or classic in a JVM of its own.

Attributes

`bootclasspath` *(all, Path, N)*
: The bootstrap* classpath to use.

`bootclasspathref` *(all, Reference, N)*
: A reference to a bootstrap classpath defined elsewhere in the buildfile.

`classpath` *(all, Path, N)*
: The classpath to use. This is added to Ant's classpath unless `fork="true"`.

`classpathref` *(all, Reference, N)*
: A reference to a classpath defined elsewhere in the buildfile.

`debug` *(all, boolean, N)*
: If `true`, compile source with debug information. Defaults to `false`.

`defaultexcludes` *(all, boolean, N)*
: Determines whether to use default excludes, as described in Chapter 4 under "FileSet DataType." Defaults to `true`.

`depend` *(all, boolean, N)*
: If `true`, enables dependency checking for compilers that support it, such as `jikes` and `classic`. Defaults to `false`.

`deprecation` *(all, boolean, N)*
: If `true`, display deprecation warnings. Defaults to `false`.

`destdir` *(all, File, N)*
: The destination directory for class files.

`encoding` *(all, String, N)*
: Character encoding of source files.

`excludes` *(all, String, N)*
: A comma-separated list of file patterns to exclude. These are in addition to the default excludes.

`excludesfile` *(all, File, N)*
: The name of a file containing one exclude pattern per line.

`extdirs` *(all, Path, N)*
: Override the usual location for Java-installed optional packages.

`failonerror` *(1.3, 1.4, boolean, N)*
: If `true`, the build fails when errors occur. Defaults to `true`.

* When using Sun's JVM, the bootstrap classpath includes those classes implementing the Java 2 Platform. These are found in the *rt.jar* and *i18n.jar* files in the *jre/lib* directory.

fork *(1.4, boolean, N)*
If true, execute the Java compiler as a separate process. When set, this attribute overrides the build.compiler property, and Ant executes the actual *javac* executable in JAVA_HOME*/bin* rather than the compiler's Main class. Defaults to false.

includeantruntime *(1.3, 1.4, boolean, N)*
If true, include the Ant runtime libraries in the classpath. Defaults to true.

includejavaruntime *(1.3, 1.4, boolean, N)*
If true, include the default runtime libraries from the executing VM. Defaults to false.

includes *(all, String, N)*
A comma-separated list of file patterns to include.

includesfile *(all, File, N)*
The name of a file containing one include pattern per line.

memoryinitialsize *(1.4, String, N)*
Works only when fork=true. Specifies the initial memory size for the VM—for instance 64000000, 64000k, or 64m.

memorymaximumsize *(1.4, String, N)*
Works only when fork=true. Specifies the maximum memory size for the VM.

nowarn *(1.4, boolean, N)*
If true, pass the -nowarn switch to the compiler. Defaults to false.

optimize *(all, boolean, N)*
If true, instruct the compiler to optimize the code. Defaults to false.

source *(1.4.1, String, N)*
If specified, the text from this attribute is passed as the **-source** command-line option to the underlying *javac* executable. Legal values are 1.3 and 1.4. Passing 1.4 allows JDK 1.4 to use its new assertion facility.

srcdir *(all, Path, *)*
Location of the source code files.

target *(all, String, N)*
Generate class files for a specific VM version, such as 1.1 or 1.2.

verbose *(all, boolean, N)*
If true, instruct the compiler to produce verbose output. Defaults to false.

The srcdir attribute is required unless nested <src> elements are specified.

Content

0..n nested patternset *elements:* <exclude>, <include>, <patternset> *(all);* <excludesfile>, <includesfile> *(1.4)*
Used in place of their corresponding attributes, these specify the set of included and excluded source files.

0..n nested path *elements:* <bootclasspath>, <classpath>, <extdirs>, *and* <src> *(all)*
Used in place of their corresponding attributes.

Example Usage

Compile all Java source files in the com.oreilly.antbook package and subpackages, placing results in ${builddir}:

```
<javac srcdir="${srcdir}"
       destdir="${builddir}"
       includes="com/oreilly/antbook/**"/>
```

javadoc

all

Invokes the javadoc utility — **org.apache.tools.ant.taskdefs.Javadoc**

Invokes the javadoc utility. Unlike other Ant tasks, this task performs no dependency analysis, so all documentation is generated with each usage.

Older versions of javadoc simply ignore attributes that are not supported.

Attributes

access *(1.4, Enum, N)*
: One of public, protected, package, or private. Defaults to protected, meaning that all protected and public classes and members are included in the output. These directly correspond to JavaDoc's *-public*, *-protected*, *-package*, and *-private* command-line flags.

additionalparam *(all, String, N)*
: Additional parameters for the JavaDoc command line. Use " for parameters requiring quotes.

author *(all, boolean, N)*
: If true, include @author tags. Defaults to true.

bootclasspath *(all, Path, N)*
: The bootstrap classpath to use.

bootclasspathref *(all, Reference, N)*
: A reference to a bootstrap classpath defined elsewhere in the buildfile.

bottom *(all, String, N)*
: HTML to include in the bottom of each page.

charset *(all, String, N)*
: Charset for cross-platform viewing of generated documentation.

classpath *(all, Path, N)*
: The classpath to use.

classpathref *(all, Reference, N)*
: A reference to a classpath defined elsewhere in the buildfile.

defaultexcludes *(1.4, boolean, N)*
: Determines whether to use default excludes, as described in Chapter 4 under "FileSet DataType." Defaults to true.

destdir *(all, File, *)*
: Destination directory for generated documentation.

`docencoding` *(all, String, N)*
Output character encoding name—for example, "UTF-8" .

`doclet` *(all, String, N)*
The class name of a custom doclet. This corresponds to JavaDoc's *-doclet* parameter.

`docletpath` *(all, Path, N)*
The classpath for the custom doclet.

`docletpathref` *(all, Reference, N)*
A reference to a doclet classpath defined elsewhere in the buildfile.

`doctitle` *(all, String, N)*
The HTML to include on the package index page.

`encoding` *(all, String, N)*
Character encoding of source files.

`excludepackagenames` *(1.4, String, N)*
A comma-separated list of packages to exclude.

`extdirs` *(all, String, N)*
Override the usual location for Java installed optional packages.

`failonerror` *(all, boolean, N)*
If `true`, the build fails when the command returns anything other than 0. Defaults to `false`.

`footer` *(all, String, N)*
The HTML to include in the footer of each generated page.

`group` *(all, String, N)*
Group-specified packages together in an overview page. This attribute is specified as a comma-delimited string. Each entry contains a title for the HTML page, followed by a space, followed by a colon-delimited list of Java package names. This follows the syntax specified by JavaDoc's *-group* command-line parameter.

`header` *(all, String, N)*
The HTML to include in the header of each generated page.

`helpfile` *(all, File, N)*
The file the help link links to.

`link` *(all, String, N)*
Create links to JavaDoc output at the given URL.

`linkoffline` *(all, String, N)*
A space-separated list of two URLs. Link to docs at the first URL using the package list at the second URL.

`locale` *(all, String, N)*
The locale name to use, such as `en_US`.

`maxmemory` *(all, String, N)*
The maximum heap size available to the Java VM.

`nodeprecated` *(all, boolean, N)*
If `true`, do not include `@deprecated` tags. Defaults to `false`.

`nodeprecatedlist` *(all, boolean, N)*
If `true`, do not include the deprecated list. Defaults to `false`.

`nohelp` *(all, boolean, N)*
: If `true`, do not generate a help link. Defaults to `false`.

`noindex` *(all, boolean, N)*
: If `true`, do not generate an index page. Defaults to `false`.

`nonavbar` *(all, boolean, N)*
: If `true`, do not generate a navigation bar. Defaults to `false`.

`notree` *(all, boolean, N)*
: If `true`, do not generate a class hierarchy. Defaults to `false`.

`old` *(all, boolean, N)*
: If `true`, emulate the JDK 1.1 doclet. Defaults to `false`.

`overview` *(all, File, N)*
: The name of a file containing HTML overview documentation.

`package` *(all, boolean, N)*
: If `true`, show package classes and members. Defaults to `false`.

`packagelist` *(all, String, N)*
: The name of a file containing packages to process.

`packagenames` *(all, String, *)*
: A comma-separated list of package names, such as `com.foo.*,com.bar.*`.

`private` *(all, boolean, N)*
: If `true`, show all classes and members. Defaults to `false`.

`protected` *(all, boolean, N)*
: If `true`, show protected classes and members. Defaults to `true`.

`public` *(all, boolean, N)*
: If `true`, show only public classes and members. Defaults to `false`.

`serialwarn` *(all, boolean, N)*
: If true, generate warning about `@serial` tag. Defaults to `false`.

`sourcefiles` *(all, String, *)*
: A comma-separated list of source files.

`sourcepath` *(all, Path, *)*
: The location of source code files.

`sourcepathref` *(all, Reference, *)*
: A reference to a source path defined elsewhere.

`splitindex` *(all, boolean, N)*
: If `true`, split the JavaDoc index page into one HTML page per letter. Defaults to `false`.

`stylesheetfile` *(all, File, N)*
: The name of a CSS file to use.

`use` *(all, boolean, N)*
: If `true`, create class and package usage pages. Defaults to `false`.

`useexternalfile` *(1.4, boolean, N)*
: If `true`, source filenames and package names are written to a temporary file before executing the `javadoc` command, making the command line shorter. Defaults to `false`.

`verbose` *(all, boolean, N)*
: Defaults to `false`.

`version` *(all, boolean, N)*
  If `true`, include `@version` tags. Defaults to `true`.

`windowtitle` *(all, String, N)*
  Specifies the HTML page title.

Content

0..n nested `path` *elements:* `<bootclasspath>`, `<classpath>`, *and* `<sourcepath>` *(1.3, 1.4)*
  Used in place of their corresponding attributes.

0,1 nested elements containing HTML: `<bottom>`, `<doctitle>`, `<footer>`, *and* `<header>` *(1.4)*
  Used in place of their corresponding attributes.

0,1 nested `<doclet>` *elements (1.3, 1.4)*
  References a custom doclet. The following attributes are supported for `<doclet>` elements.

  `name` *(all, String, Y)*
    The class name of the doclet.

  `path` *(all, Path, N)*
    The classpath to the doclet.

  `pathref` *(all, Reference, N)*
    A reference to a classpath defined elsewhere in the buildfile.

  `<doclet>` accepts any number of nested `<param>` elements. These have `name` and `value` attributes, and are used to pass command-line parameters to the doclet. For example:

```
<doclet name="MyDoclet" path="${mydoclet.path}">
  <param name="-loglevel" value="verbose"/>
  <param name="-outputdir" value="${mydoclet.output}"/>
</doclet>
```

0..n nested `<excludepackage>` *and* `<package>` *elements (1.4)*
  Use each in place of one entry in the list specified by the `excludepackagenames` and `packagenames` attributes, respectively. For example:

```
<package name="com.oreilly.util.*"/>
<excludepackage name="com.oreilly.test.*"/>
```

0..n nested `<group>` *elements (1.3, 1.4)*
  Used in place of the group attribute. Following are the valid `<group>` element attributes.

  `title` *(all, String, *)*
    The group title.

  `packages` *(all, String, *)*
    A colon-delimited list of packages to include in the group.

  `<group>` supports 0..n nested `<title>` and `<package>` elements. These may be used in place of their corresponding attributes.

0..n nested `<link>` *elements (1.3, 1.4)*
  Used in place of the `link` attribute. Following are the valid `<link>` element attributes.

  `href` *(all, String, Y)*
    The URL for the external documentation to link to.

  `offline` *(all, boolean, N)*
    If `true`, the link is not available when JavaDoc is being generated. Defaults to `false`.

packagelistloc *(all, File, *)*
The location of the directory containing the package list file.

packagelistloc is required if offline=true.

0..n nested <source> *elements. (1.4)*
Each is used in place of one entry in the list specified by the sourcefiles attribute. Following is the valid <source> element attribute:

file *(all, File, Y)*
The source file to document.

Example Usage

This example creates documentation in the *docs* directory. The directory must already exist or the build fails. It also shows how to include HTML content using the <bottom> element. The same technique works for <doctitle>, <footer>, and <header>.

```
<javadoc excludepackagenames="com.oreilly.test.*"
         destdir="docs"
         windowtitle="My Documentation">
  <package name="com.oreilly.antbook.*"/>
  <package name="com.oreilly.util.*"/>
  <sourcepath location="${srcdir}"/>
  <classpath location="${builddir}"/>
  <bottom>
    <![CDATA[<em>Copyright (C) 2001, O'Reilly</em>
    <br>All Rights Reserved]]>
  </bottom>
</javadoc>
```

mail

all

Sends email **org.apache.tools.ant.taskdefs.SendEmail**

Sends SMTP email.

Attributes

files *(all, String, *)*
A comma-separated list of filenames. Each specifies a text file to include in the mail body.

from *(all, String, Y)*
The sender's email address.

mailhost *(all, String, N)*
The mail server hostname.

message *(all, String, *)*
The message content.

subject *(all, String, N)*
The mail subject.

tolist *(all, String, Y)*
A comma-separated list of recipient email addresses.

Either files or message is required.

Content

None.

Example Usage

Send email with build results:

```
<property name="my.mailhost" value="mail.oreilly.com"/>

<mail from="ant@foobar.com"
      tolist="developers@foobar.com"
      subject="Build Results"
      mailhost="${my.mailhost}"
      files="buildlog.txt"/>
```

See Also

Use the `mimemail` optional task listed in Chapter 8 when binary attachments are required.

mkdir

all

Creates a directory — org.apache.tools.ant.taskdefs.Mkdir

Creates a directory if it does not already exist. Also creates parent directories as needed.

Attributes

`dir` *(all, File, Y)*
: The directory to create.

Content

None.

Example Usage

This task is commonly used in a `prepare` target that other targets depend on. This ensures that necessary destination directories are created before other targets are executed.

```
<target name="prepare">
  <mkdir dir="${builddir}"/>
  <mkdir dir="${deploydir}/docs"/>
</target>

<target name="compile" depends="prepare">
  ...
</target>
```

See Also

See the `delete` task for information on removing files and directories.

move

all

Moves files and directories **org.apache.tools.ant.taskdefs.Move**

Moves one or more files and directories.

Attributes

`file` *(all, File, *)*
: Specifies a single file to move. Use nested `<fileset>`s to move multiple files and directories.

`filtering` *(all, boolean, N)*
: If `true`, token filtering using any global buildfile filters takes place. Nested filters are always applied, regardless of this attribute. Defaults to `false`.

`flatten` *(all, boolean, N)*
: If `true`, the directory structure of the source files is not preserved, moving all files to a single destination directory. A nested `<mapper>` can achieve the same results. Defaults to `false`.

`includeemptydirs` *(all, boolean, N)*
: If `true`, empty directories are also moved. Defaults to `true`.

`overwrite` *(all, boolean, N)*
: If `true`, files are moved even when destination files are newer. Defaults to `false`.

`todir` *(all, File, *)*
: The directory to move files to.

`tofile` *(all, File, *)*
: The file to move to.

Either `file` or a nested fileset element is required. When the `file` attribute is used, one of either `tofile` or `todir` is required. When a nested fileset is used, only `todir` is allowed: it's also required.

Content

0..n nested `<fileset>` *elements (all)*
: Selects files to move. The `todir` attribute is required when `<fileset>`s are present.

0..n nested `<filterset>` *elements (1.4)*
: Defines token filters for text substitution as files are moved. See the `filter` task for more info.

0,1 nested `<mapper>` *elements (1.3, 1.4)*
: Defines how filenames are transformed when moved. By default, an identity transformation is performed, meaning that filenames are not modified.

Example Usage

Moves all *.class* files to new location:

```
<move todir="${builddir}/foo">
  <!-- the files to move -->
  <fileset dir="${builddir}">
    <include name="**/*.class"/>
  </fileset>
</move>
```

See Also

See the copy task.

parallel

1.4

Contains nested tasks — org.apache.tools.ant.taskdefs.Parallel

This is a container for other tasks. Each contained task executes in its own thread, potentially improving overall build performance. The main build process blocks until all nested tasks are complete. If any nested task fails, the `parallel` task also fails once all threads are complete.

> Use `parallel` only when the contained tasks are independent of one another. For instance, do not execute a code generator in parallel with a task that attempts to compile the generated code. Unless you are comfortable with multithreading concepts, avoid this task.

The `sequential` task is used in conjunction with `parallel` in order to execute groups of tasks sequentially.

Attributes

None.

Content

Any task, including nested `parallel` tasks.

Example Usage

In this example, the client and server portion of an application are independent of each other and can be compiled concurrently. Before compiling the client, however, some critical files are copied and code is generated using a custom Java program. While all of this is happening inside of the `<sequential>` task, the server code is compiling.

```
<parallel>
  <sequential>
    <!-- copy some critical files first... -->
    <copy ... />

    <!-- run a code generator -->
    <java ... />

    <!-- now compile the client code -->
    <javac srcdir="${client_srcdir}"
           destdir="${client_builddir}"
           includes="com/oreilly/client/**"/>
  </sequential>

  <!-- compile the server code in parallel with everything
       contained in the <sequential> task -->
```

```
    <javac srcdir="${server_srcdir}"
           destdir="${server_builddir}"
           includes="com/acme/server/**"/>
</parallel>
```

See Also

The sequential task.

patch

all

Applies a diff file — **org.apache.tools.ant.taskdefs.Patch**

Applies a `diff` file to originals. CVS includes the `patch` command-line utility, which must be located on the path for this task to execute.

Attributes

`backups` *(all, boolean, N)*
: If `true`, keep backup copies of unpatched files. Defaults to `false`.

`ignorewhitespace` *(all, boolean, N)*
: If `true`, ignore whitespace differences when applying the patch file. Defaults to `false`.

`originalfile` *(all, File, N)*
: The file to patch.

`patchfile` *(all, File, Y)*
: The file containing the `diff` output.

`quiet` *(all, boolean, N)*
: If `true`, work silently unless an error occurs. Defaults to `false`.

`reverse` *(all, boolean, N)*
: If `true`, assume patch file was created with old and new files swapped. Defaults to `false`.

`strip` *(all, int, N)*
: Strips the smallest prefix containing this number of leading slashes from filenames. Equivalent to `patch`'s `-p` option.

Content

None.

Example Usage

Apply the diff included in *foo.patch*, guessing filenames from the diff output:

```
<patch patchfile="foo.patch"/>
```

See Also

See the cvs task.

pathconvert 1.4

Converts Ant paths to platform-specific paths org.apache.tools.ant.taskdefs.PathConvert

Converts Ant paths, or `filesets`, into platform-specific paths, storing the result in a property.

Attributes

`dirsep` *(1.4, String, *)*

The character used as a directory separator, such as ":". Defaults to `File.separator` on the current JVM.

`pathsep` *(1.4, String, *)*

The character used as a path separator, such as "/". Defaults to `File.pathSeparator` on the current JVM.

`property` *(1.4, String, Y)*

The property in which to store the converted path.

`refid` *(1.4, Reference, *)*

A reference to the path to convert.

`targetos` *(1.4, String, *)*

A shortcut for defining both `pathsep` and `dirsep`. Legal values are `unix` and `windows`. `dirsep` and `pathsep` values are then chosen in conformance with specified operating systems.

Must specify either `targetos` or both `dirsep` and `pathsep`. Either the `refid` attribute or a nested `<path>` element is required.

Content

0..n nested `<map>` *elements (1.4)*

Each specifies the mapping of path prefixes between Unix and Windows. Ant applies only the first matching `<map>` element. Following are the valid `<map>` attributes in this context.

from (1.4, String, Y)

The prefix to map, such as `C:`. This is case-insensitive when Ant runs on Windows, and case-sensitive when Ant runs on Unix.

to (1.4, String, Y)

The replacement to use when `from` matches—for example, `/usr`.

0,1 nested `<path>` *elements (1.4)*

A path element used in place of the `refid` attribute.

Example Usage

The following example defines a `fileset`:

```
<fileset id="sources1" dir="src"
         includes="**/*.java"
         excludes="**/test/**/*.java"/>
```

Here is how `pathconvert` converts the `fileset` into a Unix-style path, storing the result in the `p1` property:

```
<pathconvert targetos="unix" property="p1" refid="sources1"/>
```

The value of the p1 property is now something like:

```
/home/aidan/src/com/oreilly/Book.java:/home/aidan/src/com/oreilly/Chapter.java
```

property

all

Sets properties in the current project **org.apache.tools.ant.taskdefs.Property**

Sets properties in the project. Properties specified by users always take precedence over properties defined by this task. The same is true for properties defined by parent projects that invoke this project using the ant task.

Attributes

`classpath` *(1.3, 1.4, Path, N)*
: The classpath to use when looking up a resource.

`classpathref` *(1.3, 1.4, Reference, N)*
: A reference to a classpath defined elsewhere in the buildfile.

`environment` *(1.3, 1.4, String, *)*
: A prefix used for retrieving environment variables. We use this in the upcoming example to retrieve the value of `TOMCAT_HOME`. This was also covered in Chapter 4 under "Environment DataType."

`file` *(all, File, *)*
: The name of a properties file. This defines a set of properties (name-value pairs) according to the contents of the properties file.

`location` *(all, File, *)*
: Sets the property value to an absolute filename. If this attribute contains an absolute path, any "/" and "\" characters are converted to current system conventions. If the path is relative to the project, it is expanded to an absolute path.

`name` *(all, String, N)*
: The name of the property to set.

`refid` *(all, Reference, *)*
: A reference to a path or property defined elsewhere in the project.

`resource` *(all, String, *)*
: The Java resource name of a properties file. Uses a `ClassLoader` to load the properties file.

`value` *(all, String, *)*
: An explicit value for the property.

When `name` is specified, one of `value`, `location`, or `refid` is required. Otherwise, one of `resource`, `file`, or `environment` is required.

Content

0,1 nested `<classpath>` *elements (1.3, 1.4)*
: May be used in place of the `classpath` attribute.

Example Usage

Define the `builddir` and `srcdir` properties, relative to the project base directory:

```
<property name="builddir" value="build"/>
<property name="srcdir" value="src"/>
```

The following example defines two properties based on the contents of *test.properties* in the `com.oreilly.antbook` package:

```
<property resource="com/oreilly/antbook/test.properties">
  <classpath>
    <pathelement path="${srcdir}"/>
  </classpath>
</property>
<!-- display the property values... -->
<echo message="book.title = ${book.title}"/>
<echo message="book.author = ${book.author}"/>
```

This example first retrieves all environment variables, prefixing them with `env.`. It then assigns the value of the `TOMCAT_HOME` environment variable to the `tomcat.home` property:

```
<property environment="env"/>
<property name="tomcat.home" value="${env.TOMCAT_HOME}"/>
```

record 1.4

Creates a listener to the build process — **org.apache.tools.ant.taskdefs.Recorder**

Creates a listener to the current build process, recording output to a file. Multiple recorders can exist for the same file.

Attributes

`action` *(1.4, Enum, N)*
: Defines whether the recorder should start or stop recording. Legal values are `start` and `stop`. Defaults to `start` when this task is first encountered. On subsequent calls, the recorder state remains unchanged.

`append` *(1.4, boolean, N)*
: If `true`, append to the file when this recorder is first created, rather than replacing the file. Defaults to `true`. Subsequent calls during the same build always append to the file.

`loglevel` *(1.4, Enum, N)*
: Determines the logging level. Legal values are `error`, `warn`, `info`, `verbose`, and `debug`. The level may be changed with each recorder instance.

`name` *(1.4, String, Y)*
: The name of the file to log to.

Content

None.

Example Usage

This example shows how to write detailed logging information to a file while code compiles.

```
<record name="javac.log" loglevel="debug"
        action="start" append="false"/>
<javac srcdir="${srcdir}" destdir="${builddir}"
       includes="com/oreilly/antbook/**">
</javac>
<record name="javac.log" action="stop"/>
```

rename

This task was deprecated in Ant 1.2; use the move task instead.

replace **all**

Performs string replacement **org.apache.tools.ant.taskdefs.Replace**

Performs string replacement in one or more files. The original files are replaced rather than copied.

Attributes

defaultexcludes *(all, boolean, N)*
: Determines whether to use default excludes, as described in Chapter 4 under "FileSet DataType." Defaults to true.

dir *(all, File, *)*
: The base directory used when specifying multiple files.

excludes *(all, String, N)*
: A comma-separated list of file patterns to exclude. These are in addition to the default excludes.

excludesfile *(all, File, N)*
: The name of a file containing one exclude pattern per line.

file *(all, File, *)*
: An individual file to perform replacements in.

includes *(all, String, N)*
: A comma-separated list of file patterns to include.

includesfile *(all, File, N)*
: The name of a file containing one include pattern per line.

propertyfile *(1.3, 1.4, File, *)*
: Specifies a properties file containing properties referenced by nested <replacefilter> elements.

summary *(1.4, boolean, N)*
: If true, display a summary report of this operation. Defaults to false.

`token` *(all, String, *)*
: The token to replace.

`value` *(all, String, N)*
: The new value for the token. Defaults to an empty string.

Exactly one of `file` or `dir` is required. The `token` attribute is required if a nested `<replacetoken>` element is used. The `propertyfile` attribute is required if the `property` attribute of a nested `<replacefilter>` element is specified.

Content

0..n nested `patternset` *elements:* `<exclude>`, `<include>`, `<patternset>` *(all);* `<excludesfile>`, `<includesfile>` *(1.4)*

Used in place of their corresponding attributes, these specify the set of included and excluded source files.

0..n nested `<replacefilter>` *elements (1.3, 1.4)*

Allows multiple replacements, and works in conjunction with the `propertyfile` attribute. `<replacefilter>` attributes are as follows:

`token` *(1.3, 1.4, String, Y)*
: The token to search for.

`value` *(1.3, 1.4, String, *)*
: The replacement text.

`property` *(1.3, 1.4, String, *)*
: The name of a property whose value is used as the replacement text.

Either `value` or `property` may be specified, or neither.

0,1 nested `<replacetoken>` *and* `<replacevalue>` *elements (all)*

Used in place of the `token` and `value` attributes, supporting multiline text.

Example Usage

Replace all occurrences of `@builddate@` with the current date:

```
<replace file="${builddir}/replaceSample.txt"
         token="@builddate@"
         value="${DSTAMP}"/>
```

This next example performs a multiline token replacement. It uses XML `<![CDATA[ ... ]]>` to represent literal text containing a newline character:

```
<replace file="${builddir}/replaceSample.txt">
  <replacetoken><![CDATA[Token line 1
Token line 2]]></replacetoken>
  <replacevalue><![CDATA[Line 1
Line 2]]></replacevalue>
</replace>
```

Use a properties file containing token replacement values. Apply to all source files:

```
<replace dir="${srcdir}" includes="**/*.java" propertyfile="tokens.properties">
  <replacefilter token="@vendor@" property="vendor.name"/>
  <replacefilter token="@version@" property="version.name"/>
</replace>
```

rmic

all

Invokes the rmic compiler

org.apache.tools.ant.taskdefs.Rmic

Invokes the `rmic` compiler, generating stubs and skeletons for Java Remote Method Invocation.

Attributes

`base` *(all, File, Y)*
: The location in which to store compiled files.

`classname` *(all, String, N)*
: Run `rmic` on this class.

`classpath` *(all, Path, N)*
: The classpath to use.

`classpathref` *(all, Reference, N)*
: A reference to a classpath defined elsewhere in the buildfile.

`debug` *(1.3, 1.4, boolean, N)*
: If `true`, pass `-g` to `rmic`. Defaults to `false`.

`defaultexcludes` *(all, boolean, N)*
: Determines whether to use default excludes, as described in Chapter 4 under "FileSet DataType." Defaults to `true`.

`excludes` *(all, String, N)*
: A comma-separated list of file patterns to exclude. These are in addition to the default excludes.

`excludesfile` *(all, File, N)*
: The name of a file containing one exclude pattern per line.

`extdirs` *(1.4, Path, N)*
: Override the usual location for Java-installed optional packages.

`filtering` *(all, boolean, N)*
: If `true`, token filtering should take place. Defaults to `false`.

`idl` *(1.3, 1.4, boolean, N)*
: Instructs `rmic` to produce IDL output files.

`idlopts` *(1.3, 1.4, String, N)*
: Additional arguments when `idl=true`.

`iiop` *(1.3, 1.4, boolean, N)*
: When `true`, generate portable RMI/IIOP stubs. Defaults to `false`.

`iiopopts` *(1.3, 1.4, String, N)*
: Additional arguments when `iiop=true`.

`includeantruntime` *(1.4, boolean, N)*
: If `true`, include the Ant runtime libraries in the classpath. Defaults to `true`.

`includejavaruntime` *(1.4, boolean, N)*
: If `true`, include the default runtime libraries from the executing VM. Defaults to `false`.

`includes` *(all, String, N)*
: A comma-separated list of file patterns to include.

`includesfile` *(all, File, N)*
: The name of a file containing one include pattern per line.

`sourcebase` *(all, File, N)*
: When specified, passes the `-keepgenerated` option to `rmic`. The generated source file is moved to the specified directory.

`stubversion` *(all, String, N)*
: Set this to `1.1` to pass the `-v1.1` option to `rmic`.

`verify` *(all, boolean, N)*
: When `true`, verify that classes implement `Remote` before passing them to `rmic`. Defaults to `false`.

Content

0..n nested `patternset` *elements:* `<exclude>`, `<include>`, `<patternset>` *(all);* `<excludesfile>`, `<includesfile>` *(1.4)*
: Used in place of their corresponding attributes, these specify the set of included and excluded source files.

0,1 nested `<classpath>` *elements (all)*
: May be used in place of the `classpath` and `classpathref` attributes.

0..n nested `<extdirs>` *elements (1.4)*
: May be used in place of the `extdirs` attribute.

Example Usage

Run the `rmic` compiler for all classes in the `com.oreilly.remote` package:

```
<rmic base="${builddir}" includes="com/oreilly/remote/*.class"/>
```

sequential 1.4

Contains ordered tasks — org.apache.tools.ant.taskdefs.Sequential

This is a container task designed for use with the `parallel` task. It ensures that a group of tasks are executed in order.

Attributes

None.

Content

Any nested tasks.

Example Usage

See the example for the `parallel` task.

See Also

The `parallel` task.

signjar

all

Executes jarsigner **org.apache.tools.ant.taskdefs.SignJar**

Executes the `jarsigner` command-line tool.

Attributes

`alias` *(all, String, Y)*
: Specifies the alias to sign under.

`internalsf` *(all, boolean, N)*
: If `true`, include the *.SF* file inside the signature block. Defaults to `false`.

`jar` *(all, String, Y)*
: The JAR file to sign.

`keypass` *(all, String, *)*
: The password for the private key.

`keystore` *(all, String, N)*
: The keystore location.

`sectionsonly` *(all, boolean, N)*
: If `true`, don't compute the hash of the entire manifest. Defaults to `false`.

`sigfile` *(all, String, N)*
: The name of the *.SF* or *.DSA* file.

`signedjar` *(all, String, N)*
: The name of the signed JAR file.

`storepass` *(all, String, Y)*
: The password for keystore integrity.

`storetype` *(all, String, N)*
: The keystore type.

`verbose` *(all, boolean, N)*
: If `true`, produce verbose output. Defaults to `false`.

`keypass` is required if the private key password is different than the keystore password.

Content

0..n nested `<fileset>` *elements (1.4)*
: Use in place of the `jar` attribute to sign multiple files.

Example Usage

```
<signjar jar="${builddir}/server.jar" alias="oreilly"
         storepass="${password}"/>
```

sleep 1.4

Pauses the build org.apache.tools.ant.taskdefs.Sleep

Pause the build for a specified amount of time.

Attributes

`failonerror` *(1.4, boolean, N)*
: If `true`, the build fails when any error occurs while sleeping. Defaults to `true`.

`hours` *(1.4, int, N)*
: The number of hours.

`milliseconds` *(1.4, int, N)*
: The number of milliseconds.

`minutes` *(1.4, int, N)*
: The number of minutes.

`seconds` *(1.4, int, N)*
: The number of seconds.

Content

None.

Example Usage

```
<!-- start a web server, then wait a few seconds for it to initialize -->
<sleep seconds="10"/>
<!-- now start the client unit tests -->
```

sql all

Executes SQL statements org.apache.tools.ant.taskdefs.SQLExec

Executes SQL statements using JDBC.

Attributes

`autocommit` *(all, boolean, N)*
: If `true`, set the JDBC `autocommit` flag. Defaults to `false`.

`classpath` *(all, Path, N)*
: The classpath to use when loading the JDBC driver.

`classpathref` *(all, Reference, N)*
: A reference to a classpath defined elsewhere in the buildfile.

`delimiter` *(1.4, String, N)*
: A string separating SQL statements. Defaults to "`;`".

`delimitertype` *(1.4, Enum, N)*
: Legal values are `row` and `normal`. Defaults to `normal`, meaning that any occurrence of the delimiter terminates the SQL command. `row` means the delimiter must appear on a line by itself.

`driver` *(all, String, Y)*
: The class name of the JDBC driver.

`onerror` *(all, Enum, N)*
: Controls what happens when a statement fails. Defaults to `abort`. Legal values are as follows:

  `continue`
  : This task attempts to continue executing statements even after one or more statements fail.

  `abort`
  : The transaction is explicitly rolled back by the task when errors occur, just prior to aborting the build.

  `stop`
  : The build fails without attempting to rollback a failed transaction. Nonetheless, the database should roll back the transaction once the JVM exits.

`output` *(all, File, N)*
: The output file for result sets when `print=true`. Defaults to `System.out`.

`password` *(all, String, Y)*
: The database password.

`print` *(all, boolean, N)*
: If `true`, print all result sets. Defaults to `false`.

`rdbms` *(all, String, N)*
: Specifies an RDBMS brand, and restricts execution of this task to that RDBMS. This should equal the value returned from the `getDatabaseProductName()` method of `DatabaseMetaData`.

`showheaders` *(all, boolean, N)*
: If `true`, show header columns when printing result sets. Defaults to `true`.

`src` *(all, File, *)*
: A file containing SQL statements to execute.

`url` *(all, String, Y)*
: The database connection URL.

`userid` *(all, String, Y)*
: The database user ID.

`version` *(all, String, N)*
: Specifies a version number. The task is only executed if the RDBMS version matches this value. The product version is obtained from `DatabaseMetaData`.

The `src` attribute is not required if the SQL statements to be executed are specified as text content of the tag.

Content

Text content (all)
: Used in place of the `src` attribute for SQL statements. The character specified by the `delimiter` attribute separates multiple statements. Lines beginning with `//`, `--`, or `REM` are comments.

0,1 nested `<classpath>` *elements (all)*
: May be used in place of the `classpath` attribute.

0..n nested `<fileset>` *elements (1.4)*

Used in place of the `src` attribute to specify multiple files containing SQL statements. The files are executed in the order listed.

0..n nested `<transaction>` *elements (all)*

Each defines a block of commands for execution within a single transaction. One attribute is supported:

`src` *(all, String, *)*

The name of a file containing SQL statements

The `src` attribute may be omitted if SQL statements are nested as text within the `<transaction>` element.

Example Usage

Executes the statement(s) contained in *report.sql*:

```
<sql driver="${db.driver}"
     url="${db.url}"
     userid="${db.userid}"
     password="${db.password}"
     src="report.sql"/>
```

Execute the SQL statements specified as the content of the `sql` task:

```
<sql driver="${db.driver}"
     url="${db.url}"
     userid="${db.userid}"
     password="${db.password}">
  SELECT *
  FROM ReportTbl;

  // additional statements follow...
  SELECT ... ;
</sql>
```

style

all

Performs XSLT transformations — **org.apache.tools.ant.taskdefs.XSLTProcess**

Performs XSLT transformations. XSLT stylesheets define how XSLT processors transform XML into other text formats.

Attributes

`basedir` *(all, File, N)*

Specifies where to find the XML files to transform. Defaults to the project's base directory.

`classpath` *(1.4, Path, N)*

The classpath to use when looking up the XSLT processor.

`classpathref` *(1.4, Reference, N)*

A reference to a classpath defined elsewhere in the buildfile.

`defaultexcludes` *(all, boolean, N)*

Determines whether to use default excludes, as described in Chapter 4 under "FileSet DataType." Defaults to `true`.

`destdir` *(all, File, *)*
: Specifies where transformation results are stored.

`excludes` *(all, String, N)*
: A comma-separated list of file patterns to exclude. These are in addition to the default excludes.

`excludesfile` *(all, File, N)*
: The name of a file containing one exclude pattern per line.

`extension` *(all, String, N)*
: The default file extension used for transformation results. Defaults to `.html`.

`force` *(1.4, boolean, N)*
: If `true`, create target files even if they are newer than their source XML or XSLT files. The default is `false`.

`in` *(1.3, 1.4, File, N)*
: Specifies a single XML file for transformation. Used in conjunction with the `out` attribute.

`includes` *(all, String, N)*
: A comma-separated list of file patterns to include.

`includesfile` *(all, File, N)*
: The name of a file containing one include pattern per line.

`out` *(1.3, 1.4, File, N)*
: Specifies the filename for the transformation result. Used in conjunction with the `in` attribute.

`processor` *(all, String, N)*
: The XSLT processor to use. The default (and recommended) value is `trax`. Legal values are as follows:

    `trax`
    : Supports any processor compatible with Sun's JAXP 1.1.

    `xslp`
    : Is deprecated.

    `xalan`
    : Supports Apache Xalan Version 1.x.

`style` *(all, String, Y)*
: The XSLT stylesheet name.

The `destdir` attribute is required unless the `in` and `out` attributes are specified.

Content

0..n nested `patternset` *elements:* `<exclude>`, `<include>`, `<patternset>` *(all);* `<excludesfile>`, `<includesfile>` *(1.4)*
: Used in place of their corresponding attributes, these specify the set of included and excluded XML files.

0,1 nested `<classpath>` *elements (1.4)*
: May be used in place of the `classpath` attribute.

0..n nested `<param>` *elements (1.3, 1.4)*

Each passes a parameter to the XSLT stylesheet using the following attributes:

`name` *(1.3, 1.4, String, Y)*

The XSLT parameter name.

`expression` *(1.3, 1.4, String, Y)*

The parameter value. Literal text must be passed in single quotes, or the stylesheet treats it as an expression.*

Example Usage

Transform *customers.xml* using *customers.xslt*, placing results in the build directory:

```
<style destdir="${builddir}" style="customers.xslt">
  <param name="date" expression="${DSTAMP}"/>
  <include name="customers.xml"/>
</style>
```

tar

all

Creates a tar file — **org.apache.tools.ant.taskdefs.Tar**

Creates a tar archive.

Attributes

`basedir` *(all, File, N)*

Specifies the base directory from which to add files to the tar file.

`defaultexcludes` *(all, boolean, N)*

Determines whether to use default excludes, as described in Chapter 4 under "FileSet DataType." Defaults to `true`.

`excludes` *(all, String, N)*

A comma-separated list of file patterns to exclude. These are in addition to the default excludes.

`excludesfile` *(all, File, N)*

The name of a file containing one exclude pattern per line.

`includes` *(all, String, N)*

A comma-separated list of file patterns to include.

`includesfile` *(all, File, N)*

The name of a file containing one include pattern per line.

`longfile` *(1.3, 1.4, String, N)*

Controls handling of files with long (>100 character) filenames. Legal values are `truncate`, `fail`, `warn`, `omit`, and `gnu`. Defaults to `warn`.

`tarfile` *(all, File, Y)*

The tar file to create.

* Although the Ant manual says that literal text must be escaped with single quotes, this does not appear to be the case. The stylesheet always seems to treat the value as text, rather than as an expression.

Content

0..n nested patternset *elements:* <exclude>, <include>, <patternset> *(all);* <excludesfile>, <includesfile> *(1.4)*

Used in place of their corresponding attributes, these specify the set of included and excluded source files.

0..n nested <tarfileset> *elements (1.3, 1.4)*

Each support all fileset attributes and content (includes, excludes, etc.), as well as the following additional attributes:

mode *(1.3, 1.4, String, N)*

A 3-digit octal string specifying user, group, and other modes.

username *(1.3, 1.4, String, N)*

The username for the tar entry.

group *(1.3, 1.4, String, N)*

The group name for the tar entry.

Example Usage

Creates a tar archive containing all class files in the build directory:

```
<tar tarfile="${dist}/classes.tar"
     basedir="${builddir}"
     includes="**/*.class"/>
```

See Also

See the gzip task.

taskdef

all

Adds a task **org.apache.tools.ant.taskdefs.Taskdef**

Adds a task to the current project. This is used to define tasks not already defined in the *ant.jar*'s *default.properties* file.

Attributes

classname *(all, String, *)*

The class that implements the task.

classpath *(all, Path, N)*

The classpath to use.

file *(1.4, File, N)*

The name of a properties file containing one or more task definitions. Each line is formatted like this:

```
taskname=full.package.name.TaskClass
```

name *(all, String, *)*

The name of the task.

resource *(1.4, String, N)*

The Java resource name of a properties file containing one or more task definitions. This is identical to the file attribute, except it uses a ClassLoader to locate the properties file.

The name and classname attributes are required unless the file or resource attributes are specified.

Content

0,1 nested <classpath> *elements (all)*
May be used in place of the classpath attribute.

Example Usage

Defines a custom task that can then be used throughout a project:

```
<taskdef name="mycodegen" classname="com.foobar.tasks.MyCodeGen"/>
```

touch

all

Updates the timestamp — **org.apache.tools.ant.taskdefs.Touch**

Updates the timestamp of one or more files.

Attributes

datetime *(all, String, N)*
The new modification time for the file(s), in the format MM/DD/YYYY HH:MM AM or PM. Defaults to the current time.

file *(all, File, *)*
Name of a file to touch. The file is created if it does not exist. To touch directories, use nested <fileset> elements.

millis *(all, long, N)*
The new modification time for the file, expressed as the number of milliseconds since January 1, 1970.

The file attribute is required unless a nested <fileset> is specified.

Content

0..n nested <fileset> *elements (1.4)*
Specifies files and directories to touch.

Example Usage

Update the timestamp of *build.xml* with the current time:

```
<touch file="build.xml"/>
```

Change the timestamp of all files and directories in the build directory:

```
<touch datetime="06/25/1999 6:15 AM">
  <fileset dir="${builddir}"/>
</touch>
```

tstamp

all

Sets timestamp properties **org.apache.tools.ant.taskdefs.Tstamp**

Sets the DSTAMP, TSTAMP, and TODAY properties. Additionally, each property is formatted using java.text.SimpleDateFormat according to the formats listed in Table 7-4.

Table 7-4. tstamp formats

Property	Format	Example
DSTAMP	yyyyMMdd	20010916
TSTAMP	HHmm	1923
TODAY	MMMM d yyyy	September 16 2001

Attributes

None.

Content

0..n nested <format> *elements (1.3, 1.4)*

Supports custom formats. The results of each are placed in a property. Following are the <format> element attributes:

property *(1.3, 1.4, String, Y)*

The name of the property to place the formatted timestamp in.

pattern *(1.3, 1.4, String, Y)*

The format pattern as defined by java.text.SimpleDateFormat.

offset *(1.3, 1.4, int, N)*

The numeric offset to the current time.

unit *(1.3, 1.4, String, N)*

Defines what the offset parameter is affecting. Legal values are: millisecond, second, minute, hour, day, week, month, and year.

locale *(1.4, String, N)*

The locale used when constructing the SimpleDateFormat object. See the documentation for java.util.Locale.

Example Usage

Produce three properties containing the current time, one hour prior to the current time, and one minute after the current time. All are formatted like September 16 2001 07:37 PM:

```
<tstamp>
  <format property="now"
          pattern="MMMM d yyyy hh:mm aa"/>
  <format property="hour_earlier"
          pattern="MMMM d yyyy hh:mm aa"
          offset="-1"
          unit="hour"/>
  <format property="minute_later"
          pattern="MMMM d yyyy hh:mm aa"
```

```
        offset="1"
        unit="minute"/>
</tstamp>

<!-- now display one of the values -->
<echo>now = ${now}</echo>
```

typedef 1.4

Adds custom DataType definitions **org.apache.tools.ant.taskdefs.Typedef**

Adds one or more custom DataType definitions to the current project.

Attributes

`name` *(1.4, String, *)*
: The name of the DataType to add.

`classname` *(1.4, String, *)*
: The Java class implementing the DataType.

`file` *(1.4, File, N)*
: A properties file containing DataType definitions. Each line is of the form:

```
name=classname
```

`resource` *(1.4, String, N)*
: The Java resource name of a properties file. Uses a `ClassLoader` to load the properties file.

`classpath` *(1.4, Path, N)*
: The classpath to use.

The `name` and `classname` attributes are required unless the `file` or `resource` attribute is specified.

Content

0,1 nested `<classpath>` *elements (1.4)*
: May be used in place of the `classpath` attribute.

Example Usage

The following example creates the custom DataType `customer`, which is implemented by the class `com.oreilly.domain.Customer`.

```
<typedef name="customer" classname="com.oreilly.domain.Customer"/>
```

unjar

The `unjar`, `unwar`, and `unzip` tasks are identical. The `org.apache.tools.ant.taskdefs.Expand` class implements them all. See the section on `unzip` for attributes and examples.

untar

all

Expands a tar file **org.apache.tools.ant.taskdefs.Untar**

Expands a tar archive.

Attributes

`dest` *(all, File, Y)*
: The destination directory.

`overwrite` *(1.4, boolean, N)*
: If `true`, overwrite files even if they are newer than those in the tar file. Defaults to `true`.

`src` *(all, File, Y)*
: The tar file to expand.

Content

None.

Example Usage

```
<untar src="foo.tar" dest="${builddir}"/>
```

See Also

See the `tar` task.

unwar

The `unjar`, `unwar`, and `unzip` tasks are identical. The `org.apache.tools.ant.taskdefs.Expand` class implements them all. See the section on `unzip` for attributes and examples.

unzip (also unjar and unwar)

all

Expands a file **org.apache.tools.ant.taskdefs.Untar**

Unzips a ZIP file, a JAR file, or a WAR file.

Attributes

`dest` *(all, File, Y)*
: The destination directory.

`src` *(all, File, Y)*
: The file to expand.

`overwrite` *(1.4, boolean, N)*
: If `true`, overwrite files even if they are newer than those in the archive. Defaults to `true`.

Content

None.

Example Usage

```
<unzip src="dist.jar" dest="${builddir}"/>
```

See Also

The jar, war, and zip tasks.

uptodate

all

Sets a property if files are up-to-date **org.apache.tools.ant.taskdefs.UpToDate**

Sets a property if one or more target files are up-to-date with respect to corresponding source files. The property is set if the target is newer than all source files.

Attributes

property *(all, String, Y)*
: The property to set.

targetfile *(all, File, *)*
: A target file to check.

value *(1.4, String, N)*
: The value to set the property to. Defaults to true.

The targetfile attribute is required unless a nested <mapper> is specified.

Content

0..n nested <srcfiles> *elements (all)*
: Each is a fileset defining a set of source files to compare.

0,1 nested <mapper> *elements (1.3, 1.4)*
: Defines how source files relate to target files. If not specified, this task uses a merge mapper whose to attribute is set to the value of the uptodate task's targetfile attribute.

Example Usage

The following example sets the jar_ok property if *classes.jar* is newer than the *.class* files found in the project directory and all its subdirectories.

```
<uptodate property="jar_ok" targetfile="${builddir}/classes.jar">
  <srcfiles dir="${builddir}" includes="**/*.class"/>
</uptodate>
```

This next example assumes we have a custom code generator that creates *.java* files based on *.template* files. It uses a nested <mapper> and sets the codegen_uptodate property whenever all *.java* files are up-to-date with respect to their corresponding *.template* files.

```
<uptodate property="codegen_uptodate">
  <srcfiles dir="src" includes="**/*.template"/>
  <mapper type="glob" from="*.template" to="*.java"/>
</uptodate>
```

See Also

mappers are discussed in Chapter 4.

war — all

Creates a WAR file — org.apache.tools.ant.taskdefs.War

Creates a Web Application Archive (WAR) file. WAR files are the deployment mechanism for servlets.

Attributes

`basedir` *(all, File, N)*
: Specifies the base directory from which to add files to the WAR file.

`compress` *(all, boolean, N)*
: If `true`, compress the WAR file. Defaults to `true`.

`defaultexcludes` *(all, boolean, N)*
: Determines whether to use default excludes, as described in Chapter 4 under "FileSet DataType." Defaults to `true`.

`encoding` *(1.4, String, N)*
: Specifies the character encoding for filenames inside the JAR file. Defaults to UTF-8. The Ant specification warns that changing this attribute probably renders the JAR file unusable by Java.

`excludes` *(all, String, N)*
: A comma-separated list of file patterns to exclude. These are in addition to the default excludes.

`excludesfile` *(all, File, N)*
: The name of a file containing one exclude pattern per line.

`filesonly` *(1.4, boolean, N)*
: If `true`, do not create empty directories. Defaults to `false`.

`includes` *(all, String, N)*
: A comma-separated list of file patterns to include.

`includesfile` *(all, File, N)*
: The name of a file containing one include pattern per line.

`manifest` *(all, File, N)*
: The name of the manifest file to use.

`update` *(1.4, boolean, N)*
: If `true`, update the existing WAR file when changes are made, rather than erasing and creating it from scratch. Defaults to `false`.

`warfile` *(all, File, Y)*
: The name of the WAR file to create.

`webxml` *(all, File, Y)*
: The name of the deployment descriptor. It is placed in the *WEB-INF* directory and renamed to *web.xml*.

`whenempty` *(all, Enum, N)*
: The behavior used when no files to include are found. Defaults to `create`. Legal values are as follows:

    `fail`
    : Abort the build.

`skip`
: Don't create the WAR file.

`create`
: Create an empty WAR file when no include files are present.

Content

0..n nested `patternset` *elements:* `<exclude>`, `<include>`, `<patternset>` *(all);* `<excludesfile>`, `<includesfile>` *(1.4)*
: Used in place of their corresponding attributes, these specify the set of included and excluded source files.

0..n nested `<classes>` *elements (all)*
: `zipfileset` elements defining which files are placed in the *WEB-INF/classes* directory of the WAR file.

0..n nested `<fileset>` *elements (all)*
: `fileset` elements defining which files are placed in top-level directory of the WAR file.

0..n nested `<lib>` *elements (all)*
: `zipfileset` elements defining which files are placed in the *WEB-INF/lib* directory of the WAR file.

0..n nested `<metainf>` *elements (1.4)*
: `zipfileset` elements defining which files are placed in the *META-INF* directory of the WAR file.

0..n nested `<webinf>` *elements (all)*
: `zipfileset` elements defining which files are placed in the *WEB-INF* directory of the WAR file.

0..n nested `<zipfileset>` *elements (1.3, 1.4)*
: `zipfileset` elements defining which files are placed in top-level directory of the WAR file.

Example Usage

The following example creates a WAR file named *ecom.war*. Files in the *src/docroot* directory are placed in the root directory of the WAR file. All class files are placed under *WEB-INF/classes*, and JAR files are placed under *WEB-INF/lib*.

```
<war warfile="${builddir}/ecom.war"
     webxml="src/metadata/web.xml">
  <fileset dir="src/docroot"/>
  <classes dir="${builddir}" includes="**/*.class"/>
  <lib dir="${builddir}" includes="*.jar"/>
</war>
```

See Also

See the `zip` task for a description of `zipfileset`.

zip

all

Creates a ZIP file **org.apache.tools.ant.taskdefs.Zip**

Creates a ZIP file.

Attributes

`basedir` *(all, File, N)*
: Specifies the base directory from which to add files to the ZIP file.

`compress` *(all, boolean, N)*
: If `true`, compress the ZIP file. Defaults to `true`.

`defaultexcludes` *(all, boolean, N)*
: Determines whether to use default excludes, as described in Chapter 4 under "FileSet DataType." Defaults to `true`.

`encoding` *(1.4, String, N)*
: Specifies the character encoding for filenames inside the ZIP file. Defaults to whatever encoding the current VM uses.

`excludes` *(all, String, N)*
: A comma-separated list of file patterns to exclude. These are in addition to the default excludes.

`excludesfile` *(all, File, N)*
: The name of a file containing one exclude pattern per line.

`filesonly` *(1.4, boolean, N)*
: If `true`, do not create empty directories. Defaults to `false`.

`includes` *(all, String, N)*
: A comma-separated list of file patterns to include.

`includesfile` *(all, File, N)*
: The name of a file containing one include pattern per line.

`update` *(1.4, boolean, N)*
: If `true`, update the existing ZIP file when changes are made, rather than erasing and creating it from scratch. Defaults to `false`.

`whenempty` *(all, Enum, N)*
: The behavior used when no files match. Defaults to `create`. Legal values are as follows:

  `fail`
  : Abort the build.

  `skip`
  : Don't create the ZIP file.

  `create`
  : Create an empty ZIP file when no files are present.

`zipfile` *(all, File, Y)*
: The name of the ZIP file to create.

Content

0..n nested patternset *elements:* <exclude>, <include>, <patternset> *(all);* <excludesfile>, <includesfile> *(1.4)*

Used in place of their corresponding attributes, these specify the set of included and excluded source files.

0..n nested <fileset> *elements (all)*

fileset elements defining which files are placed in the ZIP file.

0..n nested <zipfileset> *elements (1.3, 1.4)*

Each is a zipfileset, which is an extension of fileset.

zipfileset adds the following attributes to fileset:

fullpath *(String, N)*

Can only be set for a single file. Specifies the full pathname for a file once it is added to the archive.

prefix *(String, N)*

If specified, all files are prefixed with this path when placed in the archive.

src *(File, *)*

Specifies an existing ZIP file whose contents will be extracted and then inserted into the new ZIP file.

Exactly one of dir or src is required. (dir is inherited from fileset.)

Example Usage

Create a ZIP file containing all source code:

```
<zip zipfile="${builddir}/src.zip" basedir="src"/>
```

See Also

See the ear, jar, tar, and war tasks, all of which are based on the same code that zip uses.

CHAPTER 8

Optional Tasks

This chapter lists optional tasks available with Ant Versions 1.2, 1.3, and 1.4. The presentation follows the same format as is used in Chapter 7.

Task Summary

Table 8-1 summarizes all of Ant's optional tasks.

Table 8-1. Optional task summary

Task name	Ant versions	Synopsis
`antlr`	1.3, 1.4	Runs the ANTLR parser and translator generator tool.
`blgenclient`	1.4	Creates a client JAR file from an existing *ejb-jar* file. The name is derived from "Borland Generated Client."
`cab`	all	Creates Microsoft *.cab* archives.
`cccheckin`	1.3, 1.4	Performs a Rational ClearCase *checkin* command.
`cccheckout`	1.3, 1.4	Performs a ClearCase *checkout* command.
`ccmcheckin`	1.4	Performs a Continuus[a] *ci* command.
`ccmcheckintask`	1.4	Performs a Continuus *ci default* command.
`ccmcheckout`	1.4	Performs a Continuus *co* command.
`ccmcreatetask`	1.4	Performs a Continuus *create_task* command.
`ccmreconfigure`	1.4	Performs a Continuus *reconfigure* command.
`ccuncheckout`	1.3, 1.4	Performs a ClearCase *uncheckout* command.
`ccupdate`	1.3, 1.4	Performs a ClearCase *update* command.
`csc`	1.3, 1.4	Compiles C# source code.
`ddcreator`	all	Creates serialized EJB deployment descriptors from text files.
`depend`	1.3, 1.4	Determines which class files are out-of-date based on analysis of content, in addition to comparing class file timestamps to source file timestamps.
`ejbc`	all	Executes BEA WebLogic Server's *ejbc* tool, generating code necessary to deploy EJB components in that environment.

Table 8-1. Optional task summary (continued)

Task name	Ant versions	Synopsis
ejbjar	all	Creates *ejb-jar* files compatible with EJB 1.1.
ftp	all	Implements a basic FTP client.
icontract	1.4	Executes the iContract Design By Contract preprocessor.
ilasm	1.3, 1.4	Assembles .NET Intermediate Language files.
iplanet-ejbc	1.4	Compiles EJB stubs and skeletons for iPlanet Application Server Version 6.0.
javacc	all	Executes the JavaCC compiler compiler on a grammar file.
javah	1.3, 1.4	Executes the *javah* tool, generating Java Native Interface (JNI) headers from one or more Java classes.
jdepend	1.4	Executes the JDepend tool.
jjtree	all	Executes the JJTree preprocessor for JavaCC.
jlink	all	Builds a JAR or ZIP file, optionally merging contents of existing JAR and ZIP archives.
jpcoverage	1.4	Executes the JProbe Coverage tool.
jpcovmerge	1.4	Merges several JProbe Coverage snapshots into one.
jpcovreport	1.4	Creates a report from a JProbe Coverage snapshot.
junit	all	Executes unit tests using the JUnit testing framework.
junitreport	1.3, 1.4	Creates a formatted report based on several XML files from the `junit` task.
maudit	1.4	Executes the WebGain Quality Analyzer to analyze Java source code for programming errors.
mimemail	1.4	Sends SMTP mail with MIME attachments.
mmetrics	1.4	Executes the WebGain Quality Analyzer on a set of Java files, reporting on code complexity and other metrics.
mparse	all	Executes the now obsolete Metamata MParse compiler compiler on a grammar file.
native2ascii	all	Converts files with native encoding to ASCII containing escaped Unicode characters.
netrexxc	all	Compiles a set of NetRexx files.
p4change	1.3, 1.4	Requests a new changelist from a Perforce server.
p4counter	1.4	Gets and sets a Perforce counter value.
p4edit	1.3, 1.4	Opens files from Perforce for editing.
p4have	1.3, 1.4	Lists Perforce files in the current client view.
p4label	1.3, 1.4	Creates a label for files in the current Perforce workspace.
p4reopen	1.4	Moves files between Perforce changelists.
p4revert	1.4	Reverts opened Perforce files.
p4submit	1.3, 1.4	Checks files in to a Perforce depot.
p4sync	1.3, 1.4	Synchronizes a workspace with the Perforce depot.
propertyfile	1.3, 1.4	Creates or edits Java properties files.
pvcs	1.4	Extracts files from a PVCS repository.
renameext	all	Renames filename extensions. This task was deprecated in Ant 1.3. Use the `move` task with a glob `mapper` instead.

Table 8-1. Optional task summary (continued)

Task name	Ant versions	Synopsis
`rpm`	1.4	Builds a Linux RPM file.
`script`	all	Executes a BSF script.
`sound`	1.3, 1.4	Plays a sound file at the end of the build process.
`starteam`	all	Checks out files from StarTeam.
`stylebook`	1.3, 1.4	Executes the Apache Stylebook documentation generator.
`telnet`	1.3, 1.4	Executes a telnet session.
`test`	1.3, 1.4	Executes a unit test in the `org.apache.testlet` framework.
`vsscheckin`	1.4	Checks in files to Visual SourceSafe.
`vsscheckout`	1.4	Checks out files from Visual SourceSafe.
`vssget`	all	Gets files from Visual SourceSafe.
`vsshistory`	1.4	Shows history for files and projects in Visual SourceSafe.
`vsslabel`	1.3, 1.4	Assigns a label to files and projects in Visual SourceSafe.
`wljspc`	all	Precompiles JSP files using BEA WebLogic Server's JSP compiler.
`wlrun`	all	Starts an instance of the BEA WebLogic Server.
`wlstop`	all	Stops an instance of the BEA WebLogic Server.
`xmlvalidate`	1.4	Verifies that XML documents are well-formed and optionally valid, using any SAX parser.

[a] Although the Ant tasks still refer to Continuus commands, the product is now known as Telelogic Synergy, available at *http://www.telelogic.com*.

Optional Task Reference

The remainder of this chapter provides detailed information on each of Ant's optional tasks. Attribute descriptions are formatted exactly like the previous chapter.

antlr — 1.3, 1.4

Runs the ANTLR parser — **org.apache.tools.ant.taskdefs.optional.ANTLR**

Runs the ANTLR parser and translator generator tool. ANTLR must be installed for this task to run. It is available at *http://www.antlr.org*. This task compares the grammar file against the target files, running ANTLR only if the grammar file is newer.

Attributes

`dir` *(1.3, 1.4, File, N)*
: The working directory for the forked JVM. Only valid when `fork=true`.

`fork` *(1.3, 1.4, boolean, N)*
: If `true`, run ANTLR in its own JVM. Defaults to `false`.

`outputdirectory` *(1.3, 1.4, File, N)*
: The destination directory for the generated files. Defaults to the directory containing the grammar file.

`target` *(1.3, 1.4, File, Y)*
: The name of the grammar file.

Content

None.

blgenclient

1.4

Creates a client JAR file — org.apache.tools.ant.taskdefs.optional.ejb.BorlandGenerateClient

Creates a client JAR file from an existing *ejb-jar* file. `blgenclient` is derived from "Borland Generated Client." It is designed for use with Borland Application Server v4.5.

Attributes

`classpath` *(1.4, Path, N)*
: The classpath used by the `java` task. Only valid when mode is `java`.

`classpathref` *(1.4, Reference, N)*
: A reference to a classpath defined elsewhere in the buildfile. Only valid when mode is `java`.

`clientjar` *(1.4, File, N)*
: The name of the client JAR to create. If omitted, the task appends `client` to the filename. For instance, *foo.jar* becomes *fooclient.jar*.

`debug` *(1.4, boolean, N)*
: If `true`, the task passes the `-trace` command-line option to the underlying command. Defaults to `false`.

`ejbjar` *(1.4, File, Y)*
: The *ejb-jar* file from which to generate the client JAR.

`mode` *(1.4, String, N)*
: Specifies how the command is launched. Defaults to `java`. Legal values are as follows:

  `fork`
  : Use the exec core task.

  `java`
  : Use the `java` core task.*

Content

0,1 nested `<classpath>` *elements (1.4)*
: A `path` element used in place of the `classpath` or `classpathref` attributes.

* Even in "java" mode, this task forks a new JVM.

cab **all**

Creates Microsoft CAB files **org.apache.tools.ant.taskdefs.optional.Cab**

Creates Microsoft CAB archives. On Windows platforms, you must include the Microsoft *cabarc* tool on the path. On non-Windows platforms, you can use *libcabinet*, available at *http://trill.cis.fordham.edu/~barbacha/cabinet_library/*.

Attributes

`basedir` *(all, File, Y)*
: The directory from which to archive files.

`cabfile` *(all, File, Y)*
: The name of the CAB file to create.

`compress` *(all, boolean, N)*
: If `true`, compress files. Defaults to `true`.

`defaultexcludes` *(all, boolean, N)*
: Determines whether to use default excludes. Defaults to `true`.

`excludes` *(all, String, N)*
: A comma-separated list of file patterns to exclude.

`excludesfile` *(all, File, N)*
: The name of a file containing one exclude pattern per line.

`includes` *(all, String, N)*
: A comma-separated list of file patterns to include.

`includesfile` *(all, File, N)*
: The name of a file containing one include pattern per line.

`options` *(all, String, N)*
: Specifies additional command-line arguments for the underlying *cabarc* command.

`verbose` *(all, boolean, N)*
: If `true`, the task instructs the *cabarc* command to operate in verbose mode. Defaults to `false`.

Content

0..n nested `patternset` *elements:* `<exclude>`, `<include>`, `<patternset>` *(all);* `<excludesfile>`, `<includesfile>` *(1.4)*
: Used in place of their corresponding attributes, these specify the set of included and excluded source files.

0..n nested `<fileset>` *elements (all)*
: `fileset` elements specifying files included in the CAB archive.

cccheckin **1.3, 1.4**

Performs a ClearCase checkin **org.apache.tools.ant.taskdefs.optional.clearcase.CCCheckin**

Performs a ClearCase *checkin* command.

Attributes

`cleartooldir` *(1.3, 1.4, String, N)*
: Specifies the directory in which *cleartool* is located.

`comment` *(1.3, 1.4, String, *)*
: A comment to use when checking in the file.

`commentfile` *(1.3, 1.4, String, *)*
: A file containing a comment used when checking in the file.

`identical` *(1.3, 1.4, boolean, N)*
: If `true`, the task checks in the file even if it is identical to its original. Defaults to `false`.

`keepcopy` *(1.3, 1.4, boolean, N)*
: If `true`, the task keeps a copy of the file with a *.keep* extension. Defaults to `false`.

`nowarn` *(1.3, 1.4, boolean, N)*
: If `true`, the task does not show warning messages. Defaults to `false`.

`preservetime` *(1.3, 1.4, boolean, N)*
: If `true`, the task preserves the file-modification time. Defaults to `false`.

`viewpath` *(1.3, 1.4, String, N)*
: The path to the ClearCase view file or directory.

The `comment` and `commentfile` attributes are optional, but you cannot specify both.

Content

None.

cccheckout 1.3, 1.4

Performs a ClearCase checkout org.apache.tools.ant.taskdefs.optional.clearcase.CCCheckout

Performs a ClearCase *checkout* command.

Attributes

`branch` *(1.3, 1.4, String, N)*
: Specifies the branch used when checking out files.

`cleartooldir` *(1.3, 1.4, String, N)*
: Specifies the directory in which *cleartool* is located.

`comment` *(1.3, 1.4, String, *)*
: A comment to use when checking out the file.

`commentfile` *(1.3, 1.4, String, *)*
: A file containing a comment used when checking out the file.

`nodata` *(1.3, 1.4, boolean, N)*
: If `true`, the task checks out the file but does not create a file containing editable data. Defaults to `false`.

`nowarn` *(1.3, 1.4, boolean, N)*
: If `true`, the task does not show warning messages. Defaults to `false`.

`out` *(1.3, 1.4, String, N)*
: Specifies a different filename to check the file out to.

`reserved` *(1.3, 1.4, boolean, Y)*
: If `true`, the task checks out the file as reserved. Defaults to `true`.

`version` *(1.3, 1.4, boolean, N)*
: If `true`, the task allows checking out a version other than latest. Defaults to `false`.

`viewpath` *(1.3, 1.4, String, N)*
: The path to the ClearCase view file or directory.

The `comment` and `commentfile` attributes are optional, but you cannot specify both.

Content

None.

ccmcheckin 1.4

Performs a Continuus ci — **org.apache.tools.ant.taskdefs.optional.ccm.CCMCheckin**

Performs a Continuus *ci* command. This and other `ccm` tasks are wrappers around the Continuus Source Manager product. Although these tasks still refer to Continuus, the product was purchased by Telelogic in September 2000, and is now known as Telelogic Synergy. It is available at *http://www.telelogic.com*.

Attributes

`ccmdir` *(1.4, String, N)*
: The directory containing the *ccm* executable. The task searches the path if this is not specified.

`comment` *(1.4, String, N)*
: A comment for the file. Defaults to "Checkin " + current date and time.

`file` *(1.4, File, Y)*
: The file to check in.

`task` *(1.4, String, N)*
: The Continuus task number used when checking in the file.

Content

None.

ccmcheckintask 1.4

Performs a Continuus ci default — **org.apache.tools.ant.taskdefs.optional.ccm.CCMCheckinDefault**

Performs a Continuus *ci default* command.

Attributes

`ccmdir` *(1.4, String, N)*
: The directory containing the *ccm* executable. The task searches the path if this is not specified.

`comment` *(1.4, String, N)*
A comment to use when checking in the file(s).

`task` *(1.4, String, N)*
The Continuus task number used when checking in the file.

Content

None.

ccmcheckout 1.4

Performs a Continuus co **org.apache.tools.ant.taskdefs.optional.ccm.CCMCheckout**

Performs a Continuus *co* command.

Attributes

`ccmdir` *(1.4, String, N)*
The directory containing the *ccm* executable. The task searches the path if no directory is specified.

`comment` *(1.4, String, N)*
A comment used when checking out the file.

`file` *(1.4, File, Y)*
The file to check out.

`task` *(1.4, String, N)*
The Continuus task number used when checking out the file.

Content

None.

ccmcreatetask 1.4

Performs a Continuus create_task **org.apache.tools.ant.taskdefs.optional.ccm.CCMCreateTask**

Performs a Continuus *create_task* command.

Attributes

`ccmdir` *(1.4, String, N)*
The directory containing the *ccm* executable. The task searches the path if this is not specified.

`comment` *(1.4, String, N)*
A comment for the operation.

`platform` *(1.4, String, N)*
The */plat* command-line option.

`release` *(1.4, String, N)*
The */release* command-line option.

`resolver` *(1.4, String, N)*
The */resolver* command-line option.

`subsystem` *(1.4, String, N)*
The */subsystem* command-line option.

`task` *(1.4, String, N)*
The Continuus task number to use.

Content

None.

ccmreconfigure 1.4

Performs a Continuus reconfigure **org.apache.tools.ant.taskdefs.optional.ccm.CCMReconfigure**

Performs a Continuus *reconfigure* command.

Attributes

`ccmdir` *(1.4, String, N)*
The directory containing the *ccm* executable. The task searches the path if this is not specified.

`ccmproject` *(1.4, String, Y)*
The name of the project for this command.

`recurse` *(1.4, boolean, N)*
If `true`, the task recursively processes subprojects. Defaults to `false`.

`verbose` *(1.4, boolean, N)*
If `true`, the task prints verbose information. Defaults to `false`.

Content

None.

ccuncheckout 1.3, 1.4

Performs a ClearCase uncheckout **org.apache.tools.ant.taskdefs.optional.clearcase.CCUnCheckout**

Performs a ClearCase *uncheckout* command.

Attributes

`cleartooldir` *(1.3, 1.4, String, N)*
Specifies the directory in which *cleartool* is located.

`keepcopy` *(1.3, 1.4, boolean, N)*
If `true`, the task keeps a copy of the file with a *.keep* extension. Defaults to `false`.

`viewpath` *(1.3, 1.4, String, N)*
Path to the ClearCase view file or directory.

Content

None.

ccupdate **1.3, 1.4**

Performs a ClearCase update **org.apache.tools.ant.taskdefs.optional.clearcase.CCUpdate**

Performs a ClearCase *update* command.

Attributes

`cleartooldir` *(1.3, 1.4, String, N)*
: Specifies the directory in which *cleartool* is located.

`currenttime` *(1.3, 1.4, boolean, *)*
: If `true`, the task sets the file-modification time to the current system time. Defaults to `false`.

`graphical` *(1.3, 1.4, boolean, N)*
: If `true`, the task shows the GUI window. Defaults to `false`.

`log` *(1.3, 1.4, String, N)*
: The name of a log file ClearCase should write to.

`overwrite` *(1.3, 1.4, boolean, N)*
: If `true`, the task overwrites hijacked files.* Defaults to `false`.

`preservetime` *(1.3, 1.4, boolean, *)*
: If `true`, the task preserves the file-modification time from the Version Object Base (VOB). Defaults to `false`.

`rename` *(1.3, 1.4, boolean, N)*
: If `true`, indicates that hijacked files should be renamed with a *.keep* extension. Defaults to `false`.

`viewpath` *(1.3, 1.4, String, N)*
: Specifies the path to the ClearCase view file or directory.

The `currenttime` and `preservetime` attributes are optional, but you cannot specify both.

Content

None.

csc **1.3, 1.4**

Compiles C# code **org.apache.tools.ant.taskdefs.optional.dotnet.CSharp**

Compiles C# source code. Currently works on platforms containing the *csc.exe* executable, i.e., various flavors of Windows.

* ClearCase considers a file "hijacked" when you modify it without checking it out.

Attributes

`additionalmodules` *(1.3, 1.4, String, N)*
A semicolon-delimited list of additional modules, which are DLLs containing metadata. This is equivalent to *csc*'s */addmodule* parameter.

`debug` *(1.3, 1.4, boolean, N)*
If `true`, include debug information. Defaults to `true`.

`defaultexcludes` *(1.3, 1.4, boolean, N)*
Determines whether to use default excludes. Defaults to `true`.

`definitions` *(1.3, 1.4, String, N)*
List of definitions passed to *csc.exe*, delimited by "`;`", "`:`", or "`,`"—for instance, `DEBUG;BETA_TEST`.

`docfile` *(1.3, 1.4, File, N)*
The name of a file for generated XML documentation.

`excludes` *(1.3, 1.4, String, N)*
A comma-separated list of file patterns to exclude.

`excludesfile` *(1.3, 1.4, File, N)*
The name of a file containing one exclude pattern per line.

`extraoptions` *(1.3, 1.4, String, N)*
Extra options passed directly to the *csc.exe* command.

`failonerror` *(1.3, 1.4, boolean, N)*
If `true`, the task fails the build when the compile returns an error. Defaults to `true`.

`fullpaths` *(1.4, boolean, N)*
If `true`, the task prints the full path of files when errors occur. Defaults to `true`.

`includedefaultreferences` *(1.3, 1.4, boolean, N)*
If `true`, the task includes common assemblies found in .NET beta 1, and in links in *mscore.dll*. Defaults to `true`.

`includes` *(1.3, 1.4, String, N)*
A comma-separated list of file patterns to include.

`includesfile` *(1.3, 1.4, File, N)*
The name of a file containing one include pattern per line.

`incremental` *(1.3, 1.4, boolean, N)*
If `true`, the task instructs *csc.exe* to perform an incremental build. Defaults to `false`.

`mainclass` *(1.3, 1.4, String, N)*
The name of the main class for executables.

`noconfig` *(1.4, boolean, N)*
If `true`, the task passes the */noconfig* flag to *csc.exe*. Defaults to `false`.*

`optimize` *(1.3, 1.4, boolean, N)*
If `true`, the task instructs *csc.exe* to apply optimizations. Defaults to `false`.

* Although this attribute is documented in the Ant user manual, its implementation method is protected instead of public, preventing its use in Ant 1.4.

`outputfile` *(1.3, 1.4, File, N)*
: The target filename, such as *mygui.exe*.

`referencefiles` *(1.3, 1.4, Path, N)*
: A path of references to include.

`references` *(1.3, 1.4, String, N)*
: A semicolon-delimited list of *.dll* files to refer to.

`srcdir` *(1.3, 1.4, File, N)*
: A directory containing source code.

`targettype` *(1.3, 1.4, String, N)*
: Specifies the type of target. Allowable values are `exe`, `module`, `winexe`, and `library`. Defaults to exe.

`unsafe` *(1.3, 1.4, boolean, N)*
: If `true`, the task enables the `unsafe` keyword. Defaults to `false`.

`utf8output` *(1.4, boolean, N)*
: If `true`, the task uses UTF-8 encoding for output files. Defaults to `false`.

`warnlevel` *(1.3, 1.4, int, N)*
: A warning level, ranging from 1..4, where 4 is strictest. Defaults to 3.

`win32icon` *(1.3, 1.4, File, N)*
: The filename of an icon to use, such as *foo.ico*.

`win32res` *(1.4, File, N)*
: The filename of a Win32 resource, such as *foo.res*.

Content

0..n nested `patternset` *elements:* `<exclude>`, `<include>`, `<patternset>` *(1.3, 1.4);* `<excludesfile>`, `<includesfile>` *(1.4)*
: Used in place of their corresponding attributes, these specify the set of included and excluded source files.

ddcreator **all**

Creates EJB deployment descriptors **org.apache.tools.ant.taskdefs.optional.ejb.DDCreator**

Creates serialized EJB deployment descriptors from text files. This task is designed for BEA WebLogic Server 4.5.1.

Attributes

`classpath` *(all, String, N)*
: The classpath used when running the `weblogic.ejb.utils.DDCreator` class.

`defaultexcludes` *(all, boolean, N)*
: Determines whether to use default excludes. Defaults to `true`.

`descriptors` *(all, String, Y)*
: The base directory containing text deployment descriptors.

`dest` *(all, String, Y)*
: The destination directory.

`excludes` *(all, String, N)*
: A comma-separated list of file patterns to exclude.

`excludesfile` *(all, File, N)*
: The name of a file containing one exclude pattern per line.

`includes` *(all, String, N)*
: A comma-separated list of file patterns to include.

`includesfile` *(all, File, N)*
: The name of a file containing one include pattern per line.

Content

0..n nested `patternset` *elements:* `<exclude>`, `<include>`, `<patternset>` *(all);* `<excludesfile>`, `<includesfile>` *(1.4)*
: Used in place of their corresponding attributes, these specify the set of included and excluded source files.

depend 1.3, 1.4

Finds /removes out-of-date files with dependencies **org.apache.tools.ant.taskdefs.optional.depend.Depend**

Determines which class files are out of date based on analysis of content, in addition to comparing class file timestamps to source file timestamps. It then removes class files that are out of date, either because source files are newer or because some logical dependency has changed. For instance, changing source code for a base class causes all derived classes to be removed, because they have a logical dependency on their base class.

Attributes

`cache` *(1.3, 1.4, File, N)*
: A directory in which this task caches dependency information. If omitted, a cache is not used.

`classpath` *(1.4, Path, N)*
: Specifies where additional (with respect to `destdir`) classes and JAR files are located. This task checks dependencies against classes specified by this attribute. You should not include third-party libraries and JDK libraries in this path, because they rarely change and will slow down dependency analysis. This is useful if you wish to check dependencies against a utility JAR file, for example.

`classpathref` *(1.4, Reference, N)*
: A reference to a classpath defined elsewhere in the buildfile.

`closure` *(1.3, 1.4, boolean, N)*
: If `true`, the task deletes only class files that directly depend on out-of-date classes. Otherwise, indirect dependencies are considered as well. Defaults to `false`.

`defaultexcludes` *(1.3, 1.4, boolean, N)*
: Determines whether to use default excludes. Defaults to `true`.

`destdir` *(1.3, 1.4, Path, N)*
: Directory in which class files are found. If omitted, defaults to the value specified by `srcdir`.

`dump` *(1.4, boolean, N)*
: If `true`, the task writes dependency information to the logging output. Defaults to `false`.

`excludes` *(1.3, 1.4, String, N)*
: A comma-separated list of file patterns to exclude.

`excludesfile` *(1.3, 1.4, File, N)*
: The name of a file containing one exclude pattern per line.

`includes` *(1.3, 1.4, String, N)*
: A comma-separated list of file patterns to include.

`includesfile` *(1.3, 1.4, File, N)*
: The name of a file containing one include pattern per line.

`srcdir` *(1.3, 1.4, Path, Y)*
: The directory containing source files.

Content

0,1 nested `<classpath>` *elements (1.4)*
: The `Path` element used in place of the `classpath` and `classpathref` attributes.

0..n nested `patternset` *elements:* `<exclude>`, `<include>`, `<patternset>` *(1.3, 1.4);* `<excludesfile>`, `<includesfile>` *(1.4)*
: Used in place of their corresponding attributes, these specify the set of included and excluded source files.

ejbc

all

Executes WebLogic ejbc tool **org.apache.tools.ant.taskdefs.optional.ejb.Ejbc**

Executes BEA WebLogic Server's *ejbc* tool, generating code necessary to deploy EJB components in that environment. This task is designed for WebLogic 4.5.1.

Attributes

`classpath` *(all, String, N)*
: The classpath to use. This must include all necessary supporting classes, such as the remote and home interfaces for the bean(s).

`defaultexcludes` *(all, boolean, N)*
: Determines whether to use default excludes. Defaults to `true`.

`descriptors` *(all, String, Y)*
: A base directory containing serialized deployment descriptors.

`dest` *(all, String, Y)*
: A destination directory for generated classes, stubs, and skeletons.

`excludes` *(all, String, N)*
: A comma-separated list of file patterns to exclude.

`excludesfile` *(all, File, N)*
: The name of a file containing one exclude pattern per line.

`includes` *(all, String, N)*
A comma-separated list of file patterns to include.

`includesfile` *(all, File, N)*
The name of a file containing one include pattern per line.

`keepgenerated` *(1.3, 1.4, String, N)*
If `true`, keep the generated Java source code. Defaults to `false`. Note that this is a `String` attribute, not a Boolean; legal values are `true` and `false`.

`manifest` *(all, String, Y)*
The name of the manifest file to create.

`src` *(all, String, Y)*
The base of the source tree, containing home interfaces, remote interfaces, and bean implementation classes.

Content

0..n nested `patternset` *elements:* `<exclude>`, `<include>`, `<patternset>` *(all);* `<excludesfile>`, `<includesfile>` *(1.4)*
Used in place of their corresponding attributes, these specify the set of included and excluded deployment descriptors.

ejbjar — all

Creates EJB JAR files — **org.apache.tools.ant.taskdefs.optional.ejb.EjbJar**

Creates *ejb-jar* files compatible with EJB 1.1. This task supports a set of generic attributes and nested elements, along with several vendor-specific nested elements.

Attributes

`basejarname` *(all, String, *)*
The base name used for generated JAR filenames.

`basenameterminator` *(all, String, N)*
Used to determine filenames based on deployment descriptor names. For instance, suppose this attribute is set to "`-`". With this value, a deployment descriptor named *Customer-ejb-jar.xml* results in a base name of `Customer`. This attribute is only used when `basejarname` is specified. Defaults to "`-`".

`classpath` *(1.3, 1.4, Path, N)*
A classpath used to locate classes that are added to the *ejb-jar* file.

`defaultexcludes` *(all, boolean, N)*
Determines whether to use default excludes. Defaults to `true`.

`descriptordir` *(all, File, N)*
The base of a directory tree containing deployment descriptors. Defaults to the value specified by `srcdir`.

`destdir` *(all, File, Y)*
A destination directory for generated JAR files. Files are placed in subdirectories corresponding to deployment descriptor subdirectories.

excludes *(all, String, N)*
A comma-separated list of file patterns to exclude.

excludesfile *(all, File, N)*
The name of a file containing one exclude pattern per line.

flatdestdir *(all, boolean, N)*
Used instead of destdir when generated JAR files should not be placed into subdirectories.

genericjarsuffix *(all, String, N)*
The name appended to the base name of the deployment descriptor when generating generic *ejb-jar* files. Defaults to *-generic.jar*.

includes *(all, String, N)*
A comma-separated list of file patterns to include.

includesfile *(all, File, N)*
The name of a file containing one include pattern per line.

manifest *(1.4, File, N)*
Specifies a manifest file to include.

naming *(1.4, Enum, *)*
Configures how the JAR file name is determined. Defaults to descriptor. Legal values are as follows:

ejb-name
The JAR filename is based on the EJB name. For example, a Customer bean results in *Customer.jar*.

directory
The JAR filename is based the last part of a directory containing the deployment descriptor. For example, *com/oreilly/sales/accounting-ejb-jar.xml* becomes *sales.jar*.

descriptor
The JAR filename is based on the deployment descriptor name. For example, *com/oreilly/sales/accounting-ejb-jar.xml* becomes *accounting.jar*.

basejarname
Only legal when the basejarname attribute is set. When it is set, the ejbjar task uses the basejarname attribute value when determining JAR filenames. For example, when basejarname is "Book", the resulting JAR is *Book.jar*.

srcdir *(all, File, Y)*
A directory containing class files comprising the beans.

The basejarname attribute is only allowed when naming="basejarname".

Content

0..n nested patternset *elements:* <exclude>, <include>, <patternset> *(all);* <excludesfile>, <includesfile> *(1.4)*
Used in place of their corresponding attributes, these specify the set of included and excluded deployment descriptors.

0,1 nested <classpath> *elements (1.3, 1.4)*
Used in place of the classpath attribute.

0..n nested `<dtd>` *elements (1.3, 1.4)*

Specifies local locations for DTD references in XML files. This is useful because loading DTDs from a local file is faster than loading DTDs remotely, and works when disconnected from a network or running behind a firewall. This element requires the following two attributes:

`location` *(1.3, 1.4, String, Y)*

The local copy of the DTD. This is either a filename or a Java resource name.

`publicid` *(1.3, 1.4, String, Y)*

The public ID of the DTD.

0..n nested `<support>` *elements (1.3, 1.4)*

`fileset` elements specifying additional files to include in the generated JAR files. When generating multiple JAR files, these support files are added to each one.

The `ejbar` task supports numerous vendor-specific nested elements. These account for deployment differences across various EJB servers.

0,1 nested `<borland>` *elements (1.4)*

Supports Borland Application Server Version 4.5. Generates and compiles stubs and skeletons, creates the JAR file, then verifies its contents. Attributes are as follows:

`classpath` *(1.4, Path, N)*

Classpath used when generating stubs and skeletons. This is appended to the classpath specified in the `ejbjar` parent class. A nested `<classpath>` element is also supported.

`debug` *(1.4, boolean, N)*

If `true`, run the Borland tools in debug mode. Defaults to `false`.

`destdir` *(1.4, File, Y)*

The base directory for generated JAR files.

`generateclient` *(1.4, boolean, N)*

If `true`, generate the corresponding client JAR file. Defaults to `false`.

`suffix` *(1.4, String, N)*

The text appended to the base name of the deployment descriptor. This is used when generating the JAR filename. Defaults to `-ejb.jar`.

`verify` *(1.4, boolean, N)*

If `true`, verify the generated JAR files. Defaults to `false`.

`verifyargs` *(1.4, String, N)*

The extra arguments used when `verify=true`.

0,1 nested `<iplanet>` *elements. (1.4)*

Supports iPlanet Application Server (iAS) Version 6.0. Attributes are as follows:

`classpath` *(1.4, Path, N)*

Classpath used when generating stubs and skeletons. This is appended to the classpath specified in the `ejbjar` parent class. A nested `<classpath>` element is also supported.

`debug` *(1.4, boolean, N)*

If `true`, log debugging information as the `ejbjar` task runs. Defaults to `false`.

`destdir` *(1.4, File, Y)*

The base directory for generated JAR files.

`iashome` *(1.4, File, N)*
The home directory for the iAS distribution, used to locate the *ejbc* utility when it is not on the path.

`keepgenerated` *(1.4, boolean, N)*
If `true`, keep generated Java source files. Defaults to `false`.

`suffix` *(1.4, String, N)*
Appended to each generated JAR filename. Defaults to *.jar*.

0,1 nested `<jboss>` *elements (1.4)*
Supports the JBoss server. Since JBoss supports hot deployment, it does not require generated stubs and skeletons. This task searches for *jboss.xml* and *jaws.xml*, adding them to the generated JAR file. One attribute is supported:

`destdir` *(1.4, File, Y)*
Base directory for generated JAR files.

0,1 nested `<weblogic>` *elements (all)*
Supports the *weblogic.ejbc* compiler. The following attributes are supported:

`args` *(all, String, N)*
The additional arguments for *weblogic.ejbc.*

`classpath` *(all, Path, N)*
The classpath used when running the *weblogic.ejbc* tool.

`compiler` *(all, String, N)*
Select a different Java compiler.

`destdir` *(all, File, Y)*
The base directory for generated JAR files.

`genericjarsuffix` *(all, String, N)*
The filename suffix used when generating an intermediate, temporary JAR file. Defaults to *-generic.jar*.

`keepgenerated` *(all, boolean, N)*
If `true`, keep generated Java files. Defaults to `false`.

`keepgeneric` *(all, boolean, N)*
If `true`, keep the intermediate generic JAR files. Defaults to `false`.

`newCMP` *(1.3, 1.4, boolean, N)*
If `true`, use the new method for locating CMP descriptors. Defaults to `false`.

`noEJBC` *(1.4, boolean, N)*
If `true`, do not run *weblogic.ejbc* on the JAR file. Defaults to `false`.

`rebuild` *(1.3, 1.4, boolean, N)*
If `true`, force execution of *weblogic.ejbc* without checking file timestamps. Defaults to `true`.

`suffix` *(all, String, N)*
Appended to each generated JAR filename. Defaults to *.jar*.

`wlclasspath` *(1.3, 1.4, Path, N)*
Use this attribute to avoid a WebLogic 6.0 warning that is issued when home and remote interfaces for a bean are located on the classpath used to run *weblogic.ejbc*. Set this attribute to include the standard WebLogic classes, and use the `classpath` attribute to include bean-related classes.

0,1 nested `<weblogictoplink>` *elements (all)*

Used when using TOPLink with WebLogic for CMP. This task supports all of the `<weblogic>` attributes, plus the following additional attributes:

`toplinkdescriptor` *(all, String, Y)*

The name of the locally stored TOPLink deployment descriptor file. This is relative to the `descriptordir` attribute of the containing `ejbjar` task.

`toplinkdtd` *(all, String, N)*

The location of the TOPLink DTD file. A local file path or URL is recommended, but not required. Defaults to the DTD found at *http://www.objectpeople.com*.

ftp **all**

Implements an FTP client **org.apache.tools.ant.taskdefs.optional.net.FTP**

Implements a basic FTP client. This task depends on *netcomponents.jar*, available at *http://www.savarese.org/oro/downloads*.

Attributes

`action` *(all, String, N)*

The FTP command to execute. Legal values are `send`, `put`, `recv`, `get`, `del`, `delete`, `list`, and `mkdir`. Defaults to `send`.

`binary` *(all, boolean, N)*

If `true`, use binary-mode transfers instead of text-mode. Defaults to `true`.

`depends` *(all, boolean, N)*

If `true`, transfer only new or changed files. Defaults to `false`.

`ignorenoncriticalerrors` *(1.4, boolean, N)*

If `true`, ignore noncritical error codes sent by some FTP servers. Defaults to `false`.

`listing` *(all, File, *)*

Name of a file to store output from the `list` action.

`newer` *(all, boolean, N)*

An alias for `depends`.

`passive` *(1.3, 1.4, boolean, N)*

If `true`, use passive-mode transfers. Defaults to `false`.

`password` *(all, String, Y)*

The login password for the FTP server.

`port` *(all, int, N)*

The port number. Defaults to 21.

`remotedir` *(all, String, N)*

A directory on the remote server.

`separator` *(all, String, N)*

The file separator on the FTP server. Defaults to "`/`".

`server` *(all, String, Y)*

The URL of the remote server.

`skipfailedtransfers` *(1.4, boolean, N)*
: If `true`, continue transferring files even if some failures occur. Defaults to `false`.

`userid` *(all, String, Y)*
: The login ID for the FTP server.

`verbose` *(all, boolean, N)*
: If `true`, operate in verbose mode. Defaults to `false`.

The `listing` attribute is required when `action="list"`.

Content

0..n nested `<fileset>` *elements (all)*
: Specifies files and directories to include and exclude from transfers.

icontract 1.4

Executes iContract preprocessor org.apache.tools.ant.taskdefs.optional.IContract

Executes the iContract Design By Contact preprocessor. iContract is available at *http://www.reliable-systems.com/tools/*. This task uses whatever Java compiler the `javac` task uses. You can specify an alternate Java compiler by setting the `build.compiler` property.

Attributes

`builddir` *(1.4, File, N)*
: The destination for compiled instrumented classes. The Ant user manual warns against using the same directory for instrumented and uninstrumented classes, because this breaks dependency checking.

`classdir` *(1.4, File, N)*
: The source directory containing compiled, uninstrumented classes.

`classpath` *(1.4, Path, N)*
: The classpath used when instrumenting and compiling files.

`classpathref` *(1.4, Reference, N)*
: A reference to a classpath defined elsewhere in the buildfile.

`controlfile` *(1.4, File, *)*
: The name of the control file passed to iContract.

`defaultexcludes` *(1.4, boolean, N)*
: Determines whether to use default excludes. Defaults to `true`.

`excludes` *(1.4, String, N)*
: A comma-separated list of file patterns to exclude.

`excludesfile` *(1.4, File, N)*
: The name of a file containing one exclude pattern per line.

`failthrowable` *(1.4, String, N)*
: The class name of an exception or error to throw when an assertion is violated. Defaults to `java.lang.Error`.

`includes` *(1.4, String, N)*
: A comma-separated list of file patterns to include.

`includesfile` *(1.4, File, N)*
: The name of a file containing one include pattern per line.

`instrumentdir` *(1.4, File, Y)*
: The destination directory for instrumented source files.

`invariant` *(1.4, boolean, N)*
: If `true`, instrument for invariants. Defaults to `true` unless `controlfile` is specified.

`post` *(1.4, boolean, N)*
: If `true`, instrument for postconditions. Defaults to `true` unless `controlfile` is specified.

`pre` *(1.4, boolean, N)*
: If `true`, instrument for preconditions. Defaults to `true` unless `controlfile` is specified.

`quiet` *(1.4, boolean, N)*
: If `true`, execute in quiet mode. Defaults to `false`.

`repbuilddir` *(1.4, File, N)*
: The destination directory for compiled repository classes. Defaults to the value specified by `repositorydir`.

`repositorydir` *(1.4, File, Y)*
: The destination directory for repository source files.

`srcdir` *(1.4, File, Y)*
: The location of original Java source files.

`targets` *(1.4, File, N)*
: The name of a file that this task creates, listing all classes that iContract will instrument. If specified, the file is not deleted after execution. Otherwise, a temporary file is created, then deleted after execution.

`updateicontrol` *(1.4, boolean, N)*
: If `true`, update the properties file for iControl in the current directory, or create a new one if necessary. Defaults to `false`.

`verbosity` *(1.4, String, N)*
: A comma-separated list of verbosity levels. Any combination of `error*`, `warning*`, `note*`, `info*`, `progress*`, and `debug*` is allowed. Defaults to `error*`.

The `controlfile` attribute is required if `updateicontrol=true`.

Content

0..n nested `patternset` *elements:* `<exclude>`, `<excludesfile>`, `<include>`, `<includesfile>`, *and* `<patternset>` *(1.4)*
: Used in place of their corresponding attributes, these specify the set of included and excluded source files.

0,1 nested `<classpath>` *elements (1.4)*
: May be used in place of the `classpath` and `classpathref` attributes.

ilasm 1.3, 1.4

Assembles .NET Intermediate Language files **org.apache.tools.ant.taskdefs.optional.dotnet.Ilasm**

Assembles .NET Intermediate Language files. Works only on Windows; *csc.exe* and *ilasm.exe* must be on the path.

Attributes

`debug` *(1.3, 1.4, boolean, N)*
: If `true`, include debug information. Defaults to `true`.

`defaultexcludes` *(1.3, 1.4, boolean, N)*
: Determines whether to use default excludes. Defaults to `true`.

`excludes` *(1.3, 1.4, String, N)*
: A comma-separated list of file patterns to exclude.

`excludesfile` *(1.3, 1.4, File, N)*
: The name of a file containing one exclude pattern per line.

`extraoptions` *(1.3, 1.4, String, N)*
: Extra options passed directly to the *csc.exe* command.

`failonerror` *(1.3, 1.4, boolean, N)*
: If `true`, fail the build when this task fails. Defaults to `true`.

`includes` *(1.3, 1.4, String, N)*
: A comma-separated list of file patterns to include.

`includesfile` *(1.3, 1.4, File, N)*
: The name of a file containing one include pattern per line.

`keyfile` *(1.4, File, N)*
: The name of a file containing a private key.

`listing` *(1.3, 1.4, boolean, N)*
: If `true`, produce a listing to the current output stream. Defaults to `false`.

`outputfile` *(1.3, 1.4, File, N)*
: The target filename, such as *mygui.exe*.

`owner` *(1.3, 1.4, String, N)*
: Specifies the */owner* parameter to *ilasm.exe*.

`resourcefile` *(1.3, 1.4, File, N)*
: The name of a resource file to include.

`srcdir` *(1.3, 1.4, File, N)*
: The directory containing sources.

`targettype` *(1.3, 1.4, String, N)*
: Specifies the type of target. Allowable values are exe and `library` (to create a DLL). Defaults to exe.

`verbose` *(1.3, 1.4, boolean, N)*
: If `true`, operate in verbose mode. Defaults to `false`.

Content

0..n nested patternset *elements:* <exclude>, <include>, <patternset> *(1.3, 1.4);* <excludesfile>, <includesfile> *(1.4)*

Used in place of their corresponding attributes, these specify the set of included and excluded source files.

iplanet-ejbc 1.4

Compiles EJB stubs for iPlanet server **org.apache.tools.ant.taskdefs.optional.ejb.IPlanetEjbcTask**

Compiles EJB stubs and skeletons for iPlanet Application Server Version 6.0.

Attributes

classpath *(1.4, Path, N)*
The classpath used when generating stubs and skeletons.

debug *(1.4, boolean, N)*
If true, log additional debugging information. Defaults to false.

dest *(1.4, File, Y)*
The base directory in which generated stubs and skeletons are placed. The class files for beans, home interfaces, and remote interfaces must also exist in this directory, and the directory must exist before the task is executed.

ejbdescriptor *(1.4, File, Y)*
Location of the EJB 1.1 deployment descriptor, generally named *ejb-jar.xml*.

iasdescriptor *(1.4, File, Y)*
The iPlanet EJB deployment descriptor, generally named *ias-ejb-jar.xml*.

iashome *(1.4, File, N)*
The home directory for the iPlanet distribution.

keepgenerated *(1.4, boolean, N)*
If true, this task keeps generated Java source code. Defaults to false.

Content

0,1 nested <classpath> *elements (1.4)*
May be used in place of the classpath attribute.

javacc all

Executes JavaCC on a grammar file **org.apache.tools.ant.taskdefs.optional.javacc.JavaCC**

Executes the Java Compiler Compiler (JavaCC) on a grammar file. JavaCC is available at *http://www.webgain.com/products/java_cc/*.

Attributes

buildparser *(all, boolean, N)*
If specified, the task sets the BUILD_PARSER grammar option to the value of this attribute.

`buildtokenmanager` *(all, boolean, N)*
: If specified, the task sets the `BUILD_TOKEN_MANAGER` grammar option to the value of this attribute.

`cachetokens` *(all, boolean, N)*
: If specified, the task sets the `CACHE_TOKENS` grammar option to the value of this attribute.

`choiceambiguitycheck` *(all, int, N)*
: If specified, the task sets the `CHOICE_AMBIGUITY_CHECK` grammar option to the value of this attribute.

`commontokenaction` *(all, boolean, N)*
: If specified, the task sets the `COMMON_TOKEN_ACTION` grammar option to the value of this attribute.

`debuglookahead` *(all, boolean, N)*
: If specified, the task sets the `DEBUG_LOOKAHEAD` grammar option to the value of this attribute.

`debugparser` *(all, boolean, N)*
: If specified, the task sets the `DEBUG_PARSER` grammar option to the value of this attribute.

`debugtokenmanager` *(all, boolean, N)*
: If specified, the task sets the `DEBUG_TOKEN_MANAGER` grammar option to the value of this attribute.

`errorreporting` *(all, boolean, N)*
: If specified, the task sets the `ERROR_REPORTING` grammar option to the value of this attribute.

`forcelacheck` *(all, boolean, N)*
: If specified, the task sets the `FORCE_LA_CHECK` grammar option to the value of this attribute.

`ignorecase` *(all, boolean, N)*
: If specified, the task sets the `IGNORE_CASE` grammar option to the value of this attribute.

`javacchome` *(all, File, Y)*
: The directory containing the JavaCC distribution.

`javaunicodeescape` *(all, boolean, N)*
: If specified, the task sets the `JAVA_UNICODE_ESCAPE` grammar option to the value of this attribute.

`lookahead` *(all, int, N)*
: If specified, the task sets the `LOOKAHEAD` grammar option to the value of this attribute.

`optimizetokenmanager` *(all, boolean, N)*
: If specified, the task sets the `OPTIMIZE_TOKEN_MANAGER` grammar option to the value of this attribute.

`otherambiguitycheck` *(all, int, N)*
: If specified, the task sets the `OTHER_AMBIGUITY_CHECK` grammar option to the value of this attribute.

`outputdirectory` *(all, File, N)*
: The destination directory for generated files. Defaults to the directory containing the grammar file.

`sanitycheck` *(all, boolean, N)*
: If specified, the task sets the `SANITY_CHECK` grammar option to the value of this attribute.

`static` *(all, boolean, N)*
: If specified, the task sets the `STATIC` grammar option to the value of this attribute.

`target` *(all, File, Y)*
: The grammar file to process.

`unicodeinput` *(all, boolean, N)*
: If specified, the task sets the `UNICODE_INPUT` grammar option to the value of this attribute.

`usercharstream` *(all, boolean, N)*
: If specified, the task sets the `USE_CHAR_STREAM` grammar option to the value of this attribute.

`usertokenmanager` *(all, boolean, N)*
: If specified, the task sets the `USER_TOKEN_MANAGER` grammar option to the value of this attribute.

Content

None.

javah — 1.3, 1.4

Executes javah tool — org.apache.tools.ant.taskdefs.optional.Javah

Executes the *javah* tool, generating Java Native Interface (JNI) headers from one or more Java classes. This task uses the default Java compiler, unless the `build.compiler` property is set to something else, as explained in the `javac` task description in Chapter 7.

Attributes

`bootclasspath` *(1.3, 1.4, Path, N)*
: The bootstrap classpath to use.

`bootclasspathref` *(1.3, 1.4, Reference, N)*
: Reference to a bootstrap classpath defined elsewhere in the buildfile.

`class` *(1.3, 1.4, String, Y)*
: A comma-separated list of class names to process.

`classpath` *(1.3, 1.4, Path, N)*
: The classpath to use.

`classpathref` *(1.3, 1.4, Reference, N)*
: A reference to a classpath defined elsewhere in the buildfile.

`destdir` *(1.3, 1.4, File, *)*
: The destination directory for generated files.

`force` *(1.3, 1.4, boolean, N)*
: If `true`, the task always writes output files. Defaults to `false`.

`old` *(1.3, 1.4, boolean, N)*
: If `true`, the task uses JDK 1.0–style header files. Defaults to `false`.

`outputfile` *(1.3, 1.4, File, *)*
: If specified in place of `destdir`, the task concatenates all output into this single file.

`stubs` *(1.3, 1.4, boolean, N)*
: Used when `old=true`. If `true`, the task generates C declarations. Defaults to `false`.

`verbose` *(1.3, 1.4, boolean, N)*
: If `true`, the task executes *javah* in verbose mode. Defaults to `false`.

Exactly one of either `outputfile` or `destdir` is required.

Content

0,1 nested `<bootclasspath>` *elements (1.3, 1.4)*
: May be used in place of the `bootclasspath` or `bootclasspathref` attributes.

0..n nested `<class>` *elements (1.3, 1.4)*
: May be used in place of the `class` attribute to specify classes to generate. Each `<class>` element has a required `name` attribute. For example:

```
<class name="com.oreilly.util.Foobar"/>
```

0,1 nested `<classpath>` *elements (1.3, 1.4)*
: The `path` element used in place of the `classpath` or `classpathref` attributes.

jdepend 1.4

Executes JDepend tool **org.apache.tools.ant.taskdefs.optional.jdepend.JDependTask**

Executes the JDepend tool. JDepend analyzes Java source files, producing design quality metrics for each package. This task requires JDepend Version 1.2 or later, which is available at *http://www.clarkware.com/software/JDepend.html.*

Attributes

`classpath` *(1.4, Path, N)*
: The classpath to use.

`classpathref` *(1.4, Reference, N)*
: A reference to a classpath defined elsewhere in the buildfile.

`dir` *(1.4, File, N)*
: The working directory for the JVM.

`fork` *(1.4, boolean, N)*
: If `true`, the task forks a new JVM instance. Defaults to `false`.

`haltonerror` *(1.4, boolean, N)*
: If `true`, the task halts the build when errors occur. Defaults to `false`.

`jvm` *(1.4, String, N)*
: The command used to invoke the JVM. Ignored if `fork=false`. Defaults to `java`.

`outputfile` *(1.4, File, N)*
: The task sends output to this file, or to the current output stream if omitted.

Content

0,1 nested `<classpath>` *elements (1.4)*
A path element used in place of the `classpath` or `classpathref` attributes.

0..n nested `<jvmarg>` *elements (1.4)*
Command-line arguments as described in Chapter 4. Only valid when `fork=true`.

1..n nested `<sourcespath>` *elements (1.4)*
The path elements defining where Java source files are located.

jjtree

all

Executes JJTree preprocessor — org.apache.tools.ant.taskdefs.optional.javacc.JJTree

Executes the JJTree preprocessor for the Java Compiler Compiler (JavaCC), which is available at *http://www.webgain.com/products/java_cc/*.

Attributes

`buildnodefiles` *(all, boolean, N)*
If specified, the task sets the `BUILD_NODE_FILES` grammar option to the value of this attribute.

`javacchome` *(all, File, Y)*
The directory containing the JavaCC distribution.

`multi` *(all, boolean, N)*
If specified, the task sets the `MULTI` grammar option to the value of this attribute.

`nodedefaultvoid` *(all, boolean, N)*
If specified, the task sets the `NODE_DEFAULT_VOID` grammar option to the value of this attribute.

`nodefactory` *(all, boolean, N)*
If specified, the task sets the `NODE_FACTORY` grammar option to the value of this attribute.

`nodepackage` *(all, String, N)*
If specified, the task sets the `NODE_PACKAGE` grammar option to the value of this attribute.

`nodeprefix` *(all, String, N)*
If specified, the task sets the `NODE_PREFIX` grammar option to the value of this attribute.

`nodescopehook` *(all, boolean, N)*
If specified, the task sets the `NODE_SCOPE_HOOK` grammar option to the value of this attribute.

`nodeusesparser` *(all, boolean, N)*
If specified, the task sets the `NODE_USES_PARSER` grammar option to the value of this attribute.

`outputdirectory` *(all, File, N)*
The destination directory for the generated file. If omitted, output goes to the directory containing the grammar file.

`static` *(all, boolean, N)*
    If specified, the task sets the `STATIC` grammar option to the value of this attribute.

`target` *(all, File, Y)*
    The JJTree grammar file to process.

`visitor` *(all, boolean, N)*
    If specified, the task sets the `VISITOR` grammar option to the value of this attribute.

`visitorexception` *(all, String, N)*
    If specified, the task sets the `VISITOR_EXCEPTION` grammar option to the value of this attribute.

Content

None.

jlink **all**

Creates/merges JAR or ZIP files **org.apache.tools.ant.taskdefs.optional.jlink.JlinkTask**

Builds a JAR or ZIP file, optionally merging contents of existing JAR and ZIP archives. When duplicate files exist, the first is accepted and subsequent entries are ignored. When merging archives, existing *META-INF* directories are ignored.

Attributes

`addfiles` *(all, Path, *)*
    A list of files for addition to the archive. These are added as individual files, even if they are JAR or ZIP archives. Use the `mergefiles` attribute or nested element to merge contents of existing JAR or ZIP archives.

`compress` *(all, boolean, N)*
    If `true`, compress the output. Defaults to `false`.

`defaultexcludes` *(all, boolean, N)*
    Determines whether to use default excludes. Defaults to `true`.

`excludes` *(all, String, N)*
    A comma-separated list of file patterns to exclude.

`excludesfile` *(all, File, N)*
    The name of a file containing one exclude pattern per line.

`includes` *(all, String, N)*
    A comma-separated list of file patterns to include.

`includesfile` *(all, File, N)*
    A comma-separated list of file patterns to include.

`mergefiles` *(all, Path, *)*
    A list of files for addition to the archive. Contents of *.jar* and *.zip* files are merged into the output archive, rather than added as JAR and ZIP files.

`outfile` *(all, File, Y)*
    The target archive—for example, *myproj.jar*.

At least one of addfiles or mergefiles is required, or else the corresponding nested elements are.

Content

0..n nested patternset *elements:* <exclude>, <include>, <patternset> *(all);* <excludesfile>, <includesfile> *(1.4)*

Used in place of their corresponding attributes, these specify the set of included and excluded source files.

0..n nested <addfiles> *elements. (all)*

The Path elements used in place of the addfiles attribute. Entries are added as individual files, even if they end in *.jar* or *.zip*. For example, *utils.jar* is added to the resulting archive as an individual file, without being expanded. When paths point to directories, all files found in subdirectories are recursively added.

0..n nested <mergefiles> *elements. (all)*

May be used in place of the mergefiles attribute. Entries are added as individual files unless they end in *.jar* or *.zip*. In those cases, the contents of the archives are extracted and then added to the new archive. *META-INF* directories are ignored.

jpcoverage 1.4

Executes JProbe Coverage tool **org.apache.tools.ant.taskdefs.optional.sitraka.Coverage**

Executes the JProbe Coverage tool, which runs a class and analyzes which lines of code are executed. This task is designed to work with JProbe Suite Server Side Version 3.0, which is available at *http://www.sitraka.com*.

Attributes

applet *(1.4, boolean, N)*

If true, indicates that the classname attribute specifies an applet. Defaults to false.

classname *(1.4, String, Y)*

The class to analyze.

exitprompt *(1.4, String, N,)*

Controls when the console prompt displays "Press Enter to close this window." Legal values are always, never, and error. Defaults to never.

finalsnapshot *(1.4, String, N)*

Configures the type of snapshot to take when the program ends. Legal values are none, coverage, and all. Defaults to coverage.

home *(1.4, File, Y)*

The directory in which JProbe is installed.

inputfile *(1.4, File, N)*

A JProbe Coverage parameter file. If specified, all other attributes are ignored.

javaexe *(1.4, File, N)*

The path to the java executable. Only used when vm="java2".

recordfromstart *(1.4, Enum, N)*
: Configures the analysis performed when the program starts. Legal values are none, coverage, and all. Defaults to coverage.

seedname *(1.4, String, N)*
: The base name for temporary snapshot files. If this attribute is foo, files are named *foo.jpc*, *foo1.jpc*, *foo2.jpc*, etc. Defaults to snapshot.

snapshotdir *(1.4, File, N)*
: The destination directory for snapshots. Defaults to the project base directory.

tracknatives *(1.4, boolean, N)*
: If true, the task tracks native methods. Defaults to false.

vm *(1.4, Enum, N)*
: Specifies the JVM for the task to run. Legal values are jdk117, jdk118, and java2.

warnlevel *(1.4, int, N)*
: Specifies the warning level, ranging from 0..3. Defaults to 0, which yields the least amount of warnings.

workingdir *(1.4, File, N)*
: The working directory for the JVM.

Content

0..n nested <arg> *elements (1.4)*
: The command-line application arguments as described in Chapter 4.

0,1 nested <classpath> *elements (1.4)*
: The path element specifying the classpath.

0..n nested <jvmarg> *elements (1.4)*
: The command-line JVM arguments as described in Chapter 4.

0,1 nested <filters> *elements (1.4)*
: Defines JProbe filters for classes and methods. For example:

```
<filters>
<include class="com.oreilly.*" method="*"/>
<exclude class="com.oreilly.test.*" method="*"/>
</filters>
```

This supports one attribute:

defaultexclude *(1.4, boolean, N)*
: If true, exclude all classes and methods. Defaults to true.

<filters> supports the following nested elements:

0..n nested <include> *elements (1.4)*
: Defines which classes and methods are included. The following attributes are supported:

class *(1.4, String, N)*
: A regular expression specifying which classes to include or exclude.

enabled *(1.4, boolean, N)*
: If true, this element is enabled. Defaults to true.

method *(1.4, String, N)*
: A regular expression specifying which methods to include or exclude.

0..n nested `<exclude>` *elements (1.4)*

Defines which classes and methods are excluded. The following attributes are supported:

`class` *(1.4, String, N)*

A regular expression specifying which classes to include or exclude.

`enabled` *(1.4, boolean, N)*

If `true`, this element is enabled. Defaults to `true`.

`method` *(1.4, String, N)*

A regular expression specifying which methods to include or exclude.

0,1 nested `<socket>` *elements (1.4)*

Defines the host and port number for remote viewing. Attributes are as follows:

`host` *(1.4, String, N)*

The host to connect to. Defaults to `localhost`.

`port` *(1.4, int, N)*

The port number. Defaults to 4444.

0,1 nested `<triggers>` *elements (1.4)*

Defines JProbe triggers, which are actions to take when certain events occur. The following nested elements are supported:

0..n nested `<method>` *elements (1.4)*

Each defines a new trigger. The following attributes are supported:

`action` *(1.4, String, Y)*

The action to perform. Must be one of `clear`, `exit`, `pause`, `resume`, `snapshot`, or `suspend`.

`event` *(1.4, String, Y)*

The event that triggers the action. Must be either `enter` or `exit`.

`name` *(1.4, String, Y)*

The name of the method(s) as a simple regular expression. An example would be `com.oreilly.util.DateUtil.getCurrentTime`.

`param` *(1.4, String, N)*

The optional parameter appended to the end of the *-jp_trigger* flag.

jpcovmerge 1.4

Combines JProbe Coverage snapshots **org.apache.tools.ant.taskdefs.optional.sitraka.CovMerge**

Merges several JProbe Coverage snapshots into one.

Attributes

`home` *(1.4, File, Y)*

The directory in which JProbe is installed.

`tofile` *(1.4, File, Y)*

The output filename.

`verbose` *(1.4, boolean, N)*

If `true`, operate in verbose mode. Defaults to `false`.

Content

1..n nested `<fileset>` *elements (1.4)*
: `fileset` elements defining the list of snapshots to merge.

jpcovreport 1.4

Generates printable JProbe report **org.apache.tools.ant.taskdefs.optional.sitraka.CovReport**

Generates a printable report of a JProbe Coverage snapshot.

Attributes

`filters` *(1.4, String, N)*
: A comma-delimited list of filters, each formatted like `<package>.class:?`, in which `?` can be `I` for Include, or `E` for Exclude.

`format` *(1.4, Enum, N)*
: The format of the report. Legal values are `xml`, `html`, or `text`. Defaults to `html`.

`home` *(1.4, File, Y)*
: The directory in which JProbe is installed.

`includesource` *(1.4, boolean, N)*
: If `true`, include source code in the report. Only applies when `format="xml"` and `type="verydetailed"`. Defaults to `true`.

`percent` *(1.4, int, N)*
: The threshold for printing methods, ranging from 0..100. Defaults to 100.

`snapshot` *(1.4, File, Y)*
: The name of the snapshot to report on.

`tofile` *(1.4, File, Y)*
: The name of the report to generate.

`type` *(1.4, Enum, N)*
: The type of report to generate. Legal values are `executive`, `summary`, `detailed`, and `verydetailed`. Defaults to `detailed`.

Content

0..n nested `<sourcepath>` *elements (1.4)*
: The `Path` elements specifying where source files are found.

0,1 nested `<reference>` *elements (1.4)*
: Applicable only when `format="xml"`. Specifies additional classes to check for coverage information. `<reference>` elements can contain the following content:

  0,1 nested `<classpath>` *elements (1.4)*
  : The `Path` element defining where to find classes.

  0,1 nested `<filters>` *elements (1.4)*
  : The syntax of `<filters>` is defined under the `jpcoverage` task.

junit

all

Executes tests using JUnit **org.apache.tools.ant.taskdefs.optional.junit.JUnitTask**

Executes unit tests using the JUnit testing framework. This task requires JUnit 3.0 or later, available at *http://www.junit.org*.

Attributes

`dir` *(all, File, N)*
: The working directory for the JVM. Used only when `fork=true`.

`errorproperty` *(1.4, String, N)*
: A property to set when a test error occurs.

`failureproperty` *(1.4, String, N)*
: A property to set when a test failure occurs.

`fork` *(all, boolean, N)*
: If `true`, fork a new JVM for the tests. Defaults to `false`.

`haltonerror` *(all, boolean, N)*
: If `true`, stop the build if a test error occurs. Defaults to `false`.

`haltonfailure` *(all, boolean, N)*
: If `true`, stop the build if a test failure occurs. Defaults to `false`.

`jvm` *(all, String, N)*
: The command used to invoke the JVM. Defaults to `java`. Used only when `fork=true`.

`maxmemory` *(all, String, N)*
: The maximum amount of memory used when `fork=true`.

`printsummary` *(all, Enum, N)*
: Configures how statistics are printed for each test case. Legal values are `on`, `off`, and `withOutAndErr`. `withOutAndErr` is the same as `on`, except the test output is also written to both standard output and standard error. Defaults to `off`.

`timeout` *(all, int, N)*
: The maximum number of milliseconds to wait for an individual test before timing out. Used only when `fork=true`.

Content

0..n nested `<batchtest>` *elements (all)*
: Defines a collection of tests based on naming conventions. The following attributes are supported:

  `errorproperty` *(1.4, String, N)*
  : Overrides the `errorproperty` attribute specified in `junit`. Defaults to `false`.

  `failureproperty` *(1.4, String, N)*
  : Overrides the `failureproperty` attribute specified in `junit`.

  `fork` *(all, boolean, N)*
  : Overrides the `fork` attribute specified in `junit`. Defaults to `false`.

  `haltonerror` *(all, boolean, N)*
  : Overrides the `haltonerror` attribute specified in `junit`. Defaults to `false`.

`haltonfailure` *(all, boolean, N)*
: Overrides the `haltonfailure` attribute specified in `junit`. Defaults to `false`.

`if` *(all, String, N)*
: Specifies a property. Tests are only run if the specified property is set.

`todir` *(1.3, 1.4, String, N)*
: The destination directory for reports.

`unless` *(all, String, N)*
: Specifies a property. Tests are run unless the specified property is set.

0,1 nested `<classpath>` *elements (all)*
: The `path` element used when running tests.

0..n nested `<formatter>` *elements (all)*
: Configures how test results are written out. The following attributes are supported:

`type` *(all, Enum, *)*
: Specifies which predefined formatter to use. Legal values are `xml`, `plain`, and `brief`.

`classname` *(all, String, *)*
: A custom formatter class.

`extension` *(all, String, *)*
: The output filename extension. Works in conjunction with the `outfile` attribute of `<test>`.

`usefile` *(all, boolean, N)*
: If `true`, the task sends output to a file. The filename is determined by the test name, or is specified by the `outfile` attribute of the `<test>` element. Defaults to `true`.

Exactly one of `type` or `classname` must be specified. `extension` is required if `classname` is specified.

0..n nested `<jvmarg>` *elements (all)*
: The command-line arguments as described in Chapter 4. Only valid when `fork=true`.

0..n nested `<sysproperty>` *elements (1.3, 1.4)*
: The environment variables as described in Chapter 4.

0..n nested `<test>` *elements. (all)*
: Each defines a single test. The following attributes are supported:

`errorproperty` *(1.4, String, N)*
: Overrides the `errorproperty` attribute specified in `junit`. Defaults to `false`.

`failureproperty` *(1.4, String, N)*
: Overrides the `failureproperty` attribute specified in `junit`.

`fork` *(all, boolean, N)*
: Overrides the `fork` attribute specified in `junit`. Defaults to `false`.

`haltonerror` *(all, boolean, N)*
: Overrides the `haltonerror` attribute specified in `junit`. Defaults to `false`.

`haltonfailure` *(all, boolean, N)*
: Overrides the `haltonfailure` attribute specified in `junit`. Defaults to `false`.

`if` *(all, String, N)*
: Specifies a property. Tests are run only if the specified property is set.

name *(all, String, Y)*
The name of the test class.

outfile *(all, String, N)*
The base name for test result. The extension specified by <formatter> is appended to this. Defaults to TEST-, followed by the value of the name attribute.

todir *(1.3, 1.4, File, N)*
The destination directory for reports.

unless *(all, String, N)*
Specifies a property. Tests are run unless the specified property is set.

junitreport

1.3, 1.4

Creates formatted JUnit report **org.apache.tools.ant.taskdefs.optional.junit.XMLResultAggregator**

Creates a formatted report based on several XML files from the junit task. This task applies an XSLT stylesheet. Apache's Xalan XSLT Processor (*http://xml.apache.org*) is required.*

Attributes

todir *(1.3, 1.4, File, N)*
The destination directory for the XML file.

tofile *(1.3, 1.4, String, N)*
The destination XML filename. Individual XML files from the junit task are aggregated into this file. Defaults to *TESTS-TestSuites.xml*.

Content

0..n nested <fileset> *elements (1.3, 1.4)*
fileset elements selecting XML reports to merge together into the file specified by tofile. These are the output files from the junit task.

0..n nested <report> *elements (1.3, 1.4)*
Each specifies how an XSLT transformation is performed in order to generate a formatted report. The following attributes are supported:

todir *(1.3, 1.4, File, N)*
The destination directory for transformation results. Defaults to the current directory.

styledir *(1.3, 1.4, File, N)*
The directory containing *junit-frames.xsl* and *junit-noframes.xsl*. If unspecified, the task loads the files from the Ant optional tasks JAR file.

format *(1.3, 1.4, Enum, N)*
Selects which of the stylesheets to use. Legal values are frames or noframes. Defaults to frames.

* Xalan 1.2.2 is supported, but Xalan 2.x is recommended.

maudit

1.4

Finds errors using WebGain Quality Analyzer **org.apache.tools.ant.taskdefs.optional.metamata.MAudit**

Executes the WebGain Quality Analyzer to analyze Java source code for programming errors. This task is based on Metamata Audit, which was purchased by WebGain in October 2000. On January 3, 2002, WebGain Quality Analyzer was integrated into WebGain Studio, and is no longer offered as a standalone product. For more information, refer to *http://www.webgain.com*.

Attributes

`fix` *(1.4, boolean, N)*
: If `true`, automatically fix certain types of errors. Defaults to `false`.

`list` *(1.4, boolean, N)*
: If `true`, create a *.maudit* listing file for each audited file. Defaults to `false`.

`maxmemory` *(1.4, String, N)*
: The maximum memory for the JVM.

`metamatahome` *(1.4, File, Y)*
: The directory containing the Metamata distribution.

`tofile` *(1.4, File, Y)*
: The destination XML file for the audit report.

`unused` *(1.4, boolean, N)*
: If `true`, find unused declarations in search paths. Used with the `<searchpath>` nested element. Defaults to `false`.

Content

0,1 nested `<classpath>` *elements (1.4)*
: The `path` element specifying the classpath.

0,1 nested `<fileset>` *elements (1.4)*
: The `fileset` element specifying where *.java* files are found.

0..n nested `<jvmarg>` *elements (1.4)*
: The command-line arguments as described in Chapter 4. Valid only when `fork=true`.

0,1 nested `<searchpath>` *elements (1.4)*
: The `path` element specifying where to look for unused global declarations. This is required when `unused=true`. The task issues a warning when a `<searchpath>` is specified but `unused=false`.

0,1 nested `<sourcepath>` *elements (1.4)*
: The `path` element overriding the `SOURCEPATH` environment variable.

mimemail

1.4

Sends email with attachments **org.apache.tools.ant.taskdefs.optional.net.MimeMail**

Sends SMTP mail with MIME attachments. This task requires the JavaMail API and the JavaBeans Activation Framework. This differs from the core `mail` task in that it supports attachments.

Attributes

`bcclist` *(1.4, String, *)*
: A comma-delimited list of BCC recipients.

`cclist` *(1.4, String, *)*
: A comma-delimited list of CC recipients.

`failonerror` *(1.4, boolean, N)*
: If `true`, abort the build on failure. Defaults to `true`.

`from` *(1.4, String, Y)*
: The sender's email address.

`mailhost` *(1.4, String, N)*
: The mail server name. Defaults to `localhost`.

`message` *(1.4, String, *)*
: The message body.

`messagefile` *(1.4, File, *)*
: A file containing the message body.

`messagemimetype` *(1.4, String, N)*
: MIME type of attached message when using `message` or `messagefile` attributes. Defaults to `text/plain`.

`subject` *(1.4, String, N)*
: The email subject line.

`tolist` *(1.4, String, *)*
: A comma-delimited list of `TO` recipients.

Specify exactly one of `message` or `messageFile`, or specify a nested `<fileset>`. At least one of `tolist`, `cclist`, or `bcclist` must be specified.

Content

0..n nested `<fileset>` *elements (1.4)*
: `fileset` elements specifying files to attach.

mmetrics 1.4

Reports on metrics using WebGain Quality Analyzer **org.apache.tools.ant.taskdefs.optional.metamata.MMetrics**

Executes the WebGain Quality Analyzer on a set of Java files, reporting on code complexity and other metrics. See the `maudit` task for background information on the WebGain Quality Analyzer, formerly known as Metamata Quality Analyzer.

Attributes

`granularity` *(1.4, String, Y)*
: Specifies the metrics granularity. Legal values are `files`, `types`, and `methods`.

`maxmemory` *(1.4, String, N)*
: The maximum memory available to the JVM.

`metamatahome` *(1.4, File, Y)*
: The directory containing the WebGain Quality Analyzer distribution.

`tofile` *(1.4, File, Y)*
: The destination XML file for the metrics report.

Content

0,1 nested `<classpath>` *elements (1.4)*
: The `path` element specifying the classpath.

0..n nested `<fileset>` *elements (1.4)*
: The `fileset` elements specifying source files to analyze.

0..n nested `<jvmarg>` *elements (1.4)*
: The command-line JVM arguments as described in Chapter 4.

0,1 nested `<path>` *elements (1.4)*
: The `path` element specifying directories scanned for source code.

0,1 nested `<sourcepath>` *elements (1.4)*
: The `path` element overriding the `SOURCEPATH` environment variable.

mparse **all**

Executes MParse on a grammar file **org.apache.tools.ant.taskdefs.optional.metamata.MParse**

Executes the Metamata MParse compiler compiler on a grammar file. Metamata was purchased by WebGain in October 2000, and MParse is no longer available.

Attributes

`cleanup` *(1.3, 1.4, boolean, N)*
: If `true`, remove the temporary Sun JavaCC file created during transformation of the grammar file. Defaults to `false`.

`debugparser` *(1.3, 1.4, boolean, N)*
: If `true`, enable parser debugging. Defaults to `false`.

`debugscanner` *(1.3, 1.4, boolean, N)*
: If `true`, enable scanner debugging. Defaults to `false`.

`maxmemory` *(1.3, 1.4, String, N)*
: Sets the maximum memory for the JVM.

`metamatahome` *(all, File, Y)*
: The directory containing the Metamata distribution.

`target` *(all, File, Y)*
: The *.jj* grammar file to process. Its timestamp is compared to the generated *.java* file, and this task runs only if the *.jj* file is newer.

`verbose` *(1.3, 1.4, boolean, N)*
: If `true`, operate in verbose mode. Defaults to `false`.

Content

0,1 nested `<classpath>` *elements (1.3, 1.4)*
: May be used in place of the `classpath` or `classpathref` attributes.

0..n nested `<jvmarg>` *elements (1.3, 1.4)*
The command-line JVM arguments as described in Chapter 4.

0,1 nested `<sourcepath>` *elements (1.3, 1.4)*
The path element defining where source files are located.

native2ascii

all

Converts files to ASCII **org.apache.tools.ant.taskdefs.optional.Native2Ascii**

Converts files with native encoding to ASCII containing escaped Unicode characters.

Attributes

`defaultexcludes` *(all, boolean, N)*
Determines whether to use default excludes. Defaults to `true`.

`dest` *(all, File, Y)*
The destination directory for output.

`encoding` *(all, String, N)*
The character encoding of the source files. Defaults to the platform default encoding.

`excludes` *(all, String, N)*
A comma-separated list of file patterns to exclude.

`excludesfile` *(all, File, N)*
The name of a file containing one exclude pattern per line.

`ext` *(all, String, N)*
The file extension used for renaming output files. If unspecified, files are not renamed.

`includes` *(all, String, N)*
A comma-separated list of file patterns to include.

`includesfile` *(all, File, N)*
The name of a file containing one include pattern per line.

`reverse` *(all, boolean, N)*
If `true`, convert from ASCII to native. Defaults to `false`.

`src` *(all, File, N)*
The directory containing files to convert. Defaults to the project base directory.

Content

0..n nested `patternset` *elements:* `<exclude>`, `<include>`, `<patternset>` *(all);* `<excludesfile>`, `<includesfile>` *(1.4)*
Used in place of their corresponding attributes, these specify the set of included and excluded deployment descriptors.

0,1 nested `<mapper>` *elements (1.3, 1.4)*
Defines how filenames are renamed. If both `<mapper>` and the `ext` attribute are specified, the `mapper` takes precedence. `mappers` are described in Chapter 4.

netrexxc

all

Compiles NetRexx files org.apache.tools.ant.taskdefs.optional.NetRexxC

Compiles a set of NetRexx files. NetRexx is a "human-oriented" programming language that aims to be simpler than Java, yet produces Java bytecode and interacts seamlessly with Java classes. It is freely available at *http://www2.hursley.ibm.com/netrexx/*.

Attributes

`binary` *(all, boolean, N)*
: If `true`, treat literals as the binary rather than NetRexx types. Defaults to `false`.

`classpath` *(all, String, N)*
: The classpath used for compilation.

`comments` *(all, boolean, N)*
: The NetRexx compiler generates Java source code. When this flag is `true`, NetRexx comments are carried through to the generated Java code. Defaults to `false`.

`compact` *(all, boolean, N)*
: If `true`, display compact (rather than verbose) error messages. Defaults to `false`.

`compile` *(all, boolean, N)*
: If `true`, compile the generated Java code. Defaults to `true`.

`console` *(all, boolean, N)*
: If `true`, write messages to the console. Defaults to `false`.

`crossref` *(all, boolean, N)*
: If `true`, generate variable cross references. Defaults to `false`.

`decimal` *(all, boolean, N)*
: If `true`, use decimal arithmetic in the NetRexx code. Defaults to `true`.

`defaultexcludes` *(all, boolean, N)*
: Determines whether to use default excludes. Defaults to `true`.

`destdir` *(all, File, Y)*
: The directory to which NetRexx source files are copied before they are compiled.

`diag` *(all, boolean, N)*
: If `true`, generate diagnostic information about the compile. Defaults to `false`.

`excludes` *(all, String, N)*
: A comma-separated list of file patterns to exclude.

`excludesfile` *(all, File, N)*
: The name of a file containing one exclude pattern per line.

`explicit` *(all, boolean, N)*
: If `true`, variables must be explicitly declared before use. Defaults to `false`.

`format` *(all, boolean, N)*
: If `true`, try to format the generated Java source code. Otherwise, generate code so line numbers match the NetRexx source for debugging purposes. Defaults to `false`.

`includes` *(all, String, N)*
: A comma-separated list of file patterns to include.

`includesfile` *(all, File, N)*
: The name of a file containing one include pattern per line.

`java` *(all, boolean, N)*
: If `true`, generate Java source code. Defaults to `false`.

`keep` *(all, boolean, N)*
: If `true`, keep generated Java source code using the *.java.keep* filename extension. Defaults to `false`.

`logo` *(all, boolean, N)*
: If `true`, display the compiler text logo when compiling. Defaults to `true`.

`replace` *(all, boolean, N)*
: If `true`, replace generated *.java* files when compiling. Defaults to `false`.

`savelog` *(all, boolean, N)*
: If `true`, write compiler messages to the *NetRexxC.log* file in addition to the console. Defaults to `false`.

`sourcedir` *(all, boolean, N)*
: If `true`, store class files in the same directory as source files. Otherwise, use the working directory. Defaults to `true`.

`srcdir` *(all, File, Y)*
: The directory in which NetRexx sources are located.

`strictargs` *(all, boolean, N)*
: If `true`, NetRexx method calls must use parentheses even when they do not take parameters. Defaults to `false`.

`strictassign` *(all, boolean, N)*
: If `true`, assignments must match on type. Defaults to `false`.

`strictcase` *(all, boolean, N)*
: If `true`, NetRexx source is case-sensitive. Defaults to `false`.

`strictimport` *(all, boolean, N)*
: If `true`, classes must be explicitly imported. Defaults to `false`.

`strictprops` *(all, boolean, N)*
: If `true`, local properties must be explicitly referenced using `this`. Defaults to `false`.

`strictsignal` *(all, boolean, N)*
: If `true`, exceptions must be explicitly caught by type. Defaults to `false`.

`symbols` *(all, boolean, N)*
: If `true`, include debug symbols in generated class files. Defaults to `false`.

`time` *(all, boolean, N)*
: If `true`, print compilation time to the console. Defaults to `false`.

`trace` *(all, String, N)*
: When specified, enables one of the NetRexx tracing options. Legal values are `trace`, `trace1`, `trace2`, and `notrace`. Defaults to `trace2`.

`utf8` *(all, boolean, N)*
: If `true`, assume the source files use UTF-8 encoding. Defaults to `false`.

`verbose` *(all, String, Y)*
: When specified, operate in verbose mode. Defaults to `verbose3`. Legal values are `verbose1` through `verbose5`. `verbose5` outputs the most detailed information.

Content

0..n nested patternset *elements:* <exclude>, <include>, <patternset> *(all);* <excludesfile>, <includesfile> *(1.4)*

Used in place of their corresponding attributes, these specify the set of included and excluded source files when selecting files to compile.

p4change

1.3, 1.4

Requests Perforce changelist — **org.apache.tools.ant.taskdefs.optional.perforce.P4Change**

Requests a new changelist from a Perforce server.

Attributes

client *(1.3, 1.4, String, N)*
: Specifies the *p4 -c* option. Defaults to the value of the p4.client property, if set.

description *(1.3, 1.4, String, N)*
: The comment for the changelist. Defaults to AutoSubmit By Ant.

port *(1.3, 1.4, String, N)*
: Specifies the *p4 -p* option. Defaults to the value of the p4.port property, if set.

user *(1.3, 1.4, String, N)*
: Specifies the *p4 -u* option. Defaults to the value of the p4.user property, if set.

view *(1.3, 1.4, String, N)*
: The client, branch, or label view this command operates on.

Content

None.

p4counter

1.4

Gets/sets Perforce counter — **org.apache.tools.ant.taskdefs.optional.perforce.P4Counter**

Gets and sets a Perforce counter value.

Attributes

client *(1.3, 1.4, String, N)*
: Specifies the *p4 -c* option. Defaults to the value of the p4.client property, if set.

name *(1.4, String, Y)*
: The counter name. If this is the only specified attribute, the task prints the value of the counter to standard output.

port *(1.3, 1.4, String, N)*
: Specifies the *p4 -p* option. Defaults to the value of the p4.port property, if set.

property *(1.4, String, *)*
: The property to set with the retrieved counter value.

user *(1.3, 1.4, String, N)*
: Specifies the *p4 -u* option. Defaults to the value of the p4.user property, if set.

`value` *(1.4, int, *)*
: When specified, set the counter to this value.

`view` *(1.3, 1.4, String, N)*
: The client, branch, or label view this command operates on.

You cannot set both `property` and `value`, since you are *retrieving* a counter value when `property` is specified, and *setting* a counter value when `value` is specified.

Content

None.

p4edit 1.3, 1.4

Opens Perforce files — org.apache.tools.ant.taskdefs.optional.perforce.P4Edit

Opens files from Perforce for editing.

Attributes

`change` *(1.3, 1.4, String, N)*
: Assign files to this existing changelist number.

`client` *(1.3, 1.4, String, N)*
: Specifies the *p4 -c* option. Defaults to the value of the `p4.client` property, if set.

`port` *(1.3, 1.4, String, N)*
: Specifies the *p4 -p* option. Defaults to the value of the `p4.port` property, if set.

`user` *(1.3, 1.4, String, N)*
: Specifies the *p4 -u* option. Defaults to the value of the `p4.user` property, if set.

`view` *(1.3, 1.4, String, Y)*
: The client, branch, or label view this command operates on.

Content

None.

p4have 1.3, 1.4

Lists current Perforce files — org.apache.tools.ant.taskdefs.optional.perforce.P4Have

Lists Perforce files in the current client view.

Attributes

`client` *(1.3, 1.4, String, N)*
: Specifies the *p4 -c* option. Defaults to the value of the `p4.client` property, if set.

`port` *(1.3, 1.4, String, N)*
: Specifies the *p4 -p* option. Defaults to the value of the `p4.port` property, if set.

`user` *(1.3, 1.4, String, N)*
: Specifies the *p4 -u* option. Defaults to the value of the `p4.user` property, if set.

`view` *(1.3, 1.4, String, N)*
: The client, branch, or label view this command operates on.

Content

None.

p4label

1.3, 1.4

Labels Perforce files — org.apache.tools.ant.taskdefs.optional.perforce.P4Label

Creates a label for files in the current Perforce workspace.

Attributes

`client` *(1.3, 1.4, String, N)*
: Specifies the *p4 -c* option. Defaults to the value of the `p4.client` property, if set.

`desc` *(1.3, 1.4, String, N)*
: A label comment.

`lock` *(1.4, String, N)*
: If set to `locked`, causes the label to lock. Defaults to an empty string. No other values are allowed.

`name` *(1.3, 1.4, String, Y)*
: The label name.

`port` *(1.3, 1.4, String, N)*
: Specifies the *p4 -p* option. Defaults to the value of the `p4.port` property, if set.

`user` *(1.3, 1.4, String, N)*
: Specifies the *p4 -u* option. Defaults to the value of the `p4.user` property, if set.

`view` *(1.3, 1.4, String, N)*
: The client, branch, or label view this command operates on.

Content

None.

p4reopen

1.4

Moves files between Perforce changelists — org.apache.tools.ant.taskdefs.optional.perforce.P4Reopen

Moves files between Perforce changelists.

Attributes

`client` *(1.3, 1.4, String, N)*
: Specifies the *p4 -c* option. Defaults to the value of the `p4.client` property, if set.

`port` *(1.3, 1.4, String, N)*
: Specifies the *p4 -p* option. Defaults to the value of the `p4.port` property, if set.

`tochange` *(1.4, String, Y)*
: Move files to the specified changelist.

`user` *(1.3, 1.4, String, N)*
: Specifies the *p4 -u* option. Defaults to the value of the `p4.user` property, if set.

`view` *(1.3, 1.4, String, N)*
: The client, branch, or label view this command operates on.

Content

None.

p4revert 1.4

Reverts Perforce files **org.apache.tools.ant.taskdefs.optional.perforce.P4Revert**

Reverts opened Perforce files.

Attributes

`change` *(1.4, String, N)*
  The changelist to revert.

`client` *(1.3, 1.4, String, N)*
  Specifies the *p4 -c* option. Defaults to the value of the `p4.client` property, if set.

`port` *(1.3, 1.4, String, N)*
  Specifies the *p4 -p* option. Defaults to the value of the `p4.port` property, if set.

`revertonlyunchanged` *(1.4, boolean, N)*
  If `true`, revert only unchanged files. Defaults to `false`.

`user` *(1.3, 1.4, String, N)*
  Specifies the *p4 -u* option. Defaults to the value of the `p4.user` property, if set.

`view` *(1.3, 1.4, String, N)*
  The client, branch, or label view this command operates on.

Content

None.

p4submit 1.3, 1.4

Checks in Perforce files **org.apache.tools.ant.taskdefs.optional.perforce.P4Submit**

Checks files in to a Perforce depot.

Attributes

`change` *(1.3, 1.4, String, Y)*
  Submit the specified changelist.

`client` *(1.3, 1.4, String, N)*
  Specifies the *p4 -c* option. Defaults to the value of the `p4.client` property, if set.

`port` *(1.3, 1.4, String, N)*
  Specifies the *p4 -p* option. Defaults to the value of the `p4.port` property, if set.

`user` *(1.3, 1.4, String, N)*
  Specifies the *p4 -u* option. Defaults to the value of the `p4.user` property, if set.

`view` *(1.3, 1.4, String, N)*
  The client, branch, or label view this command operates on.

Content

None.

p4sync 1.3, 1.4

Synchronizes with a Perforce depot org.apache.tools.ant.taskdefs.optional.perforce.P4Sync

Synchronizes a workspace with the Perforce depot.

Attributes

`client` *(1.3, 1.4, String, N)*
: Specifies the *p4 -c* option. Defaults to the value of the `p4.client` property, if set.

`force` *(1.3, 1.4, String, N)*
: If set to a nonempty string, set the `-f` Perforce flag. Forces a refresh of files.*

`label` *(1.3, 1.4, String, N)*
: If set, the task synchronizes a workspace with files from a Perforce depot using the specified label.

`port` *(1.3, 1.4, String, N)*
: Specifies the *p4 -p* option. Defaults to the value of the `p4.port` property, if set.

`user` *(1.3, 1.4, String, N)*
: Specifies the *p4 -u* option. Defaults to the value of the `p4.user` property, if set.

`view` *(1.3, 1.4, String, N)*
: The client, branch, or label view this command operates on.

Content

None.

propertyfile 1.3, 1.4

Creates/edits property files org.apache.tools.ant.taskdefs.optional.PropertyFile

Creates or edits Java properties files. This task can add and edit entries. It does not preserve existing properties file comments.

Attributes

`comment` *(1.3, 1.4, String, N)*
: A comment to add to the properties file.

`file` *(1.3, 1.4, File, Y)*
: The name of the properties file to create or modify.

Content

0..n nested `<entry>` *elements (1.3, 1.4)*
: Each entry defines a name-value pair to write to or modify in the properties file. The following attributes are supported:

* A Boolean attribute makes more sense in this case. Ant optional tasks are not as consistent as the core tasks.

`default` *(1.3, 1.4, String, N)*
: Initial value for a property if it is not already defined. For a `date` type, the value may also be set to `now` or `never` to indicate the current time or a null time respectively. Perhaps surprisingly, if a property does not exist and both `default` and `value` are specified, `value` is assigned to the property rather than `default`.

`key` *(1.3, 1.4, String, Y)*
: The property name.

`operation` *(1.3, 1.4, Enum, N)*
: Controls how the `value` attribute modifies the property value indicated by the `key` attribute. One of `+` or `=` for all data types, and also `-` for `date` and `int` types. `+` performs addition, `=` performs assignment, and `-` performs subtraction.

`pattern` *(1.3, 1.4, String, N)*
: Controls how `date` and `int` types are formatted. Uses `SimpleDateFormat` and `DecimalFormat`, respectively.

`type` *(1.3, 1.4, Enum, N)*
: Legal values are `int`, `date`, and `string`. Defaults to `string`.

`value` *(1.3, 1.4, String, Y)*
: Specifies a value to add, subtract, or assign to/from the property specified by `key`. Works with the `operation` attribute. For the `date` type, may also be set to `now` or `never`.

Example Usage

This example creates a properties file if it does not exist, and updates several values:

```
<target name="test_propertyfile">
  <propertyfile comment="Edited by the propertyfile task"
                file="stats.properties">
    <entry key="numRuns" type="int" default="1" operation="+" value="1"/>
    <entry key="lastRun" type="date" operation="=" value="now"
           pattern="MMM dd, yyyy"/>
    <entry key="runBy" operation="="
           value="${user.name}"/>
  </propertyfile>
</target>
```

Here is what the properties file looks like after running the build four times:

```
#Edited by the propertyfile task
#Thu Jan 17 10:42:40 CST 2002
runBy=ericb
lastRun=Jan 17, 2002
numRuns=4
```

pvcs 1.4

Checks out PVCS files — **org.apache.tools.ant.taskdefs.optional.pvcs.Pvcs**

Extracts files from a PVCS repository. This task requires the PVCS Version Manager system from Merant, available at *http://www.merant.com*.

Attributes

`force` *(1.4, String, N)*
If yes, existing files are overwritten. Defaults to `no`.

`ignorereturncode` *(1.4, boolean, N)*
If `true`, do not abort the build when the command fails. Defaults to `false`.

`label` *(1.4, String, N)*
Specifies a label. When specified, only files with the specified label are extracted.

`promotiongroup` *(1.4, String, N)*
Specifies a promotion group. When specified, only files belonging to the specified promotion group are extracted.

`pvcsbin` *(1.4, String, N)*
Specifies the location of the *bin* directory of the PVCS distribution.

`pvcsproject` *(1.4, String, N)*
The project from which to extract files. Defaults to "`/`".

`repository` *(1.4, String, Y)*
The location of the PVCS repository.

`updateonly` *(1.4, boolean, N)*
If `true`, get only files if they are newer than existing local files. Defaults to `false`.

`workspace` *(1.4, String, N)*
A workspace to which files are extracted. Workspaces are configured via the PVCS client application.

Content

0..n nested `<pvcsproject>` *elements (1.4)*
Each has a required `name` attribute, specifying the name of a PVCS project from which to extract files. Use more than one element to specify multiple projects. These are in addition to any project already specified by the `pvcsproject` attribute.

renameext — 1.2 (deprecated in 1.3)

Renames file extensions

Renames filename extensions. For example, it can be used to rename **.java* to **.java.bak*. This task was deprecated in Ant 1.3. Use the `move` task with a glob `mapper` instead.

rpm — 1.4

Creates Linux RPM file — org.apache.tools.ant.taskdefs.optional.Rpm

Builds a Linux RPM file. Works only on Linux platforms.

Attributes

`cleanbuilddir` *(1.4, boolean, N)*
If `true`, remove generated files in the *BUILD* directory. Defaults to `false`.

`command` *(1.4, String, N)*
: An argument passed to the *rpm* executable. Defaults to `-bb`.

`error` *(1.4, File, N)*
: The destination file for standard error.

`output` *(1.4, File, N)*
: The destination file for standard output.

`removesource` *(1.4, boolean, N)*
: If `true`, remove the source files from the *SOURCES* directory. Defaults to `false`.

`removespec` *(1.4, boolean, N)*
: If `true`, remove the spec file from the *SPECS* directory. Defaults to `false`.

`specfile` *(1.4, String, Y)*
: The name of the spec file to use.

`topdir` *(1.4, File, N)*
: The destination directory. It contains *SPECS*, *SOURCES*, *BUILD*, and *SRPMS* subdirectories.

Content

None.

script **all**

Executes a BSF script **org.apache.tools.ant.taskdefs.optional.Script**

Executes a Bean Scripting Framework (BSF) script. This task requires IBM's Bean Scripting Framework, as well as a supported scripting language such as Rhino or Jython. BSF is available at *http://oss.software.ibm.com/developerworks/projects/bsf*. *ReleaseNotes.html*, found in the BSF distribution, indicates where supported scripting languages are available.

Attributes

`language` *(all, String, Y)*
: The script language name.

`src` *(all, String, N)*
: The location of a script source file, if the script is not inline.

Content

The `script` task accepts text content containing inline script code. This is the alternative to the `src` attribute. An XML `CDATA` section is required when scripts contain illegal XML characters such as '<' or '&', or when linefeeds must be preserved. For example:

```
<script language="javascript"><![CDATA[
  // some JavaScript code here...
  if (a < b) {
    ...
  }
]]></script>
```

sound 1.3, 1.4

Plays a sound when build ends **org.apache.tools.ant.taskdefs.optional.sound.SoundTask**

Plays a sound file at the end of the build process. The `<sound>` element must appear in one of the Ant targets that is executed during the build, but the sound is not played until the build is complete. This task relies on Sun's Java Media Framework (JMF), which is included in JDK 1.3 and later. For earlier versions of Java, JMF is available for download at *http://java.sun.com/products/java-media/sound/*.

Attributes

None.

Content

0,1 nested `<fail>` *elements (1.3, 1.4)*
    Defines the sound to play when the build fails.

0,1 nested `<success>` *elements (1.3, 1.4)*
    Defines the sound to play when the build succeeds.

Both nested elements are implemented by the same class, supporting the following attributes:

`source` *(1.3, 1.4, File, Y)*
    The name of a sound file to play. If this is a directory, one file is picked at random. For this reason, all files in the directory must be sound files. The task is tested with WAV and AIFF files.

`duration` *(1.3, 1.4, long, N)*
    The maximum number of milliseconds to play the sound.

`loops` *(1.3, 1.4, int, N)*
    The number of times to repeat the sound. Defaults to 0. If 1, the sound repeats once and therefore plays twice. Even if several iterations are requested, the total time spent by this task does not exceed the value specified by `duration`.

Example Usage

Plays applause at the end of the build, or plays a bomb exploding if an error occurs:

```
<target name="compile" depends="prepare">
  <sound>
    <!-- limit the applause to 2 seconds -->
    <success duration="2000" source="APPLAUSE.WAV"/>
    <fail source="EXPLODE.WAV"/>
  </sound>

  <javac ...> ... </javac>
</target>
```

starteam 1.3, 1.4

Checks out StarTeam files org.apache.tools.ant.taskdefs.optional.scm.AntStarTeamCheckOut

Checks out files from StarTeam, a commercial product from *http://www.starbase.com*. This task is only available to licensed users of StarTeam, and *starteam-sdk.jar* must be on the classpath.

Attributes

`excludes` *(all, String, N)*
: A space-delimited list of files to exclude from the checkout. Takes precedence over `includes`.

`foldername` *(all, String, N)*
: The subfolder in the project from which to check out files.

`force` *(all, boolean, N)*
: If `true`, overwrite existing folders. Defaults to `false`.

`includes` *(all, String, N)*
: Space-delimited list of files to include in the checkout.

`password` *(all, String, Y)*
: The password to log in with.

`projectname` *(all, String, Y)*
: The StarTeam project name.

`recursion` *(all, boolean, N)*
: If `true`, include subfolders when checking out. Defaults to `true`.

`servername` *(all, String, Y)*
: The StarTeam server name.

`serverport` *(all, String, Y)*
: The server port number.

`targetfolder` *(all, String, Y)*
: The directory to check files out to.

`username` *(all, String, Y)*
: The username to log in with.

`verbose` *(all, boolean, N)*
: If `true`, operate in verbose mode. Defaults to `false`.

`viewname` *(all, String, Y)*
: The StarTeam view name.

Content

None.

stylebook

1.3, 1.4

Executes Apache Stylebook generator **org.apache.tools.ant.taskdefs.optional.StyleBook**

Executes the Apache Stylebook documentation generator. It depends on *stylebook.jar*, available from *http://xml.apache.org*. An appropriate JAR file is also included with the Apache Xalan distribution.

Attributes

`book` *(1.3, 1.4, File, Y)*
: The book XML file to generate documentation from.

`classpath` *(1.3, 1.4, Path, N)*
: The classpath to use.

`classpathref` *(1.3, 1.4, Reference, N)*
: A reference to a classpath defined elsewhere in the buildfile.

`skindirectory` *(1.3, 1.4, File, Y)*
: A directory containing the Stylebook skin.

`targetdirectory` *(1.3, 1.4, File, Y)*
: The destination directory for the documentation.

Content

0,1 nested `<classpath>` *elements (1.3, 1.4)*
: May be used in place of the `classpath` or `classpathref` attributes.

telnet

1.3, 1.4

Creates telnet session **org.apache.tools.ant.taskdefs.optional.net.TelnetTask**

Executes a telnet session.

Attributes

`initialcr` *(1.3, 1.4, boolean, N)*
: If `true`, send a carriage return character after connecting. Defaults to `false`.

`password` *(1.3, 1.4, String, N)*
: The login password.

`port` *(1.3, 1.4, int, N)*
: The port number of the server. Defaults to 23.

`server` *(1.3, 1.4, String, Y)*
: The hostname to connect to.

`timeout` *(1.3, 1.4, int, N)*
: Number of seconds to wait before timing out. Defaults to no timeout.

`userid` *(1.3, 1.4, String, N)*
: The login name.

Content

0..n nested `<read>` *elements (1.3, 1.4)*
  Each contains a string of text to wait for from the server.

0..n nested `<write>` *elements (1.3, 1.4)*
  Each contains a string of text to send to the server.

test **1.3, 1.4**

Runs a unit test **org.apache.tools.ant.taskdefs.optional.Test**

Executes a unit test in the `org.apache.testlet` framework.

Attributes

`classpath` *(1.3, 1.4, Path, N)*
  Specifies the classpath to use.

`classpathref` *(1.3, 1.4, Reference, N)*
  A reference to a classpath defined elsewhere in the buildfile.

`forceshowtrace` *(1.3, 1.4, boolean, N)*
  If `true`, show a stack trace on any failure. Defaults to `false`.

`showbanner` *(1.3, 1.4, String, N)*
  If specified, show a banner when starting the testlet engine.

`showsuccess` *(1.3, 1.4, boolean, N)*
  If `true`, show a message when the tests succeed. Defaults to `false`.

`showtrace` *(1.3, 1.4, boolean, N)*
  If `true`, show a stack trace on errors, but not normal test failure. Defaults to `false`.

Content

0,1 nested `<classpath>` *elements (1.3, 1.4)*
  A `path` element specifying the classpath.

0..n nested `<testlet>` *elements (1.3, 1.4)*
  Each contains a class name to test. For example:

```
<testlet>com.oreilly.util.test.CustomerTestlet</testlet>
```

vsscheckin **1.4**

Checks in Visual SourceSafe files **org.apache.tools.ant.taskdefs.optional.vss.MSVSSCHECKIN**

Checks in files to Visual SourceSafe.

Attributes

`autoresponse` *(1.4, String, N)*
  Specifies the value for the `-I` flag. Legal values are `Y` and `N`. When omitted, the task passes `-I` to VSS. Otherwise, it passes `-I-Y` or `-I-N`.

`comment` *(1.4, String, N)*
  The comment applied to the files.

`localpath` *(1.4, Path, N)*
: Overrides the local working directory.

`login` *(1.4, String, N)*
: A username/password combination, formatted like `username,password`, where `,password` is optional.

`recursive` *(1.4, boolean, N)*
: If `true`, operate recursively on subprojects. Defaults to `false`.

`serverpath` *(1.4, String, N)*
: The directory in which *srcsafe.ini* resides.

`ssdir` *(1.4, String, N)*
: The directory containing *ss.exe*. Ant searches the `path` if this is omitted.

`vsspath` *(1.4, String, Y)*
: The path to the SourceSafe project, without the leading `$` character.

`writable` *(1.4, boolean, N)*
: If `true`, files are made writeable after check-in. Defaults to `false`.

Content

None.

vsscheckout 1.4

Checks out Visual SourceSafe files — **org.apache.tools.ant.taskdefs.optional.vss.MSVSSCHECKOUT**

Checks out files from Visual SourceSafe.

Attributes

`autoresponse` *(1.4, String, N)*
: Specifies the value for the `-I` flag. Legal values are `Y` and `N`. When omitted, the task passes `-I` to VSS. Otherwise, it passes `-I-Y` or `-I-N`.

`date` *(1.4, String, *)*
: The date stamp used when checking out files.

`label` *(1.4, String, *)*
: The label used when checking out files.

`localpath` *(1.4, Path, N)*
: Overrides the local working directory.

`login` *(1.4, String, N)*
: A username/password combination, formatted like `username,password`, where `,password` is optional.

`recursive` *(1.4, boolean, N)*
: If `true`, operate recursively on subprojects. Defaults to `false`.

`serverpath` *(1.4, String, N)*
: The directory in which *srcsafe.ini* resides.

`ssdir` *(1.4, String, N)*
: The directory containing *ss.exe*. Searches the `PATH` if omitted.

`version` *(1.4, String, *)*
: The version number used when checking out files.

`vsspath` *(1.4, String, Y)*
: The path to the SourceSafe project, without the leading `$` character.

One of `version`, `date`, or `label` may be specified; all are optional.

Content

None.

vssget

all

Gets Visual SourceSafe files — **org.apache.tools.ant.taskdefs.optional.vss.MSVSSGET**

Gets files from Visual SourceSafe.

Attributes

`autoresponse` *(1.3, 1.4, String, N)*
: Specifies the value for the `-I` flag. Legal values are `Y` and `N`. When omitted, the task passes `-I` to VSS. Otherwise, passes `-I-Y` or `-I-N`.

`date` *(all, String, *)*
: The date stamp used when getting files.

`label` *(all, String, *)*
: The label used when getting files.

`localpath` *(all, Path, N)*
: Overrides the local working directory.

`login` *(all, String, N)*
: A username/password combination, formatted like `username,password`, where `,password` is optional.

`quiet` *(1.4, boolean, N)*
: If `true`, operate in quiet mode. Defaults to `false`.

`recursive` *(all, boolean, N)*
: If `true`, operate recursively on subprojects. Defaults to `false`.

`serverpath` *(1.4, String, N)*
: Directory where *srcsafe.ini* resides.

`ssdir` *(all, String, N)*
: Directory containing *ss.exe*. Searches the `PATH` if omitted.

`version` *(all, String, *)*
: The version number used when getting files.

`vsspath` *(all, String, Y)*
: The path to the SourceSafe project, without the leading `$` character.

`writable` *(all, boolean, N)*
: If `true`, files are made writable after getting them. Defaults to `false`.

One of `version`, `date`, or `label` may be specified; all are optional.

Content

None.

vsshistory 1.4

Shows Visual SourceSafe project history org.apache.tools.ant.taskdefs.optional.vss.MSVSSHISTORY

Shows history for files and projects in Visual SourceSafe.

Attributes

`dateformat` *(1.4, String, N)*
: The format that is used by the `fromdate` and by the `todate` attributes. The task uses `java.text.SimpleDateFormat`, defaulting to `DateFormat.SHORT`.

`fromdate` *(1.4, String, *)*
: The start date for comparison.

`fromlabel` *(1.4, String, N)*
: The start label for comparison.

`login` *(1.4, String, N)*
: A username/password combination, formatted like `username,password`, where `,password` is optional.

`numdays` *(1.4, int, *)*
: The number of days relative to either `fromdate` or `todate`. May be a negative number.

`output` *(1.4, File, N)*
: The destination file to write the diff to.

`recursive` *(1.4, boolean, N)*
: If `true`, process projects recursively. Defaults to `false`.

`serverpath` *(1.4, String, N)*
: The directory where *srcsafe.ini* resides.

`ssdir` *(1.4, String, N)*
: The directory containing *ss.exe*. The task searches the `PATH` if omitted.

`style` *(1.4, Enum, N)*
: The format for the history report. Legal values are `brief`, `codediff`, `default`, or `nofile`. Defaults to `default`.

`todate` *(1.4, String, *)*
: The end date for comparison.

`tolabel` *(1.4, String, N)*
: The end label for comparison.

`user` *(1.4, String, N)*
: If specified, the task passes a user command (the `-U` option) to SourceSafe.

`vsspath` *(1.4, String, Y)*
: The path to the SourceSafe project, without the leading `$` character.

Various combinations of `fromdate`, `todate`, and `numdays` specify the time range for this task.

Content

None.

vsslabel

1.3, 1.4

Labels Visual SourceSafe files — org.apache.tools.ant.taskdefs.optional.vss.MSVSSLABEL

Assigns a label to files and projects in Visual SourceSafe.

Attributes

`autoresponse` *(1.4, String, N)*
: Specifies the value for the `-I` flag. Legal values are `Y` and `N`. When omitted, the task passes `-I` to VSS. Otherwise, it passes `-I-Y` or `-I-N`.

`comment` *(1.4, String, N)*
: The comment to associate with this label.

`label` *(1.3, 1.4, String, Y)*
: The label to apply to files.

`login` *(1.3, 1.4, String, N)*
: A username/password combination, formatted like `username,password`, where `,password` is optional.

`serverpath` *(1.4, String, N)*
: The directory where *srcsafe.ini* resides.

`ssdir` *(1.3, 1.4, String, N)*
: The directory containing *ss.exe*. The task searches the path if omitted.

`version` *(1.3, 1.4, String, N)*
: The version to label. Defaults to the current version.

`vsspath` *(1.3, 1.4, String, Y)*
: The path to the SourceSafe project, without the leading `$` character.

Content

None.

wljspc

all

Precompiles JSP using WebLogic compiler — org.apache.tools.ant.taskdefs.optional.jsp.WLJspc

Precompiles JSP files using BEA WebLogic Server's JSP compiler. This task requires WebLogic Version 4.5.1, and is only documented to work on Windows NT 4.0, Solaris 5.7, and Solaris 5.8.

Attributes

`classpath` *(all, Path, N)*
: The classpath used when compiling the JSPs.

`defaultexcludes` *(all, boolean, N)*
: Determines whether to use default excludes. Defaults to `true`.

`dest` *(all, File, Y)*
: The destination directory for compiled JSPs.

`excludes` *(all, String, N)*
: A comma-separated list of file patterns to exclude.

`excludesfile` *(all, File, N)*
: The name of a file containing one exclude pattern per line.

`includes` *(all, String, N)*
: A comma-separated list of file patterns to include.

`includesfile` *(all, File, N)*
: The name of a file containing one include pattern per line.

`package` *(all, String, Y)*
: The destination package for compiled JSPs.

`src` *(all, File, Y)*
: The document root directory containing the JSPs to compile.

Content

0..n nested `patternset` *elements:* `<exclude>`, `<include>`, `<patternset>` *(all);* `<excludesfile>`, `<includesfile>` *(1.4)*
: Used in place of their corresponding attributes, these specify the set of included and excluded source files.

0,1 nested `<classpath>` *elements (all)*
: May be used in place of the `classpath` attribute.

wlrun **all**

Starts WebLogic Server **org.apache.tools.ant.taskdefs.optional.ejb.WLRun**

Starts an instance of the BEA WebLogic Server. This task does not return until the server stops.

Attributes

`args` *(all, String, N)*
: Additional arguments for the WebLogic instance.

`beahome` *(1.3, 1.4, File, Y)*
: The directory containing the server's config file. Applicable only for WebLogic 6.0. The task assumes WebLogic 6.0 when this attribute is specified.

`classpath` *(all, Path, Y)*
: The classpath used to run the server. Under WebLogic 6.0, this should include all WebLogic JARs.

`domain` *(1.3, 1.4, String, Y)*
: The domain of the server. Applicable only for WebLogic 6.0.

`home` *(all, File, Y)*
: The WebLogic distribution directory.

`jvmargs` *(all, String, N)*
Additional arguments for the JVM.

`name` *(all, String, N)*
The name of the server within the WebLogic home. Defaults to `myserver`.

`password` *(1.3, 1.4, String, Y)*
The server's management password. Applicable only for WebLogic 6.0.

`pkpassword` *(1.3, 1.4, String, N)*
The private key password. Applicable only for WebLogic 6.0.

`policy` *(all, String, N)*
The name of the security policy file within the WebLogic home directory. Defaults to `weblogic.policy`.

`properties` *(all, String, Y,)*
The name of the properties file within the WebLogic home directory. Applicable only for WebLogic 4.5.1 and 5.1.

`username` *(1.3, 1.4, String, N)*
The server's management username. Applicable only for WebLogic 6.0.

`weblogicmainclass` *(all, String, N)*
The name of the WebLogic main class. Defaults to `weblogic.Server`.

`wlclasspath` *(all, Path, N)*
The classpath used by the WebLogic server. Applicable only for WebLogic 4.5.1 and 5.1.

Content

0,1 nested `<classpath>` *elements (1.3, 1.4)*
May be used in place of the `classpath` attribute.

0,1 nested `<wlclasspath>` *elements (1.3, 1.4)*
May be used in place of the `wlclasspath` attribute.

wlstop **all**

Stops WebLogic Server **org.apache.tools.ant.taskdefs.optional.ejb.WLStop**

Stops an instance of the BEA WebLogic Server.

Attributes

`beahome` *(1.3, 1.4, File, N)*
The directory containing the server's config file. The task assumes WebLogic 6.0 when this attribute is specified.

`classpath` *(all, Path, Y)*
The classpath used when executing the WebLogic shutdown command.

`delay` *(all, String, N)*
The number of seconds to wait before shutting down the server.* Defaults to `0`.

* The task uses `Integer.parseInt( )` to convert this `String` attribute value into an `int`.

password *(all, String, Y)*
The password associated with the specified user.

url *(all, String, Y)*
The URL to the port on which the server is listening to T3 connections—for example, *t3://myserver:7001*.

user *(all, String, Y)*
The username of the account used to shut down the server.

Content

0,1 nested <classpath> *elements (1.3, 1.4)*
May be used in place of the classpath attribute.

xmlvalidate 1.4

Validate XML files **org.apache.tools.ant.taskdefs.optional.XMLValidateTask**

Verifies that XML documents are well-formed, and optionally, whether they are valid, using any SAX parser.

Attributes

classname *(1.4, String, N)*
The Java class name of the SAX parser to use.

classpath *(1.4, Path, N)*
The classpath to use.

classpathref *(1.4, Reference, N)*
Reference to a classpath defined elsewhere in the buildfile.

failonerror *(1.4, boolean, N)*
If true, abort the build on failures. Defaults to true.

file *(1.4, File, N)*
The XML file to validate. Use nested <fileset> elements to specify multiple files.

lenient *(1.4, boolean, N)*
If true, verify the XML is well-formed, but do not validate. Works only when using a SAX2 parser. Defaults to false.

warn *(1.4, boolean, N)*
If true, write warnings to the log. Defaults to true.

Content

0,1 nested <classpath> *elements (1.4)*
A path element used in place of the classpath or classpathref attributes.

0..n nested <fileset> *elements (1.4)*
One or more fileset elements specifying XML files to validate, used in place of the file attribute.

APPENDIX A

The Future of Ant

Most open source projects evolve at an almost alarming rate, and Ant is no exception. Over the course of just over two years, Ant moved from a prototype build tool for building Tomcat to becoming the preferred build tool for many Java projects. On the bright side, rapid changes mean more features and more solutions for the many problems developers face in building and distributing their projects. On the dark side, rapid changes mean instability—developers have to stay on their toes to make sure releases with new features don't break the current features they're using.

The maintainers of the Ant project are aware of how their contributions can affect thousands of people's projects and work. In early 2001, they set forth on a plan to refactor Ant's design. Over time, Ant's library has become bloated. Features of some tasks overlap features of others. There is no contract between the developers of the Ant engine and developers of Ant tasks and listeners. Some implementations in the Ant engine are poorly written and need refactoring; this refactoring could affect the design in many objects. The effort for all of these changes could take months, even years. It is unacceptable to leave a working project in a state of constant development for this long. Because of this, the maintainers elected to go forward with a fork, to create Ant2.

Ant2

The maintainers of Ant are taking proposals from the user and developer base for redesign and refactoring. A new set of design requirements and functionality expectation have come from the proposals. There will be a contract defining how task developers and Ant-engine developers work together. No longer will some tasks require internal changes to Ant and vice versa, a practice that goes on too frequently with Ant1. Another change affects the *core task library*, the library of tasks shipped with Ant. There will be an attempt to manage the task library in a more "CPAN-like" manner.* A

* This refers to Perl's distributed CPAN library, which allows for any number of modules to be automatically referred to in-code without any end-user interaction.

repository of tasks will reside online, available to everyone. A buildfile would need to refer to the online library to download a JAR or class for a particular task. Developers will no longer have to manage their internal deployments of Ant.

In addition to the new design requirements, the maintainers are attempting to refactor many of Ant's old known weaknesses, especially in the XML-processing routines. Currently, Ant interprets the XML but still loads the entire buildfile into memory, which is a rather inefficient methodology. Large buildfiles can cause Ant's JVM to suck up huge amounts of system memory, degrading performance. Considering that developers may run a build 5, 10, or even 20 times a day on their machines, a 5-minute difference in build time can cost up to 3 hours of productive work.

Overall, the goal is to have a system bereft of the warts and blemishes of its predecessor. You can view the new goals and keep track of what's in and what's out by reading the documentation found in *docs/ant2*. All Ant distributions since Release 1.3 include this documentation. Expect at least a beta release version of Ant2 some time in 2002.

Ant1 RIP 2002?

So what does this mean for users of Ant1? Is it going away the day Ant2 becomes final? Not quite. Even though many of the design proposals mentioned earlier are subject to debate and change (incidentally, delaying release), one thing remains a constant in the design of Ant2: *Ant1 buildfiles will not work with Ant2*. Regardless, Ant1's life support forms its basis in its wide user base. Ant1 has become fairly entrenched within many projects and products. For example, IBM's VisualAge for Java now includes support for Ant Version 1.2 within its IDE. WebLogic 6.1 ships with the Ant 1.3 release libraries built in; all of Ant 1.3's example documentation uses Ant for building the included examples. All of the Jakarta projects use Ant1 buildfiles, although some only work with Ant Release 1.2 (but most keep up with the latest version). Given Ant1's current use and its sizeable inertia, it's unlikely that Ant1 will just go away the day Ant2 becomes Version 1.0—er, 2.0. More likely, the transition will be a slow one, if a transition takes place at all. If you're well into the life cycle of your project, it will just not make sense to change what already works for you. Because Ant1 is open source, its support can never be taken away by some company. This book and a slew of online documentation will always exist to help you maintain projects based on Ant1.

Does this mean Ant2 is unlikely to take off? This too is doubtful since Ant is part of the Jakarta project. Many of the same developers that help with Ant help with the other Jakarta subprojects. When new versions or new subprojects for Jakarta come out, there's a good chance the developers will use Ant2. Only time will tell. As with all open source tools, it's best if you keep your eyes out for changes as they happen. We've made a list here of some things that are very likely to change that may affect the way you write buildfiles now. Being considerate of Ant2's design may make a future transition easier if you plan to make one.

- If you rely on properties being immutable (their values set once and only once), you will see this design go away in Ant2 (and, to some extent, Ant 1.5). The current Ant2 design proposals call for properties that can be set and reset at any time.
- Some seemingly duplicate tasks will be consolidated into one supertask. For example, `jar`, `unjar`, `zip`, `unzip`—all of which perform operations on a ZIP-like file—will be combined into a task called `archive`.
- The concept of magic properties will go away.
- The use of SYSTEM XML entities, which allows you to dynamically include buildfile fragments using XML operators, is likely to go away in favor of a built-in Ant "include" system.
- Most importantly, regardless of how they're declared or implemented, Ant1 tasks will not work in Ant2. According to the design proposals, there will be adapters and utilities to facilitate the porting of Ant1 tasks.

Ant2 aims to be a marked improvement over Ant1. Most build and project design concepts formed with Ant1 should carry over. Everything you've learned with Ant in a "build-design" sense will not go to waste.

APPENDIX B

Ant Solutions

Over time, developers have created good, consistent solutions for builds. Unfortunately, many of these solutions remain "locked away" within their projects' buildfiles and rarely find light in articles or documentation. In Chapter 3, we organize the irssibot project in a manner that has proven successful with many other projects. Like these other projects, our example project closely ties the buildfile to file and directory organization. Due to the rather simple nature of the irssibot project, we are unable to demonstrate some other successful build designs such as those found in projects like Tomcat, the Jakarta Taglibs, and the Ant project. In this Appendix, however, we get a chance to discuss these other common build solutions as well as to clarify the ones we use in other parts of the book.

We should note that the following solutions are not patterns in the academic sense. To emphasize this difference, we've broken the solutions down into sections and started each solution with a question. If you find the question fits a problem you've come across in writing buildfiles, read the solution to see if the suggestion fits your needs.

Testing Library Availability

Q: *We use the Java SDK Version 1.4 for our Windows 2000 workstations, but our Linux boxes are still using Java SDK Version 1.2. Some of our classes use classes available only in Java SDK Version 1.4. Currently, this situation means we get build errors on the Linux machines. How do we prevent these errors without writing two different buildfiles?*

A: Use the `available` task to avoid library version problems, and to build only the necessary parts of your application, based on a developer's environment. In this case, you can determine the Java SDK Version by checking for the existence of certain classes. For the Java SDK Versions 1.4 and higher, the class `java.lang.CharSquence` is unique. This class does not exist in Java SDKs prior to 1.4. Ant's own buildfile does this type of checking. We will use Ant's buildfile to show an example.

In Ant's buildfile, the following target exists (edited to preserve space):

```
<target name="check_for_optional_packages">
    <available property="jdk1.2+" classname="java.lang.ThreadLocal" />
    <available property="jdk1.3+" classname="java.lang.StrictMath" />
    <available property="jdk1.4+" classname="java.lang.CharSequence" />
</target>
```

Later in the buildfile, we don't compile a file if the proper libraries aren't available:

```
<exclude name="${ant.package}/util/regexp/Jdk14RegexpMatcher.java"
    unless="jdk1.4+" />
```

This `exclude` is part of Ant's primary build target that compiles all of Ant's source code. It excludes the compilation of the class in `Jdk14RegexpMatcher.java` unless the Sun JDK Version 1.4 libraries are present. This solution is great when you know that the developers' environments can vary wildly, as is the case with Ant. With a few extra lines, a buildfile using `available` tasks and a combination of `exclude` DataType's with `unless` attributes enables developers to worry more about the project and to worry less about having a specific but maybe unnecessary set of libraries and tools. Conversely, build managers have the power to prevent compilation problems that you normally detect with `ClassDefNotFound` exceptions and errors; this situation is very difficult and tedious to debug in projects with large, distributed development teams.

Cleaning Up Does More Than Keep Things Neat

Q: *Our developers are having problems testing the application. For example, two builds with no code changes result in differing behaviors. Technically, this shouldn't happen, but since the compilation steps are hidden, we're never sure what's being built each time. How can we fix this?*

A: Every build should be able to return the project directory to its initial state. This may seem like "common sense," and, while this rule is followed in most build environments—including Linux's kernel build, our example in Chapter 2, Ant, and Tomcat—the reasons aren't always made clear. This pattern stems from three common build goals: distribution of the compiled project, distribution of the source, and testing.

In distributing the compiled project, the build manager desires that only the files needed to install, run, and support the finished product are made available to the end user. This is more for keeping the user's life simple and easy than for any other reason. The best solution is to have a completely separate space for creating the distribution (e.g., the *dist* directory). This gives the buildfile one location in which to place distributable components, and one location to clean up when a new distribution is needed.

Distributing the source is similar. Use a separate directory for managing the source to be packaged and distributed. Have one place to copy files and one place to delete files (i.e., one ring to rule them all). This makes more sense than trying to copy and package specific directories in the project's source code. Even better, adding and removing components from a distribution is made easier with a separate distribution staging area (this applies to distributing the binary version as well). Clean up, like with the binary distribution, is quick and easy. Just delete the directory. While you may consider distributing the source a secondary goal for your project, also consider this: by making the source distributable, you've made your project easy to be "picked up" by new developers. Long-lived projects that carry over years rarely have the same development team for their entire lifetime. Making development easier for new developers coming on to a project in midstream makes those developers reach full productivity that much faster.

Combining the solutions from the previous two rules gives us the solution to the third rule, which makes testing easier. Testing requires deterministic states of a project. By separating the distribution of a project from its work and source locations, we have an easy way to verify which version of the project we're working with. If we're ever unsure, thinking an old class file is messing things up, we delete the distribution and recreate it. No muss, no fuss. As an added bonus, we can send this easy-to-manage distribution in an easy-to-manage package (e.g., a JAR) to other developers to corroborate errors and verify test cases.

Using Ant to Consolidate Libraries

Q: *Our project uses at least 15 different JARs. The command line has reached its byte limit and the buildfile properties are ugly and hard to maintain. To make matters worse, we'll probably be adding more JARs later on. What can we do?*

A: Use the power of tasks to make your life better. Far too often, developers use powerful tools to solve the simple problems and then rely on conventions and "developer's honor" to solve the complex problems. Take, for instance, a web application that relies upon a large, common set of libraries. The quick solution for including all of the libraries is to make a `classpath` property listing each JAR file or class directory in a path. When running the web application, this list is duplicated with different directories, of course, in the startup and configuration files for the particular application server. Any changes to the library list require modification of at least two files.

We can manage many libraries as one JAR with a target such as the following:

```
<target name="makesuperjar">
  <jar jarfile="superjar.jar" destdir="${some.common.lib.dir}">
    <zipfileset src="${some.common.lib.dir}/jaxp.jar"/>
    <zipfileset src="${some.common.lib.dir}/jaxen.jar"/>
    <zipfileset src="${some.common.lib.dir}/parser.jar"/>
```

```
    <zipfileset src="${some.common.lib.dir}/netcomponents.jar"/>
    <zipfileset src="${some.common.lib.dir}/oracle816JDBC.jar"/>
  </jar>
</target>

<property name="classpath" value="${some.common.lib.dir}\superjar.jar"/>
```

Here, we've told Ant to combine all the JARs needed by an application into one superJAR for use throughout the build. We've also made distribution and installation easier by eliminating the need to track all the various libraries used by the application. Startup scripts and configuration files can now refer to *superjar.jar* with the understanding that it contains all the third-party libraries for the project in one place.

In Ant 1.2, the `jar` task cannot contain a nested `<zipfileset>` element.

The benefits from this technique extend beyond simple library management. EJBs have extraordinary library management issues. Furthermore, it doesn't help that the leading application servers handle system-wide libraries and the sharing of EJB classes differently. You may need to re-package the same classes and JARs multiple times for inclusion with a WAR or an EAR, depending on the target application server. Using the `war`, `ear`, and `jar` tasks effectively manages these issues with little management overhead.

Like every silver lining, this solution has a dark cloud. Projects like Ant, with large, distributed developer bases and a loosely managed development environment, cannot use this solution. Missing JARs causes the `jar` task to fail, and the possibility of missing JARs is part of Ant's project design. However, projects with a tightly managed library list, especially those projects with no "optional" libraries, benefit greatly from this pattern. By enforcing the library set using one JAR, the project eliminates the possibility of rogue libraries causing problems in running and testing the application. It requires that the third-party libraries are distributed with the application, which is a good thing in this case since library version and availability is important. Additionally, the pesky command-line limit, which can plague the administration of some application servers, is gone. Whether there are 2 or 20 JARs, the classpath will always be defined with one, leaving room in the command for other options and paths. We've made the build and project manager's life easier by providing one place to manage all of an application's third-party libraries, and also by enforcing the inclusion of these libraries and eliminating any confusion with versions.

Documenting the Buildfile's Targets

Q: *We have a complex buildfile. When new developers join the project, the learning curve on how to use the buildfile is high. We feel like we waste a lot of time teaching what the buildfiles do instead of better integrating the new employee with the team. We've placed some documentation on an intranet site, and this helps, but, as we all know, not everyone reads the documentation. What else can we do?*

A: Don't ignore the `description` attribute for targets. Being able to run Ant with the *-projecthelp* option and get detailed feedback is another way to shorten developers' ramp-up time on a project and increase productivity.

For example, the following target uses the `description` attribute to include some documentation:

```
<target name="do-something-really-complex"
        depends="less-complex-stuff"
        description="Perform a lot of checks and tests so you know your project
works right.  You wouldn't know this target did this unless we provided a
decription.  It's good that you know now, eh?">
...
</target>
```

Of course, there's a chance to go overboard here. Describe only the targets you want executed from the command line. While *-projecthelp* will list all targets, it separates the list into those with descriptions and those without. Most developers pick up on this quickly and know to avoid running the descriptionless targets. If you really do want to document targets that shouldn't run from the command line, include a message such as the following in those target descriptions: "DON'T RUN THIS FROM THE COMMAND LINE!"

Setting Properties Outside of the Buildfile

Q: *We've tried to make a universal buildfile, but have run into issues where certain property values will differ on each developer's workstation. We don't want developers to edit the buildfile. How do we do this?*

A: Ant's `property` task has an attribute that takes a filename. If the file is structured as a properties file (name-value pairs, one per line), Ant includes these values in the property table. If a name conflicts with a name specified in the buildfile, and the property file is included before the in-buildfile definition (this part's very important), the value overrides the buildfile's value. The key is that the first definition of a property takes precedence.

By declaring an external property file for use in the build, you give developers a way to override buildfile property values without editing the buildfile. The following buildfile snippet shows an example of how the buildfile includes an external properties file in case the `codebase` property needs to be overridden:

```
<project name="ExtenisbleProject" default="all" basedir=".">
    <property name="build.properties"/>
    <property name="codebase" value="/export/home/builduser"/>
...the rest of the properties and buildfile
...
```

This buildfile imports properties from *build.properties* before setting the properties internally. If a developer specifies a value for codebase in the *build.properties* file, that developer-specific setting takes precedence because it was defined first. Otherwise, if the developer does not specify a codebase value in his properties file, the value set for codebase inside the buildfile is used instead.

Properties files are simply text files. The following is an example of the syntax you should use to set a property (codebase in this case) in a properties file:

```
codebase=c:/src
```

Remember that Ant processes the command line first, so any value for codebase on the command line takes utmost precedence:

```
ant -Dcodebase=c:/src
```

In this case, because codebase is specified on the command line, the value c:/src is used regardless of any other settings in the buildfile or in a properties file.

Using pathconvert

Q: *I set up a bunch of paths using the* path *DataType. Now I have this task that only takes paths as an attribute. Do I need to rewrite everything using properties? I thought* path *solved this problem?*

A: When paths were first introduced, this was a legitimate gripe. Some people wrote their own tasks to handle the conversion while others suffered the pain of maintaining two sets of data, or just stuck with using properties. However, when the pathconvert task came out, all was good.

Look at this example buildfile:

```
<project name="test" default="test" basedir=".">

    <path id="classpath">
        <pathelement location="lib"/>
        <pathelement location="lib/test.jar"/>
    </path>
    <property name="somepath" value="lib:lib/test.jar"/>
    <target name="test">
        <java classname="org.oreilly.Test" fork="yes" \
          classpath="${somepath}"/>
    </target>

</project>
```

Assume for the moment that the java task must use the classpath attribute instead of a path DataType.* The only way to have both a property and DataType represent a path (without pathconvert) is to define both. In this example, that doesn't seem like a big deal, but these paths can get long and complex. You only want to define them once. The following example uses pathconvert to convert a path DataType into a property setting:

```
<project name="test" default="test" basedir=".">

    <path id="classpath">
        <pathelement location="lib"/>
        <pathelement location="lib/test.jar"/>
    </path>
    <target name="test">
        <pathconvert targetos="windows" property="somepath" \
          refid="classpath"/>
        <java classname="org.oreilly.Test" fork="yes" \
          classpath="${somepath}"/>
    </target>
</project>
```

With pathconvert, we've eliminated the need for two paths. The pathconvert task converts the path DataType into a property, which is then referenced by the java task.

Not all is perfect, however. The pathconvert task requires you to define a target operating system (or a path separator). Normally, Ant takes care of this for you, but unfortunately not in the case of pathconvert. You may want to use an extra buildfile property to denote which platform the buildfile is being processed on.

Converting DataTypes to properties isn't the only job pathconvert can do. Check out its documentation in Chapter 7 for more details.

Usage Statements

Q: *In the example from Chapter 3, you have an* all *target that builds everything. I don't want the build to do anything by default. Is there a good way to pull this off?*

A: It's not *the* way, but a good way to do this is to make a "usage statement" target. Typically this target is called help and it simply echoes messages about the common targets in the build. This behavior is similar to some Unix (and some Windows) console programs. If you're not familiar with these console programs, they normally do nothing if called from the command line with no arguments. Instead,

* This is not *that* wild of a concept. If the buildfile is part of a cascading buildfile design, the path-requiring tasks can't rely on paths stored in path DataTypes. They would all need to use a property, or the subproject buildfiles would need to redefine the paths themselves.

they display a message, starting with the text "Usage" that shows the various command-line arguments you can use with the program. Our help target does the same thing, as the following example shows:

```
<project name="usage_example" default="help" basedir=".">
    <!-- some properties -->
    <!-- some paths -->

    <target name="build-lib"/>
    <target name="build-app"/>
    <target name="deploy-app"/>
    <target name="makedoc"/>

    <target name="help">
        <echo message="Build the usage_example project"/>
        <echo message="Usage: ant [ant options] <target1> \
                        [target2 | target3 | ... ]"/>
        <echo message=""/>
        <echo message="    build-lib - build just the project's library"/>
        <echo message="    build-app - build the library and \
                             the application"/>
        <echo message="    deploy-app - ready the \
                             application for deployment"/>
        <echo message="    makedoc - generate all the \
                             documentation for the project"/>
        <echo message="    -projecthelp - (An Ant option) Display all \
                             target descriptions"/>
    </target>
</project>
```

Now, if developers just call *ant* from the command line, they'll get the message shown in the following example:

```
src%: ant
Buildfile: build.xml

help:
   [echo] Build the usage_example project
   [echo] Usage: ant [ant options] <target1> [target2 | target3 | ... ]
   [echo]    build-lib - build just the project's library
   [echo]    build-app - build the library and the application
   [echo]    deploy-app - ready the application for deployment
   [echo]    makedoc - generate all the documentation for the project
   [echo]    -projecthelp - (An Ant option) Display all target descriptions

BUILD SUCCESSFUL

Total time: 0 seconds
src%:
```

Such usage text can be a good introduction for people using your buildfiles, and having the help target as the default prevents accidental execution of other targets. Creating help targets for your buildfiles is a good habit to get into, and writing such a target doesn't take all that much effort.

Forking Processes

Q: *We need to run a Java utility on some of our files during the build. When some errors happen in this utility, we've noticed that the build just dies. We get no success or fail messages, and the log just abruptly ends. I think it may have something to do with the* `System.exit( )` *issue mentioned in Chapter 5, but we still don't know how to fix it. What do we do?*

A: Ah yes, the `System.exit( )` problem. To recap, the problem is the result of developers' misuse of the `System.exit( )` call in their code. The `System.exit( )` call speaks directly to the JVM, causing it to die immediately. Since a Java program running from Ant is running in Ant's JVM, any calls to `System.exit( )` will kill Ant's JVM. This is bad. Lucky for you, the `java` task has an attribute called `fork`.

```
<java classname="org.oreilly.SpecialTool" fork="yes"/>
```

The `fork` attribute on the `java` task gives you the ability to avoid this problem. The attribute tells the `java` task to run the class in a separate JVM. Being in a separate JVM means the program's `System.exit( )` call can't kill Ant's JVM. While this keeps your build from breaking unexpectedly, the problem isn't completely solved. The second JVM is still dying and the Java program is dying without warning. It's still in your best interest to try to solve the root problem and get rid of the `System.exit( )` call, if possible.

Using Cascading Projects and Buildfiles

Q: *We've noticed projects like JBoss and Jakarta's Taglibs do not use the project structure suggested in Chapter 3. Instead, they seem to have multiple buildfiles, one for each subproject. This seems to follow the design discussed when "cascading buildfiles" were mentioned. Just what are these things and how should I use them?*

A: There are two options as to how to build a big project that has many subprojects. One views the project as a monolithic whole, thus using one buildfile to build everything. The single buildfile defines all the targets necessary to build the project as well as all the data elements and other bits necessary for the entire build. Dependencies between subprojects in a single buildfile can be easily defined and maintained. Packaging and deployment targets can be properly related to every subproject target. The single buildfile describing this project's build is called a *monolithic buildfile*.

Some complex projects consist of many segregated subprojects making up one application or framework. The organization is such that each subproject can be built on its own, without worrying much about the other subprojects. The set of buildfiles making up this type of project's build is called a *cascading buildfile*.

For small projects or projects with complex dependencies between subprojects, a monolithic buildfile is the ideal choice. For projects that are well-defined and whose subprojects are encapsulated, a cascading buildfile system may be a better choice.

Cascading buildfiles in Ant take their cue from large Unix projects like the Linux kernel. The kernel is an example of a cascading build using makefiles. In the Java world, one of the best-organized cascading builds belongs to JBoss. JBoss consists of a root project directory containing only a buildfile. With this, you can build everything that makes up JBoss. Here's a list of subdirectories under the root directory from the JBoss 2.4.4 source tree:

```
JBoss-2.4.4-src/
     build.xml
     /contrib
     /jboss
     /jboss-j2ee
     /jbosscx
     /jbossmq
     /jnp
     /jbosspool
     /jbosstest
     /jbosssx
```

The root directory contains a buildfile, and each of the subdirectories also contains buildfiles. Since the pattern for calling buildfiles from subdirectories repeats for each level, it suffices to show you how the root buildfile calls the others. Aside from some directory name changes, everything else stays the same.

Following is the `build` target from JBoss' buildfile:

```
<target name="build" depends = "cvs-co,init">
    <ant antfile="src/build/build.xml" dir="jboss" target="main" />
    <ant antfile="src/build/build.xml" dir="jnp" target="src-install" />
    <ant antfile="src/build/build.xml" dir="jbosssx" \
         target="src-install" />
    <ant antfile="src/build/build.xml" dir="jbossmq" \
         target="src-install" />
    <ant antfile="src/build/build.xml" dir="jbosscx" \
         target="src-install" />
    <ant antfile="src/build/build.xml" dir="jbosspool" \
         target="src-install" />
    <ant antfile="src/build/build.xml" dir="jboss-j2ee" \
         target="src-install" />
</target>
```

As you can see, the target uses the `ant` task to call each subproject's buildfile. If we call *ant build* in JBoss' main source directory, Ant will try to build the entire project. The `ant` task is considered successful only when its target buildfile is successful. Thus, for the `build` target to be successful, all the other buildfiles it calls must also be successful.

So far, this cascading buildfile looks simple, but there are some rules you should understand about calling buildfiles in this manner. Some attributes can change how Ant behaves in ways you might not expect.

The first rule deals with properties and property scope. Remember that you can set properties on the command line or in the buildfile via the `<property>` data element. By default, any property from the parent buildfile or from the command line propagates to any child buildfiles called by the `ant` task. If a property is re-declared in the subproject buildfile, it doesn't matter. Immutability of properties still applies; the root buildfile's properties (and the command-line properties) stand. If, however, we add the following `inheritall` attribute to the first `ant` task, we do not see this "immutable property" behavior:

```
<ant antfile="src/build/build.xml" dir="jboss" \
    inheritAll="false" target="main" />
```

By setting `inheritall` to `false`, we are telling Ant *not* to make the current buildfile's properties available to the subproject's buildfile, with one exception: command-line properties. Just think of command-line properties as being set in stone. These properties cannot be changed and they cannot be ignored.

The second rule of cascading buildfiles is, unfortunately, less flexible than the property rule. DataType references (DataTypes with `id` attributes) do not propagate down the project tree. Period. Other than converting paths to properties with the `pathconvert` task (see earlier), there's nothing else you can do to alleviate this limitation.

Both of these rules point to a general solution, which remains true for a lot of programming: document everything and document it well. If your project uses cascading buildfiles, comment the buildfiles and write READMEs that explain why some properties make it to the third-level subproject and some don't. Explain why some paths are redefined in every buildfile. This also helps you when you have to make changes to a buildfile you haven't touched in three months.

Index

We'd like to hear your suggestions for improving our indexes. Send email to *index@oreilly.com*.

C

D

E

F

G

T

U

V

W

X

Z

About the Authors

Jesse Tilly started his professional software career in 1997. He is now a senior developer at Radiant Systems in Atlanta, where he's worked since 2000. Aside from his standard development duties helping to implement an ASP-based property management system, Jesse designed and created the configuration management system in use by his team at Radiant. He did the same with his projects at USWeb/CKS, DocuCorp International, and IBM. Jesse has published articles about Ant, and is an active participant of the Ant community on the Apache Software Foundation Ant mailing lists. He can be reached by email at *tillyj@bellsouth.net*.

Eric M. Burke is a mentor and consultant who specializes in Java, XML, and eXtreme Programming. He uses Ant on a daily basis for compiling code, running tests, and deploying software. He also enjoys carpentry and woodworking projects in the evenings, and writes books even later at night. Eric is a principal software engineer for Object Computing, Inc. in St. Louis, MO, and is the author of O'Reilly's *Java and XSLT*. He can be reached at *burke_e@yahoo.com*.

Colophon

Our look is the result of reader comments, our own experimentation, and feedback from distribution channels. Distinctive covers complement our distinctive approach to technical topics, breathing personality and life into potentially dry subjects.

The animal on the cover of *Ant: The Definitive Guide* is a horned lizard. There are 13 species of the horned lizard in North America. Horned lizards prefer a dry, warm climate, such as the desert or a dry woodland, and they can be found in Texas, Oklahoma, Kansas, and New Mexico. Adults grow to 3–5 inches. They depend on their environment to control their body temperature, and use burrows and shade to prevent overheating. The horned lizard has a wide, flat body ideal for desert camouflage, and a short neck and short legs. It has spines on its body and prominent horns on its head. It is also known as the horny "toad."

Despite the horned lizards' fierce appearance, they are not aggressive. Their primary diet consists of ants, although they sometimes eat beetles, grasshoppers, and other insects, which they catch with their long tongues. The horned lizards' first line of defense from predators is their camouflage, but they are also known to hiss and inflate their bodies to appear more intimidating. As a last resort, they have the ability to squirt blood from the corners of their eyes in an attempt to confuse attackers. In Texas and Oklahoma, horned lizards are considered a threatened species. It is illegal to possess a horned lizard without a scientific permit. More information on the conservation of horned lizards is available at *http://www.hornedlizards.org*.

Colleen Gorman was the production editor and proofreader, and Mary Brady was the copyeditor for *Ant: The Definitive Guide*. Linley Dolby and Jane Ellin provided quality control. Nancy Crumpton wrote the index.

Hanna Dyer designed the cover of this book, based on a series design by Edie Freedman. The cover image is a 19th-century engraving from the Dover Pictorial Archive. Emma Colby produced the cover layout with QuarkXPress 4.1 using Adobe's ITC Garamond font. David Futato designed the interior layout. This book was converted into FrameMaker 5.5.6 with a format conversion tool created by Erik Ray, Jason McIntosh, Neil Walls, and Mike Sierra that uses Perl and XML technologies. The text font is Linotype Birka; the heading font is Adobe Myriad Condensed; and the code font is LucasFont's TheSans Mono Condensed. The illustrations that appear in the book were produced by Robert Romano and Jessamyn Read using Macromedia FreeHand 9 and Adobe Photoshop 6. The tip and warning icons were drawn by Christopher Bing. This colophon was written by Colleen Gorman.